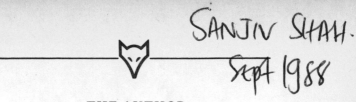

THE AUTHOR

David Widgery was born in London in 1947, and qualified as a doctor in 1974. Since then he has worked mainly in the East End of London, and is currently a general practitioner in a Limehouse group practice.

He is the author of three previous books: *The Left in Britain 1956–68* (1976), *Health in Danger* (1979) and *Beating Time* (1986), and is a regular contributor to *New Society* and *Socialist Worker*.

David Widgery lives with the fashion historian Juliet Ash and two children in Hackney.

THE
NATIONAL
HEALTH:
A Radical Perspective

David Widgery

THE HOGARTH PRESS
LONDON

To Ruth . . . again
and to A.E.L. and W.D.S.

Published in 1988 by
The Hogarth Press
30 Bedford Square, London WC1B 3RP

Copyright © David Widgery 1988

A CIP catalogue record for this book is available
from the British Library.

ISBN 0 7012 0806 6

Photoset in Linotron Plantin by
Rowland Phototypesetting Ltd
Bury St Edmunds, Suffolk
Printed in Finland by
Werner Söderström Oy

Contents

List of Abbreviations

AHA	Area Health Authority
AIDS	Acquired Immune Deficiency Syndrome
ASTMS	Association of Scientific, Technical and Managerial Staffs
BMA	British Medical Association
BMJ	*British Medical Journal*
BUPA	British United Provident Association
CHC	Community Health Council
COHSE	Confederation of Health Service Employees
CPN	Community Psychiatric Nurse
DHA	District Health Authority
DHSS	Department of Health and Social Security
DPP	Director of Public Prosecutions
EBS	Emergency Bed Service
EGA	Elizabeth Garrett Anderson Hospital
FPC	Family Practitioner Committee
FPS	Family Practitioner Service
GLC	Greater London Council
GMBATU	General, Municipal, Boilermakers' and Allied Trades' Union
GMC	General Medical Council
GMWU	General and Municipal Workers' Union
GNP	Gross National Product
GP	General Practitioner
LAS	London Ambulance Service
LASH	London Alliance of Stewards for Health Workers
MDU	Medical Defence Union
MIND	National Institute for Mental Health
MPU	Medical Practitioners' Union
NACODS	National Association of Colliery Overmen, Deputies and Shotfirers
NALGO	National Association of Local Government Officers

NGA	National Graphical Association
NHS	National Health Service
NUM	National Union of Mineworkers
NUPE	National Union of Public Employees
PPP	Private Patients Plan
RAWP	Resources Allocation Working Party
RCGP	Royal College of General Practitioners
RCN	Royal College of Nursing
RHA	Regional Health Authority
SDP	Special Duty Payment
T&GWU	Transport and General Workers' Union
TUC	Trades Unions Congress

Acknowledgements

To the Royal Free Hospital, the Suffragettes' Medical School, and Dame Frances Gardner, for teaching me medicine, to Doctors Sherlock, McIntyre and Bouchier for inspiring me about medicine, to Dr Mike Leibson of Bethnal Green and Doctors Margaret Hayton, Elizabeth Hodgetts and Joanna Shawcross of Bow for employing me to practise it and my partners at Gill Street for their tolerance and good humour.

To Dr Trevor Turner, Mrs Wendy Love, Barry Hassell, Alasdair Hatchett and Jack Robertson for their timely information.

To Ana Ransom, Jenny Uglow and Robert Lacey for their invaluable help in preparing the text.

To Giuseppe Verdi, my companion throughout.

Introduction

A typical day in the life of a Tower Hamlets GP, I suppose. Forty patients seen in a day that starts at nine a.m. and doesn't finish till seven, a dozen referral letters (three trying to get patients moved up outpatient waiting lists and two about housing problems), two delegations of relatives worried about elderly relatives, a near-row with a hospital registrar who will 'look at' an ill patient but can't guarantee admission, one asthma attack averted with a nebuliser and a wrestling match to fit an IUD for a Somalian mother of five who nearly bites through her blouse in fear but who can't understand a word of my attempted reassurance.

Well, at least there were no drunks in the waiting room or manic depressives trying to climb through the carpark window. Down the corridor, the health visitors (30 per cent annual turnover in Tower Hamlets) dash in and out of the local estates supporting isolated mothers and in the afternoon a Community Psychiatric Nurse (with over a decade's training and experience but paid less than a City PA) tries to sort out the psychiatric crises. And back in reception, they're chasing ambulances which haven't turned up and patient names from ninety national origins which are perpetually going astray. We all work under constant pressure with inadequate resources, so it's impossible to get the work in perspective.

And when you watch a blow-dried Tory Minister of Health and Social Security telling you that the NHS has never had it so good, you know you're going a bit crazy. 'We are building a better health service and providing more care for those in need,' boasted the Conservative election manifesto in June 1987. Well, the daily evidence under my professional nose was quite the reverse. Our health district has the highest birth rate in Britain, mainly due to the high fertility of recent immigrants from Bangladesh and Vietnam, an exceptionally high proportion of poorly maintained council housing, record teenage and adult unemployment, and a large percentage of the single elderly. The District Psychologist describes the 'degrees of isolation, depression and child behavioural problems' as 'the worst I have seen anywhere.' Certainly the proportion of young children registered 'at risk' is unusually high. And yet the district has been subjected to a successive loss of revenue and beds which have forced hospital care into fewer and fewer centres which are under siege by the demands of routine clinical work.

The service cuts which the Government require get more horrific each financial year. In 1987/88, the closure of a vital paediatric unit, an Accident and Emergency Department which sees 50,000 East Enders a year, and the loss of 120 acute beds, has only been staved off by an interim saving plan on hospital prescribing devised by the consultants and inconvenient to both patients and GPs. Next year, it looks like total collapse for us and probably another fifty health districts in similar straits.

If the service and the care is better, and, amazingly, in some areas it is, that reflects the determination of the staff and the considerable patience and good-humoured co-operation of their patients rather than central Government policies. These pay lip service to the problems but continue to decant medical money out of the city centres in an 'equalisation process' which in reality robs a bankrupt Peter in an effort to aid a penniless Paul.

The gap I experience between Government rhetoric and my working reality is not particular to an inner city GP. Later in the same week an obstetrician in the neighbourhood health district reports to a medical committee on which I sit that the new Homerton Hospital, which only opened this year, has had to transfer two women in established labour across London. One first-time mother, Valerie Brasington, said, 'After three hours I was transferred to a completely different hospital which I had never seen before. By the time I arrived at the Westminster, contractions were coming every two minutes. I was very tense and upset.' In some ways the new Homerton Hospital is a tremendous improvement on the dank, dingy Salvationist maternity hospital it replaced. The problem is, as community and local medical bodies have warned all along, that it is far too small: instead of the needed increase in maternity beds, the newly opened hospital has twenty-two fewer beds than the units it replaced. And Part 2 of the project, the promise on which the closures were sold, has now been mysteriously cancelled. Meanwhile a bed, a midwife and time to recover from labour can no longer be guaranteed in one of the most recently opened hospitals in Britain. Patient 'turnover' (the statistic so beloved of government health statisticians) is so high and job satisfaction so correspondingly low that 33 per cent of midwifery vacancies are unfilled.

And so it goes on. A newly appointed consultant psychiatrist struggling to build community services is, unexpectedly, found relaxing in the local. 'It's crazy,' he says, 'the District Manager has instructed us to reduce our clinical workload. They want to pay us to twiddle our thumbs.' And in the *British Medical Journal* a London renal physician whose kidney ward has just been closed, temporarily-but-probably-for-good, reflects on the destinations of his demoralised nurses (two to the private sector, two emigrating) and his own changed life: 'I have adapted to less work, spend less time in the hospital, am often home by six p.m., and read an increasing number of novels.' As for British researchers, who once led the world in medical advances, morale is exceptionally low: the most honourable advice a teaching hospital consultant can now give an aspiring Crick or Fleming is 'emigrate'. And on television I watch nurses on salaries which are a monthly insult painfully deciding to leave the RCN and join the magnificent 3 February protest strike because, as one said, 'We've tried petitions, marches and protests and they just don't take a bit of notice.'

This book comes out of such experiences. It has been written – sometimes in anger, sometimes in sorrow – in the gaps between my full-time work as an East London GP. It is an attempt to unravel just what is happening to our health service and to explain the implications to the public who rely on it. It is also an attempt to restate the socialist case for comprehensive and democratic health care. And in the process it is an attack on the public spending cuts which, in the late eighties, threaten the existence of the NHS.

This is not an easy time to advance principles about the health service, but we should not forget that such a service would never have come about if those principles had not existed in the minds of tens of thousands of people. 'The party's over,' say the new realists. 'We will simply have to lower our sights.' 'It makes the best of a bad job,' says the administrator about his plan. It reminds me of the Brecht poem: 'Those who eat their full, speak to the hungry about the wonderful times to come. Those who lead the country into the abyss, call ruling too difficult for ordinary men.' But the administrators who will carry out the gutting, and the Government which instructs them, say, as they stride into the abyss, that the public does not understand the issues. In the face of their 'realism', one starts to wonder if the nurses, doctors, laundry workers and local people who protest really are unhinged extremists?

I think not. And I think that those ordinary people who have resisted the closures will eventually be seen as wise and honourable, just as we now see the unpopular and isolated pioneers of public health measures as the clearsighted ones. 'No Government,' wrote Aneurin Bevan, 'that attempts to destroy the NHS can hope to command the support of the British people.' I hope he was right.

The first part of this book seeks to sketch out the origins of the public health service and to show how every advance has come through a productive conflict between the iron laws of finance and the social needs of people.

In the second half of the book, I have tried to give a sense of the forces the NHS has been up against since its foundation, and the implications if its present decline is not reversed. We tend to see economic depression in images of the past, of Jarrow and hunger marchers, not noticing the suffering under our noses, obscured by the television commercials and party political broadcasts. The social scientists have yet to measure the statistics of misery, but the cold who have their meters cut off, the sick in search of a hospital, the jobless school leavers, the claimants who endure insulting rules, endless waiting and humiliating cross-questioning – the human statistics – know what is happening.

I had to write this book because I do care what happens to the NHS, and I do not want to see its idealism squandered by Treasury accountants. I am an Attlee child, part of the generation shaped by Beveridge and Bevan; I got the chance to train as a doctor because of postwar educational reform and the grammar schools; I survived childhood illness in NHS hospitals; I know what even those quite modest reforms have meant to the quality of people's lives, their health and their human development. I cannot sit quietly by while the health service is dismantled before my eyes, while children leave school with no future.

After being involved in political campaigning for years, you become a little numbed, even to your own arguments. So it was almost with surprise that I realised quite how much I cared about the future of the NHS. I was in a hill-top chapel, high over the slums of Palermo, which has been ravaged by several polio epidemics. Inside the chapel was the Sicilian alternative to a health service. They relied on the power of prayer. The statue of Saint Theresa was festooned with the limbs of plastic dolls, each one symbolising the withered part of a loved one. Outside the chapel stall-owners sold tawdry mascots and religious paraphernalia. In reality, the prayers did nothing except enrich the priests on the hill, while the polio victims begged, stole or died in the alleys below. Turning to my airmail copy of the *Guardian* for a breath of liberalism, I read a news item: 'A facelift worth £5,000 carried out by a top Harley Street surgeon is top prize in a raffle for high society guests at a special ball in the Dorchester Hotel.' Both the scenes outside the chapel and the newspaper article were examples of the barbarism of societies where good health is not a right but a prize in some unearthly lottery, societies where good health is unequal because power and wealth are distributed unequally.

I, too, had had polio, in the 1956 epidemic. Through the NHS I spent five years having a series of reconstructive operations which largely cured the crippling effect of the disease. Over those painful five years I graduated from wheelchair and callipers to my first pair of shop-bought shoes. My parents could never have afforded that surgery in a private health service, an insurance-based system would never cover it, and I am doubtful about Saint Theresa. The present cuts threaten exactly that kind of surgery which ought to be available on the NHS without question, but which can be 'done without'. John Sherrard, the consultant orthopaedic surgeon at Sheffield Children's Hospital, has stated that because of staff shortages in the Sheffield area 'Spastic children will have their hips go out of date so that they will never be able to walk, children who remain ugly through curvature of the spine will get progressively worse and look twice as ugly, and others cannot go to school because they cannot wear shoes.' The same goes, only more so, for the premature babies who can't get their neonatal cots, the deteriorating renal patient hanging on for a transplant and the old lady hobbling in pain for two and a half years on the hip replacement waiting list.

My own life, as much as my politics, tells me that the level of compassion with which a society treats its sick and crippled, its old and its feeble-minded, is the real measure of that society's level of civilisation. It tells me that we need a society centred around good health rather than a health service snuffling after disease like a baffled bloodhound. It tells me not that the NHS has failed, but that it has not been given a real chance. This book will have been worth writing if it convinces more people that the health service is something worth fighting for. And that, in fighting for it, we may glimpse our potential to create a society run on a different and better basis.

1

The Early Hospitals

Only 130 years ago, Sir John Simon, perhaps the nineteenth century's most shrewd, eminent and unpopular physician, described the state of medical knowledge as scarcely beyond 'nurses' gossip and sick men's fancies and the crude compilations of a blundering empiricism.' Doctors were still examined on their knowledge of Latin rather than anatomy, and judged more by their attire than their dedication. The clinical thermometer and the stethoscope were still novelties, and the microscope's use was not fully accepted. Medicine was poised on the brink of a scientific breakthrough, but much was still shrouded in superstition. Hospitals, far from offering succour to the sick, were dreaded. 'The first requirement in a hospital,' wrote Florence Nightingale, 'is that it should do the sick no harm,' and on that criterion alone most early hospitals failed.

The rich endured their treatment in their homes, selecting their physicians from the Royal Colleges on the basis of snobbery, nepotism or their man's reputation in the voluntary hospitals, where aspiring doctors would quite literally practise on the poor. The middling classes would be more likely to depend on an apothecary, qualified by a five year apprenticeship in a pharmacy and able to charge for the medicines he supplied but not for medical advice. For the rest there were the quacks, estimated in Lincolnshire in 1864 to outnumber the trained men by a ratio of nine to one.[1]

Women, systematically excluded from the profitable business of doctoring, 'watched' the sick as servants or relatives, assisted with traditional remedies, delivered children, and laid out the dead. Death was so commonplace, disease so mysterious and suffering so natural that illness itself was best explained as the earthly evidence of divine displeasure. In the midst of such ignorance the priest was able to exercise his piety and the quack to extract his pence.

I

In 1823 the first edition of the radically-minded journal the *Lancet* announced:

> We hope the age of 'Mental Delusion' has passed and that mystery and concealment will no longer be encouraged. Indeed we trust that mystery and ignorance will shortly be considered synonymous. Ceremonies and signs have now lost their charm, hieroglyphics and serpents their power to deceive.

But when the *Lancet*'s first editor, Wakley – coroner, MP, scourge of the quacks and critic of the apothecaries – collapsed from exhaustion twenty-nine years later, scientific medicine was still struggling to find its feet. Remedies could be bought or remembered, but when they failed, when there were no relatives to help, when sickness had made them penniless or poverty had made them ill, patients would be forced into institutional medical care – either in the voluntary hospitals or in the workhouses.

Voluntary hospitals

The pioneer hospitals like St Bartholomew's and St Thomas's have their origins in medieval religious charity, but most of the voluntary hospitals were founded by civic or royal initiative in the eighteenth century. By 1800 there were forty such hospitals providing 4000 beds: even allowing for the much smaller population, only one per cent of present-day provision. Although the hospital movement clearly betokened a willingness by the rich to ease the sufferings of the sick poor, it was not without self-interest. Becoming a hospital governor was one of the ways by which the rising merchant could enter the social élite. It enabled entry into an exclusive world of fêtes and bazaars where, in the name of charity, the newly enriched encountered the nobility. Some governors had a direct financial interest in supplying the hospitals, and all subscribers were entitled to nominate prospective patients by providing them with a letter of introduction, as noted in George Eliot's novel *Middlemarch*.

The distinguished doctors who walked the hospital wards with such commotion gave their services without charge. But this honorary service in the public hospitals was a species of advertisement for their private practices, where their clients would include many of the governors themselves. Day-to-day medical supervision would be carried out by their students and juniors. The senior men, having slowly and patiently scaled the heights of professional and public esteem, were understandably reluctant to share the spoils. The teaching element in the voluntary hospitals steadily grew in importance. It became an important source of the senior doctors' incomes, not least from referrals made by ex-pupils once they themselves had qualified. The voluntary hospitals were an ideal supply of human material for teaching and research. The paupers in receipt of charity, by reason of their wretched financial and social standing, could not object to being pinched, pummelled and percussed by the legion of students who walked behind the great physicians. Charity had a way of reducing the recipient to the exact degree it enhanced the donor.

The patients, by imploring a 'ticket' from a subscriber and bribing a steward into the bargain, gained entry into a harsh world. Medical attention was brief and haphazard, depending more on the novelty of the affliction than the severity of the condition. Nurses worked very long hours with no set periods for time off, and traditionally passed the night with help from the gin bottle (although some were undoubtedly more experienced healers than the doctors). The wards were unhygienic and poorly divided, so cross-infection must have been rife. Food was dull and contained little nourishment, and was sometimes itself grubby and infested. Separation of contagious skin and fever patients was uncommon, and they were sometimes refused admission altogether, with the result that those most in need of isolation stayed free to dispense infection. The consultants' desire to impress the world with their curative powers led them to select patients with diseases in which visible improvement was likely to be swiftly registered. This led to an effective bar on the admission of the chronically sick, the old and the very poor, who then, as now, were unpopular among doctors because medical measures alone do not produce dramatic improvements. These people were shuttled to the tender mercies of the workhouses, whose patients exceeded in number the sick in the voluntary hospitals. Their lot was still more miserable.

Workhouse infirmaries

Since Elizabethan days, the Poor Law system had provided rudimentary relief for the poor. Poverty was a constant and, so the rich thought, a necessary presence in most people's lives. Low wages, seasonal work and trade depressions made saving imposs-ible, and death, disease or simply the passing of the years could expose a once diligent worker to the mercies of the parish. The able-bodied artisan only avoided relief by the earnings of children, assistance from friends and loans from traders, and all three were strictly limited. The grim workhouses kept costs to a minimum by confining all the needy in one dwelling, an unsatisfactory arrange-ment for most purposes, but especially so for a hospital. Just as the pinch of the workhouse was thought to inspire the labouring poor to work, so the starkness of medical care was expected to reveal impostors or provide an appropriate place to die for those whose illness proved genuine but who lacked strength to work. 'Our intention,' said one Assistant Commissioner, 'is to make the workhouse as like prison as possible,' and another: 'Our object . . . is to establish a discipline so severe and repulsive as to make them a terror to the poor and prevent them from entering.'[2] This deliber-ate punishment of the poor and sick was intensified as a result of the 1832–4 Poor Law Commissioners' Report and the legislation it prompted. Chadwick's skilfully biased report succeeded in estab-lishing the principle of 'less eligibility'. Poor relief was to be made deliberately unpleasant, should only be provided within work-houses, and was to be consciously cruel, tight-fisted and humiliat-ing. The intention was to separate the work-shy from the genuinely destitute by cutting off all 'outdoor' relief to the able-bodied in temporary need.

'Less eligible'

The social philosophy behind this sadism was that poverty and unemployment were healthy and natural events which strength-ened the moral fibre. Being poor was due to moral defects: a dislike of labour or a proclivity for strong drink. Unchecked pauperism might lead to desperate uprisings against authority, or, worse, infect the honest working man with dissent. As the always canny Edwin Chadwick put it, 'If a Chartist millennium is to be averted, the governing classes must free the governed from the sharp spur of their misery by improving the physical conditions of their lives.'[3]

Strictly speaking, the sick were excluded from the 'less eligible' test and were entitled to be treated at home. Nevertheless, by 1861 a total of 50,000 were under the care of workhouse medical officers.

The medical officers were selected mainly on their willingness to accept very low wages. They were expected to provide medicines out of their tiny salaries, which guaranteed parsimony in prescribing. Trained staff were scanty. Nursing was often carried out on a cost-free basis by the paupers themselves. The doctors were inferior in rank and status to the workhouse masters, whose overriding aim was to keep costs to a minimum, and who were more anxious to prevent imagined abuse than to cure the poor. The beadle, and *then* the doctor, examined the sick. The Poor Law service accommodated the bulk of sick children, mental cases, skin conditions, epileptics, diabetics, patients infected with tuberculosis, syphilis and scarlet fever, and the thousands of undiagnosed and probably unexamined chronically sick.

But although it was the Poor Law doctors who were most directly in contact with the mass of medical suffering, they were least able to protest about their conditions. If they were to escape from these low medical standards, they had best avoid a quarrel. In the meantime they had to accept that they were inferior doctors for the inferior classes. The rod was, quite literally, shaken over nurses who spoke up for their patients.

By the middle of the nineteenth century the two hospital services stood side by side: for the lucky and selected few in London and the big cities there were splendid voluntary or teaching hospitals (provided, of course, that their illness suited the doctor's interests); but the workhouse infirmaries and the Poor Law officers were ignored as long as their burden on the taxpayer was kept to an absolute minimum.

Hospital reform

Late Victorian England saw a flurry of hospital reform, building and improvement. The sheer pressure of medical need in cities thrown up so rapidly, more like standing camps than planned towns, the daily injuries inflicted by the factory system, and the growing numbers of orphans, widows, deserted wives and old people without the traditional support from their relatives, combined to demand more organised medical care. Systematic investigation of the exact state of the poor, pioneered by Booth and

Rowntree, revealed the grim reality of suffering which penetrated even the ignorant self-satisfaction of the Victorian middle class. The findings of the pioneer social investigators became a flood as they were joined by well-intentioned laymen who made it their business to find out about and to improve the real conditions of the sick and poor.

War, as always, provided its macabre exposure of the limitations of medicine: Florence Nightingale, who witnessed at first hand the collapse at Sebastopol in the Crimean War, proposed an almost military reform of nursing. She set about the reorganisation of everything from nursing education to hospital architecture, dispensing especially telling criticism of the sanitary arrangements within wards. The successive outbreaks of infectious fevers – the urban epidemics – especially the water-borne dysentery carried by the cholera *vibrio* which had the democratic tendency to afflict all classes equally, spurred the building of large isolation hospitals as well as the reforms of the water supply, public drainage and sewerage systems, and slum housing carried out by Sir John Simon in London, Percival and Ferrier in Manchester and Howard in Liverpool. But the patients and the Poor Law doctors themselves probably did most to dent the complacency of Parliament and the meanness of the Guardians, which, though periodically aroused by the writings of Dickens or the reports of Chadwick, tended to reassert itself when finance rather than sympathy was demanded. The poor, especially the Northern textile workers, who flatly refused to be punished by imprisonment in the workhouse during the regular trade depressions, had always hated the 'Bastilles', as they had dubbed them. In Bradford in 1837 and in Dewsbury and Todmorden in 1838, town-wide risings greeted the new Poor Law. And in the industrial areas workers' protests were abetted by the overseers, vestrymen and even magistrates themselves who, on principle, disliked any central direction. Although the political demands of working class radical bodies did not seem to raise the problem of their sick fellows, the increasingly organised strength and impatience of workers lent urgency to efforts at reform.

Workhouse doctors

The next generation of workhouse doctors, their status enhanced by the 1858 Act which put medical qualification and registration on a respectable footing, felt emboldened to take a stand against their exploitation by the Boards of Guardians and the bullying of the masters, and to speak up for their abused patients. In 1866 Dr Rogers formed the Poor Law Medical Officers' Association, and the *Lancet* lent its support to a national campaign for improved treatment of sick paupers with its investigation and exposure of the state of sick-wards in a number of London workhouses in 1865. With even more courage, nurses joined the protest. Joan Bateman complained about the Paddington workhouse and Matilda Beeton went further in showing how the officials in Rotherhithe had deliberately, and easily, deceived the inspectors.

The masters could sneer at ladies like Mrs Twining of the Workhouse Visiting Society, with their 'many imaginary griev-ances', who 'sometimes go to the length of bestowing unmerited tea or even indigestible lozenges and Puseyite tracts upon our protegees'.[4]

They could not, however, laugh off so easily the *Lancet*'s 'soberly sensational' findings and uncompromising conclusions:

> Patch up the present system as we may, it will still continue to be a scandal and a reproach . . . The State hospitals are in the workhouse wards. They are closed against observation, they pay no heed to public opinion, they pay no toll to science. They are under the government of men profoundly ignorant of hospital rules.[5]

Quite how far medical standards had risen by the end of the nineteenth century is hard to gauge. The authorities were less hostile to public health measures and were beginning to see state provision of basic health needs as a necessary evil, not out of any great compassion, but in the overall interests of effective produc-tion, competition and warfare. The charitable bodies, having themselves discovered the overwhelming weight of suffering, were despairing of remedying it themselves by stern advice and thin gruel alone. As the extent of poverty (a third of all Londoners were under Booth's poverty line in the 1890s) was documented in irrefutable detail, the sheer want could no longer be dismissed as unrepresentative or attributed to a deliberate unwillingness to work. But awareness of and charitable endeavour directed at the poverty of its employees did not alter the harshness of the factory system. In the last analysis low wages, long hours and unsafe working conditions, made worse by overcrowded housing and poor diet, were the fundamental cause of much ill health.

The hospital service was clearly improving, especially in the London voluntary hospitals, where antisepsis transformed the possibilities of surgery. The traditional and well-justified fear of hospitals was now tempered with a respect for the new scientific knowledge possessed somewhere within their portals. Hospitals were now more than a last resort. Evidence of the new esteem in which they were held was the opening of wards to take fee-paying middle class customers. They were elaborately screened (with thick canopies) from the eyes of their social inferiors. Great specialisation within medicine, as well as more commercial considerations, led to the establishment of a flush of specialist hospitals. The bigger hospitals provided outpatient facilities at which the poor queued for treatment. There were also dispensing clinics for those who could not afford their own practitioner, although treatment was inevitably inadequate.

General practitioners

General practitioners dispensed their medicine on the same basis as any other retail trade, set whatever fees the market could take, in direct competition with each other. In a rich district a doctor lived in style, with silk top hat, gold-headed cane and carriage. Practices with an established clientele were bought and sold, for wealthy patients, especially when chronically ill, were business assets. But many doctors were very poor and those in working class areas worked a great deal harder for very little financial return. Often young doctors without social standing or wealthy backers were exploited by the doctor who owned the practice or by the paternalistic employers or charities who retained their services. Even then, medical practitioners were not summoned lightly and illness was left until it proved serious, and relatively few of the advances in medical science had direct application in general practice yet. Minor ailments were accepted and many major ones doused with patent medicines and pain-killing draughts of opium-based cordials.

Some elementary health education was carried out in emphatic style; Robert Roberts remembers:

One local doctor whenever he was called upon by our humbler neighbours with stomach troubles would demand the family frying pan, then
go outside and smash it against a wall; a gesture which compelled
the housewife to borrow another from next door until she could
afford to buy another. She made no protest at the act; a doctor was a
demi-god.[6]

In the coalmining areas of the North, where private practice was
never workable, the 'club' system, an important antecedent to the
NHS and an influence on Aneurin Bevan, flourished. Here working
men banded together to arrange the hiring of a doctor, and
sometimes the building of his premises or a cottage hospital, by a
levy on wages; they had therefore an organised say in the kind
of medicine they received. This arrangement had elements of
workers' local initiative and even control which have subsequently
been surrendered. But the quality of care under the club system
was limited by the difficulty of gaining access to specialist opinion;
a referral usually meant a trek to London with cash and cap in
hand. Dr Danny Abse recalls being asked by a Welsh miner, 'You
from Harley Street, are you?', when he attempted to use a stethoscope as late as the 1930s.[7]

Far from welcoming the steady expansion of hospital inpatient
and clinic care, general practitioners violently resented it. Reform
of the 'abuses' of free hospital care became a burning issue; the GPs
disliked the clinics because they were providing more and more
medical care to people who, they felt, ought to pay (although they
would have disliked the hospitals still more had they charged).
They wanted consultants to be genuine specialists and to accept
patients only by referral. There was talk of gentlemen with car-
riages and private incomes spotted in hospital queues and of the
sick journeying from hospital to hospital.

The Association of General Practitioners was formed with the
aim of restricting consultants to consultation in the strict sense:
'The whole struggle between the general practitioner and the
consultant is one of bread,' wrote Dr Rentoul, a militant GP.
Financial self-interest divided the profession, put hospital and
community medicine at loggerheads and ruled out free medicine,
even though the more farsighted practitioners, especially those in
most direct contact with the poor, could see the need for such a
system.

The failure of Poor Law hospital reform

At the turn of the century, even though a brisk expansion of welfare services by the local authorities was in sight, the public provision of medicine was still third class and the treatment of those rejected by the teaching hospitals and out of financial reach of private doctoring – those in most medical need – was haphazard and often cruel. The system of using pauper nurses under the incompetent supervision of the wives of the Masters persisted because of its cheapness. Trained nurses willing to endure the very long hours and cramped quarters, and prepared to suffer the petty despotism of the Masters, could not bear to see their skills wither from want of use or be lost on patients deemed chronic or incurable by the system. As Beatrice Webb, the Fabian social reformer, pointed out about the Poor Law doctors, 'It breaks the spirit of a man who cares anything at all about his professional work to have to go on year after year merely pretending to deal with cases which have come to him only when destitution has set in.'[8] One nurse resigned because of the 'utter uselessness of nurses fighting for proper administration under untrained management . . . we stand so often entirely unsupported.'

So the scandals, or those that could not be covered up, persisted. In 1890, the sick-wards of the Bethnal Green workhouse were described by inquiring doctors as 'a crying and a notorious evil'. The workhouse medical officer described how he had to rely on the assistance of a friendly local GP to do the amputations which were still done 'underhanded', as it 'takes three men to get a leg off properly' – 590 sick paupers were crowded into wards for 495 patients, cared for by eleven nurses, only two of whom had had hospital training. On the national scale, the Webbs estimated in 1907 that the 10,000 patients in country workhouses were 'looked after' by only 654 nurses and 105 practitioners.[9]

Doctors remained poorly paid and their visits so brief that they must have been confined to a cursory look at those new patients who the nurses could persuade them were worth examining. An inspector who studied the amount of time given to workhouse duties reported of one that 'frequently he has been only in the workhouse for a few minutes' and that he had rarely been there for half an hour. Drugs were still paid for out of the doctor's own salary; this not only ruled out new or expensive drugs but even such

plus ça change

staples as quinine and digitalis if the doctor was not to end up out of pocket. Another inspector reported in 1893 that, in the workhouse hospitals, 'operations were performed where private patients would undoubtedly have anaesthetics, whereas the paupers have to suffer without them.' It was as if the poor did not feel pain so much. In the words of Dickens's upper-class gentleman, Steerforth, in *Great Expectations*, 'Why there is a pretty wide separation between them and us. They are not to be expected to be as sensitive as we are . . . they have not such fine natures and they may be thankful that, like their coarse rough skins, they are not easily wounded.'

In the workhouses the old principle of 'less eligibility' was firmly enforced; all poor relief, including that for the sick, had to be made less pleasant than even the harshest means of living outside the workhouse, and that was dismal indeed. The excuse was, as always, the prevention of fraud and the encouragement of thrift. Poverty was still attributed to fraud, indolence and idleness. It was most important, wrote Inspector Longley, that:

> the stamp of pauperism is plainly marked upon all relief given . . . the words 'Dispensary' and 'Infirmary' should never be used in forms, advertisements or addresses without the prefix 'Pauper' or 'Poor Law' or 'Workhouse', which should indeed appear as far as possible in every document supplied by Guardians to those relieved by them.[10]

The shadow of the workhouse was always present in working class life, and because there was still no public provision by right for the old or the widowed, a family prosperous at one moment could be plummeted into the deliberate miseries of the workhouse the next. In 1895, the mother of Charlie Chaplin lost her actor husband and the grim sequence commenced:

> like sand in an hourglass, our finances ran out, and hard times again pursued us . . . Instalment payments were behind, consequently Mother's sewing machine was taken away . . . There was no alternative, she was burdened with two children, and in poor health; and so she decided that the three of us should enter the Lambeth workhouse . . . there we were made to separate, Mother going in one direction to the women's ward and we in another to the children's. How well I remember the poignant sadness of the first visiting day; the shock of seeing Mother entering the visiting room garbed in workhouse clothes. How forlorn and embarrassed she looked! In one week she had aged and grown thin.[11]

Investigation at last

To many of the Victorian middle class, welfare was immoral. The poor had only themselves to blame, and to aid them in their distress was to encourage their idleness and to undermine their moral fibre. But the same class was also devoted to orderly planning and the greatest good for the greatest number (at the minimum cost, of course). The two principles came more and more openly into conflict as the *laissez-faire* approach to welfare collapsed under the sheer weight of distress caused by the very factory system which had created the wealth of Britain. The 'defenders of the filth' could bitterly deny any connection between dirt and disease, eulogise the open sewers and poisoned water as bracing and argue that dust had a positively beneficial effect on the lungs. But disease was a great leveller and no respecter of front parlours.

It was easy for the more logical to argue that the state, acting in the general interest, needed new powers, including the power, as Simon put it, 'of doing away with that form of liberty to which some communities cling, the sacred liberty to poison unto death not only themselves but their neighbours.' In the same way, the deliberately low standards of the public hospitals, the reduction of the sick to the status of the poor and the sheer complexity of parallel sources of medical care were an affront to logic. The utter failure of the treatment of tuberculosis, the very poor diet and health standards revealed by education authorities' surveys and the shocking standard of physique found among army recruits made no economic or military sense. 'How can we get an efficient army out of the stunted, anaemic, demoralised denizens of the slum basements of our great cities?' asked the Earl of Rosebery. Imperialism required 'national efficiency', and that required a break with old official Liberalism. Modern industrialists, too, saw the need for a fitter and more skilful labour force, even for collaboration with, rather than resistance to, union organisation.

In 1905 a Royal Commission set to work to report on the state of the Poor Law in an attempt to resolve some of these conflicts. The stern defenders of the 1834 spirit argued that the sick should be clearly differentiated from the poor so as to better oppress the unemployed, who, now lacking even the excuse of illness, could be put to suffer at flint-crushing and cross-cut sawing. The radicals on the Commission wanted the breaking up of the Poor Law into various separate welfare schemes for the old, the unemployed and the unhealthy, administered by the local authorities and available free to all.

Both sides agreed that moral deterrence alone was inadequate. Old-age pensions, which were introduced while the Commission sat, were approved of, and it was recommended that free hospital service should be rationalised and extended, and children with poverty-stricken or neglectful parents should be cared for publicly. Wards for the sick were to be finally separated from the workhouses and the ill diverted more often to the outpatient dispensaries. The emphasis was still on thrift and grudging aid, carefully tied to a record of past diligence. But the Commission was firmly divided over the extent of preventive welfare services for the poor, with the Webbs drafting a forceful minority report. And this split provided an official excuse for inaction. The workhouse hospitals were at an impasse, unable to go back to the deterrent pattern but unable to move forward to a national preventative service. The Webbs' blueprint for a State Medical Service, though logically sound, challenged too many vested interests.

Such a service required the loss of the voluntary hospitals' jealously-guarded independent status, and the organisation of the sick clubs and the doctors themselves by public authorities was still anathema, although already glimpsed as a possible solution by some of the more visionary doctors.

National Insurance

It was less lofty motives which had led Lloyd George to introduce National Insurance. 'I hope our competition with Germany will not be in armaments alone,' he boasted as he eyed the social benefits of the insurance scheme introduced by his European arch-rivals. His 1911 Act established a compulsory contribution towards health which would provide the wage-earner with the right of free consultation with a general practitioner who prescribed free drugs, and entitlement to sickness benefit when absent from work through illness. 'The Panel' and 'The Stamp' were born; it is from 1911 that the phrase 'getting your cards' stems, referring to the form on which the employer's contribution was affixed. The scheme faced the formidable vested interests of the private health insurance companies with whom, increasingly, the skilled artisan had contributed, as well as the doctors who were initially fiercely opposed to the Bill, reacting, as is often the case, with something little short of hysteria when any changes to their own profession were proposed. In fact, it was a splendidly convenient scheme. It provided the appearance of an alternative to a national health service, but by collaborating with, rather than replacing, the insurance giants. It was a method of replacing the Poor Law with very modest Treasury expenditure.

Although new social service for the working class might appear, if you listened to the doctors, a massive act of generosity, it was in fact paid for by that class, administered by the insurance companies (under new names), and produced a very sharp increase in income for most of the doctors who worked with the panel scheme. They could now supplement their private fee-paying work with the government's *per capita* payment for treating panel patients. As the doctor's maid puts it daintily in Arnold Bennett's *Elsie and the Child*: 'You had two voices, one for "them" and their friends and the private patients and another for Joe and the tradesmen and panel patients.'

Like Bevan, Lloyd George made much of his battles with the profession during what he called 'the wrangle in the sickroom':

> I had two hours discussion with the medical men themselves the other day. I don't think there has been anything like it since the day when Daniel went into the lions' den. I was on the dissecting table for two hours but I can assure you that they treated me with the same courtesy as the lions treated my illustrious predecessor.

And the Welsh wizard was to encounter the persistent ire of serving girls sent by their mistresses, furious about the effect that licking the employers' 3d stamp each week would have on both their fair lips and their pockets. But it is clear that even Bevan realised the conservative nature of the 1911 Bill. He memoed a civil servant in 1911:

> Insurance necessary temporary expedient. At no distant date hope State will acknowledge full responsibility in the matter of making provision for sickness, breakdown and unemployment. It really does so now, through Poor Law, but the conditions under which this system has hitherto worked have been so harsh and humiliating that working class pride revolts at accepting so degrading and doubtful a boon.

The limitations

The Lloyd George scheme was so full of expectations and limitations that, inevitably, it leaked. Only wage-earners were eligible, and venereal and alcohol-related diseases were specifically excluded, so that only about 30 per cent of the population benefited directly. It did not cover those whose general health really was bad, the wives and children of the poor and unemployed. There was no provision for hospitalisation, for which many workers continued to insure privately or by means of subscription to a voluntary hospital; nor were X-ray examination, physiotherapy or after-care nursing provided. Many drugs were excluded and there was no provision for dental care, artificial limbs, specialist eye-care or an optical service. Rather than being replaced by the Act, the insurance companies became the administrative agents for it. Because hospital and specialist care was untouched by the scheme, they were pressed into ever-worsening financial straits. The approved societies had the option to refuse cases, and protected their coffers by trying to eliminate those with known health risks.

The emphasis was still on a bare minimum coverage, the system aiming to minimise hardship during acute illness rather than forestall it. Cash benefit during illness was low. Insurance, rather than a national health service, was renewed; the companies' collectors now had access to homes to which they could market services not covered by the 1911 Act. A canvasser collecting sickness benefit for an ill patient might, after expressing his sympathies in the sick-room, sell a burial policy in the kitchen. The Government had given a great fillip to the underwriters.

Local action

Probably more important was the growing ability of local authorities to provide welfare services. School meals and medical inspection were begun, and revealed children stunted before they were ten, strangers to fresh milk and seeing meat but once a week. Between 1900 and 1913 local authority spending almost doubled. Working class radicals became more assertive, stating for the first time that free medicine and good health ought to be possessed by every citizen, by right and not for administrative convenience or to provide sturdy cannon-fodder.

In East London, Sylvia Pankhurst turned her back on the campaign for the vote and the House of Commons, 'where courage evaporates like a bubble', and organised working women and wives to arrange their own clinics, crèches and restaurants. The East London Federation of Suffragettes converted a pub into what must have been one of the first maternity centres anywhere and renamed it 'The Mother's Arms'. From there a resident nurse ran a string of mother and baby clinics, dispensed cheap maternity foods and health, sex education and hygiene talks; and in the same part of London in 1921, George Lansbury and the Labour Councillors of Poplar were imprisoned in Brixton Gaol rather than agreeing to cut down on local relief as the Tory-controlled London County Council was insisting.

Lansbury argued the socialist case for welfare: that those who had wealth ought to support those who did not. Why should working class areas, which bore the brunt of unemployment, shoulder that burden themselves when middle class residences, with more wealth, did not have any unemployed to maintain? He bellowed his case from the basement cell of his gaol to the crowds who would march across from East London every night, and, conducted by a striking policeman, serenade the imprisoned councillors in their dungeons. Poplar Council's refusal to make economies in the face of basic human need won the support of the people of Bethnal Green, who voted to follow their lead, with Stepney and Battersea not far behind. 'Poplarism' (i.e. local councils going on strike against national cuts) spread quickly. The Government backed down and then introduced a Bill that equalised rate burdens, increased unemployment benefits and administered them nationally. The patients, the poor and the unemployed were coming out of the shadows of gloom and guilt to which they had been consigned as firmly as in the workhouse. They were starting to ask for their rights.

2

The Coming of National Health

By the First World War there was the beginnings of a public medical service, even if it was operated by private medical practitioners and the insurance companies. But it was strictly limited to the (generally male) wage-earners, and access to a second opinion or specialist hospital treatment was uneven, still dependent on financial rather than medical circumstances. GPs still earned the bulk of their income from fees supplemented by part-time work for the health authorities. The voluntary hospitals' standards were improving steadily, although the attendance of the 'honorary' consultants who nominally ran them was sporadic. Over half a million, mainly the aged and chronic sick, still languished in Poor Law beds, with no fewer than 35,864 in general mixed workhouses as late as 1928. Relations between practitioner and hospital had improved, although there was still much scaremongering about GPs 'with rusty scalpels and distorted forceps running about crying out "Who can I try my skill on?"' Unhappily, the state scheme was still grafted on to a much older pattern of medical private enterprise, self-help, charity and Poor Law cruelty.

The haphazard national distribution and the maze of clubs, dispensaries, hospitals and private contracts resulted in a divided national hospital service and two very different standards of health care, clearly revealed by the First World War. Although some sort of state medical service was eventually provided on the front line, it differed widely according to the class of the injured, with officers, for example, still entitled to a Red Cross grant to pay their servants' wages during convalescence in Harrogate or on the Riviera, while private soldiers frequently died without medical aid. Civilians also suffered badly, with the tuberculosis rate in particular increasing sharply during the war.

The new dawn

Elaborate promises were made about the 'new dawn' at the end of
the First World War. Lloyd George promised not only 'a land fit
for heroes' but also the implementation of the McLean Report on
public health and the establishment of a Ministry of Health.

For two years trade boomed, wages held up at wartime levels,
and a new confidence won at the workplace by the syndicalist and
socialist trade unionists during the war seemed to press home an
advantage. Lloyd George and the Coalition pledged 'all services
relating to the care and treatment of the sick and infirm shall not be
administered as part of the Poor Law but should be a part of the
general health services of this country.' The Labour Party called
for the reconstruction 'not of this or that piece of social machinery,
but of society itself,' calling for the state to assume responsibility
for a minimum level of health care with social services paid for by
progressive taxation and administered by local authorities.

Old problems

Then a massive slump sent unemployment soaring. By the end of
1921 there were nearly two million unemployed. The National
Insurance dyke collapsed under the strain: how could a contribu-
tory scheme hold up when people were so seldom in work? The
dole, money over and above the strict level paid in contributions,
was only given in certain cases. In 1927, after the crushing of the
General Strike, even the dole was withheld if the official suspected
that the applicant was 'not genuinely seeking work', whether or not
there was any to be found. Then, finally, a family means test was
introduced. The new dawn had been brief, the old abuses and the
old stupidities were back.

The 'hungry thirties'

The 'hungry thirties' started here, in the mid-1920s: hunger for
basic human needs, for protein, for warm clothes, for dry homes,
was already stunting physiques and dragging standards of health
down. Whatever the quality of health provision, chronic poor diet
among those out of work weakened their resistance to tuberculosis,
allowed the common cold develop to epidemic proportions, and

produced sickly infants and stillborn babies. Mental depression was so common it was not even diagnosed. The medical needs for life itself were the subject of a propaganda battle. The British Medical Association produced a specimen diet as a basis for assessing the needs of the unemployed, which embarrassingly proved to be rather worse than that provided by the Scottish prison authorities to their inmates. Even so, it was estimated that one person in five lived near or below that meagre margin.

The Ministry's evidence was clearly biased. They managed to deny 'widespread manifestation of impaired health which could be attributed to insufficient nourishment' within miles of an area in the Rhondda where Lady Williams's charitable food distribution programme had reduced maternal mortality by 75 per cent. Geographical differences amplified class factors. In the old industrial areas in Wales and the North-east, entire populations were without work, while employed workers in the South improved their standards of life despite the Depression and the conditions of the rural poor probably stayed fairly constant. No one could deny the connection between class and illness. To take the single most fundamental index, the infant death rate, in 1935 it was forty-two per thousand per live births in the Home Counties, sixty-three in Glamorgan, seventy-six in Durham, seventy-seven in Scotland, ninety-two in Sunderland and 114 in Jarrow. Medical examination was becoming more widespread and more devastating in its findings. The results of the two and a half million examinations of young men completed in the last year of the First World War showed that of every nine men, only three were fit and healthy and

'two were on a definitely infirm plane of health and strength, whether from some disability or failure in development; three were incapable of undergoing more than a very moderate degree of physical exertion, and could almost (in view of their age) be described as physical wrecks; and the remaining man was a chronic invalid with a precarious hold on life.'[2]

9 per cent of schoolchildren's eyes had defects, and dental standards were appalling, a full set of teeth being a rarity in working class mouths. People only saw a dentist if pain became intolerable, and then for extractions only. Dr McGonigle found that 83 per cent of children examined in County Durham were rickety, and although the official figure was as low as 1.2 per cent,

McGonigle's higher figure was supported by a 1937 survey which found only 12 per cent of 1,638 children free from rickets, with two-thirds showing serious signs of disease. Another survey found alterations in the pelvic bones of mothers due to diet deficiency in 40 per cent of women attending the antenatal centre. Midwives, although popular because closer to the real lives of poor mothers, lacked rudimentary facilities, knew little about antisepsis and were often paid in kind. The official enquiry into the rising maternal death rate estimated that half the deaths in pregnancy were directly preventable. The Workers' Birth Control Group campaigned in the Labour Party for extension of maternity benefits with the slogan: 'It's four times as dangerous to bear a child as to go down a mine.' Against such a stark background, the piecemeal improvements in hospital care, with the Poor Law hospitals finally brought under the local authorities in 1929 and the growing integration of the voluntary hospitals, was of little avail as long as general practice remained purely palliative, with GPs operating as private entrepreneurs and still in informal competition with the hospitals. Whooping cough, for example, for which a vaccine existed, still claimed over 200 deaths in the worst years because there was no machinery for mass immunisation.

Aneurin Bevan

It was in this stark world that Aneurin Bevan, the architect of the National Health Service, grew up. He shaped his political ideas against the outline of the 'hungry thirties', in which the hideous townships, broken families and silent steelworks mocked the claims of capitalist economics. He saw Parliament as 'a public mourner for private economic crimes' and the Tories as a political party whose task was 'to beguile democracy into voting wealth back to power each election'. He knew at first hand the human suffering caused by a welfare system based on organised stinginess, where the price of lives was merely an item in the cost of things and there were no aims that could not be accounted for on a balance-sheet. The texture of his life related all of his ideas to class. The central question was: where does power lie, and how can it be obtained by the workers?

He knew the medical traditions of the South Wales miners whose lungs, eyes and limbs suffered in the pits, and who formed working men's clubs to choose and supervise their own doctors in hospitals owned by the community. He came from a world where collective action to organise society and active trade union involvement in health was assumed. His father, who died in his arms of pneumoconiosis, was a founder member of the Tredegar Working Men's Medical Aid Society. Bevan saw health as a field in which individual commercialism ran counter to most social values. To him it was illogical as well as unfair to prevent illness by private effort, or to make access to medical care dependent on the ability to pay. Illness was above all a field in which 'poverty should not be a disability' and, equally important, 'wealth not an advantage'. He wrote that 'A free health service is a triumphant example of the superiority of collective action and public initiative applied to a segment of society where commercial principles are seen at their worst.' Those who argued that a free service rather than a fee service would invite abuse were prejudging the issue. What was more likely was an initial rush of demand deriving from past neglect. In the future, Bevan shrewdly predicted, abuse was much more likely to arise where private commercial interests overlapped with the national service.

The Second World War

The need for reform was widely accepted, although the doctors and Lord Beveridge were more concerned with the efficiency of the system than with the desires of the people it served. The Second World War highlighted the unevenness of hospital standards and the rudimentary state of the pathology, blood-transfusion and ambulance services. Dispersed specialists insisted on the upgrading of the standards and services they discovered in hospitals they would never otherwise have visited. Doctors drafted into the army found that the salaried service, far from destroying their professional identity, enhanced their status and, for most of them, their standard of living. A national survey of hospitals, a medical Domesday Book, was at last carried out. The Emergency Medical Service accustomed all those in the health service to a degree of centralisation, state control and obedience which the war effort as a whole demanded.

Even before the war specialist opinion had been in favour of an extension of the Health Insurance provisions, and an influential report by the Political and Economic Planning Group in 1937 had found that 'a substantial part of the annual cost of ill health is due to delay in treatment. This delay is largely accounted for by the fact that doctors and dental fees are an expense people are loth to incur.' Churchill himself acknowledged 'that disease must be attacked in the same way that a fire engine will give its full assistance to the humble cottage as readily as it will give it to the most important mansion.' The Coalition Government had already drawn up welfare plans drawing on the rationalisations and changes in gear made during the war.

Another new dawn

The 1945 election result, an unexpected and overwhelming triumph for Labour, showed that the people who had fought and suffered the war were ungrateful to the Tory who had directed it, and were in a radical mood.

Bonfires were lit in the streets and, as Michael Foot has put it, 'no socialist who saw it will forget the blissful dawn of July 1945.' The People's War had, it seemed, led to a People's Peace. The defeats and humiliations that followed the First World War – the General Strike, the 1931 betrayal – would be repaid. But the Tories and their system swallowed their pride and lived to fight another day. Never has there been a more evident demonstration of Bevan's own favourite maxim: 'We are hard outside and soft within, the Tories are soft outside but hard within.' Even the National Health Service Bevan established was compromised. Apparently the high point of the reform, it has proved an excellent example of how the established forces can, in time, turn those reforms to their own advantage.

The Act was bold in outline; a National Health Service entirely free at the time of use, financed out of general taxation and able to organise preventative medicine, research and paramedical aids on a national basis. It entailed the taking of the voluntary hospitals into public ownership, an outrage in Tory eyes. The Bevan plan aimed at an invigoration of general practice by the establishment of health centres where groups of doctors could work in liaison with each other's special skills and experience and with nurses and social work staff.

Bevan himself was apparently well prepared to deal with

conservative pressures, and he was quite prepared for the out-
break of near-hysteria by doctors, skilfully orchestrated by
Charles Hill of the BMA, who had endeared himself to the listening public during the war as the smooth-spoken, concerned Radio
Doctor. A bargain was struck rather than a victory won.

The appointed day

Within a year of its inception, 41,200,000 people were covered by
the National Health Service. 'Workman's Insurance' had gone
national, paupers were now citizens, what had previously been
grudgingly given as assistance was now a right. The sight of people
trying on spectacles like gloves in their local Woolworth's, the
clatter of ill-fitting dentures, and the sight of nurses and sisters
selling flags and collecting money for their hospitals were abolished. In the first year 187,000,000 prescriptions were written out
by over 18,000 general practitioners, 8,500,000 dental patients
were treated and 5,250,000 pairs of glasses prescribed. 'I shudder
to think,' speculated Bevan, 'of the ceaseless cascade of medicine
which is pouring down British throats at the present time.'
Churchill did not miss the chance to suggest that Bevan ought to
be among the first to seek free psychiatric advice. But the degree
of change was more superficial than fundamental.

Firstly, the grand aims of the plans were circumscribed by the
extremely weak economic climate. It would take exceptional determination to press ahead with the building of new health centres
when the building of homes was in doubt. And although Bevan had
a keen appreciation of the limitations of reforms within the existing
social framework, he was unable and politically unwilling to
challenge them. He sought to exact the best possible compromise
within the existing balance of power by gaining the support of the
most influential section of the medical world, the consultants and
the Royal Colleges, against their GP colleagues by 'choking their
mouths with gold'. Such was the generosity of the settlement that,
as Brian Abel-Smith, the historian of British hospitals, has said,
'The most aristocratic and reactionary bodies had found it easiest to
come to terms with "socialism".' One BMA member recalled:

'We assembled at that first meeting expecting that our beautiful
profession was to be hung, drawn and quartered. Instead we were

reprieved . . . on one point after another – control by local authorities, the free choice of patient and doctor, clinical freedom – the Minister had accepted what we were demanding before we had the opportunity of asking for it.'

The workers and the soldiers had wanted a new deal, and they expected Bevan, of all people, to get one. But they had gone back to work and, in the long and winding corridors of power, the professionals had recovered the initiative.

The hospitals

The nationalisation of the hospitals was potentially a highly emotive issue, given the tenacity with which the voluntary hospitals had traditionally fought for their existence. But these hospitals were also bankrupt, and their consultants were weary of giving their services on a purely honorary basis. Their absolute medical authority no longer compensated for their non-existent salary. And, given the growing cost of medical equipment, only the state, as the war had demonstrated, was able to supply the finance which was needed to bring the outlying hospitals up to modern standards. More and more consultants required resources and ancillary technical staff and equipment which could only be provided in a hospital setting. It was in their interest to have a salaried post in a well-run hospital even if it was outside the traditional centres, especially if private work remained possible. Lord Moran, or 'Champagne Charlie' as he was known among the GPs because of his reputed love of late-night carousing with the new Minister, recalls a conversation he had with Bevan on this subject:

> *Bevan:* I find the efficiency of the hospitals varies enormously. How can that be put right?
>
> *Moran:* You will only get one standard of excellence when every hospital has a first-rate consultant staff. At present the consultants are all crowded together in the large centres of population. You've got to decentralise them.
>
> *Bevan:* That's all very well, but how are you going to get a man to leave his teaching hospital and go into the periphery? [He grinned.] You wouldn't like it if I began to direct labour.
>
> *Moran:* Oh, they'll go along if they get an interesting job and if their financial future is secured by a proper salary.
>
> *Bevan:* [after a long pause] Only the State could pay those salaries. This would mean the nationalisation of hospitals.[2]

This approach conflicted with the interests of local-government and municipal Labour Party men like Herbert Morrison and with the right wing of the Cabinet, like Hugh Dalton, who advised progress 'by stages, spread over years, and not by one bold stroke.' Bevan's move was to set up appointed Regional Hospital Boards; this in effect linked the existing interests which had run the voluntary and the municipal hospitals to the direct assistance of doctors. Although obliged to consult, the Minister had absolute power, but in practice he was to allow the consultants to run the hospitals. In an after-dinner speech, Bevan announced: 'I want for the miners, the railwaymen, the engineers, a far greater share in the management of their work and the policies that govern it, and I say no less for the doctors.' But what he was allowing was, in reality, professional self-rule, a point made in the House by Dr Stephen Taylor from the Labour benches, who feared that by the attempt to combine 'industrial democracy' with 'general democracy' there was 'a danger that we may impose on ourselves a medical dictatorship, and a very bad thing that would be.' The consultants ruled the new health service, and (although they were by no means the rapacious predators of socialist mythology) they were bound to shape the health service, above all the new generations of doctors, in their own image.

The teaching hospitals remained exempt from the new pattern of hospital government, driving a coach and four through the national system. The top doctors gained part-time sessional payment for their self-supervised sessions, to be augmented by 'merit awards' and the right to private practice, carried on, for their convenience, in the NHS hospitals. The secretly bestowed merit awards were described at the time as designed 'to ensure a practical and imaginative way of securing a reasonable differentiation of income and providing relatively high earnings for the significant minority.' They might more bluntly be described as a unique system of private bribery administered with public money in utter secrecy.

The tripartite system

The administration of the general practitioner service, the pharmaceutical service, the dental service and the ophthalmic service was to be undertaken by new bodies called Executive Councils. Health centres provided by the local authorities were to be the main feature of the primary care service. Doctors were to be paid by a mixture of capitation fee (a fee per head according to the size of their list), and salary. The sale of 'goodwill' of a practice was halted, although a sum of £66 million was allocated to compensate practitioners for the loss of that right. The remaining local services, including child care, health visiting, home nursing and the ambulance service, were the responsibility of the local authority, and the range of services was extended and made compulsory rather than optional, as it had been. In general, the role of the GP within the hospital contracted and that of the consultant was correspondingly enlarged. General practice lists increased very rapidly, but the character and resources of the family doctor's medicine hardly altered. Private practice as a whole declined as soon as it became clear that the clinical expertise of Harley Street was now freely available and the pickings of what private work survived was reserved for the hospital-based consultant. Rather than the unseemly fighting over prosperous patients, doctors from now on would be more likely to complain about having their colleagues' 'problem patients' foisted upon them. After the initial noisy resistance, GPs also fell into line. Their *per capita* payment proved an acceptable halfway house between the logical but politically unacceptable salaried system favoured by the left and the fee-for-service basis successfully insisted upon by the dental practitioners.

In hindsight, general practice and public health were grievously neglected as hospital medicine flourished. But at the time GPs seemed fairly satisfied with the new financial arrangements, and the birth of the NHS must have seemed just one aspect of the beginning of a new era of peace, prosperity and guaranteed welfare for all. The reforms of the early postwar years were underwritten by full employment, constantly rising living standards, and the alliance with the United States. We look back in a different light: the boom that buoyed up the National Health Service has long gone; the full employment and comprehensive welfare services planned by Beveridge are already a thing of the past; the 'social-democratic assumptions' are no longer taken for granted; we now face the unfinished business – over NHS financing, primary care, private practice and the drug industry – which Bevan dodged so eloquently.

The foundation of the NHS, hallowed in Labour Party mythology as the decisive battle in a terrible and hard-fought war for a new order, now seems an altogether more modest achievement, in essential continuity with pre-war liberal thinking and wartime practice. There was little that was genuinely new, much that owed its radical appearance to the optimism of the times. David Stark-Murray of the Socialist Medical Association, a man closely involved with the foundation of the NHS, notes laconically: 'In the atmosphere of 1946 when people were ready for great new moves, it seems strange that Bevan . . . did not see and did not grasp the opportunity to break with the past.'[3]

A more fundamental problem arises from the subsequent political evolution of the Labour Party. For in some ways both the organised political tendency which had been Bevanism in the fifties and the radical impetus which had created the NHS had already dispersed. Bevan's successors, like Michael Foot, may have retained and embellished the cadences of the rhetoric, but they have been either ineffectual or compromised.

And, despite rhetorical and regional similarities, Neil Kinnock's claim to the mantle of Nye is even less substantial. Whereas Bevan's response to the Conservative ascendancy of the late fifties was to sharpen his socialism, Kinnock has, oratory notwithstanding, chosen to swim with the rightward tide of political opinion in the Britain of the eighties. Bevan's argument for the NHS was not as an act of charity or even of administrative convenience, but as a historical advance which formed but one part of a larger social transformation. His achievement, as I will argue in the next chapter, was always circumscribed and limited, but it towers above anything achieved by subsequent Labour Governments in far easier economic climes. Indeed it was Labour's attack on NHS spending levels in 1976 which pioneered the long financial squeeze of the eighties.

As John Campbell, a recent biographer of Bevan rightly comments, the most important feature of Kinnock's leadership of the Labour Party is

> the steep decline over the last thirty years in the serious content of political debate. Perhaps Macmillan started it, but Wilson was Macmillan's apt pupil, and the slide into mere image politics gathered pace in the sixties. Margaret Thatcher, though no intellectual, has been a partial exception, at least marshalling her expensive public relations to project a clear view of the alternative society she would like to offer. But Labour – whether out of confusion or electoral calculation – has abjectly failed to take up the challenge.[4]

3

The NHS: Forty Years On – Part I

Forty years after Bevan founded it with such a flourish, the NHS has become a national institution as British as the Battle of Britain or Wimbledon. Like the Monarchy, it is at once beyond fundamental criticism and the subject of interminable complaint. It has become the single largest employer in the country, and in 1985 more than 75 per cent of its £18,400 million budget was spent on the wages and salaries of its 1,223,000 employees, from the eminent consultants on merit award to the night domestic staff on their pittances. It is estimated to be the largest employer in Europe, west of the Red Army. 20,193,000 outpatient visits were made to UK hospitals in 1985, and in the same year Britain's 29,655 GPs undertook 249 million consultations and dispensed over 25 million prescriptions. Over a million people per day make contact with the NHS.

Between 1948 and 1984, the expectation of life at birth rose from 66.4 years to 71.6 years for a man and from 69.3 to 77.6 for a woman. This achievement reflects a dramatic fall in infant mortality from 36 to 9 deaths for every 1,000 live births between 1948 and 1984 and the increased survival of the very old (75 and over), whose number has doubled since 1948. The death of mothers in childbirth fell to a fraction of its former level. Diseases like tuberculosis shrank in menace from being everyday killers to clinical rarities, and epidemics of polio and diphtheria were almost forgotten. The incidence of serious infectious illness has fallen sharply. As recently as 1941, 2,400 children perished from diphtheria. Medical planning, fair shares, and the idea that the healthy ought to provide for those afflicted with sickness seemed to have been accepted, even if it had taken a world war to do it.

But look again. Despite all the staff and the expenditure, preventable premature death from cardio-vascular disease continues to increase. 'About half of all strokes and a quarter of deaths from coronary heart disease in people under 70 are probably preventable by the application of existing medical knowledge,' the Royal College of General Practitioners estimated in 1981. Infectious illnesses like bacterial meningitis and TB which relate to overcrowding and poverty have begun to increase again. In 1986, the infant mortality rate went up for the first time in sixteen years. And although the number of inpatients treated has doubled (from 3.8 million in 1951 to 7.8 million in 1985), there are far fewer hospitals available, especially in the acute and psychiatric fields. There were 3,027 NHS hospitals in the UK in 1951 and only 2,341 in 1985. Bed totals have fallen from 546,000 to 404,000 over the same period. Length of inpatient stay has consequently shrunk, from an average of forty-five days in 1951 to sixteen days in 1985.

Much treatment, investigation and convalescence previously undertaken in hospital is now done on an outpatient basis. But the huge waiting lists which still dog the NHS remain, despite a spate of government initiatives, at an unsatisfactory and unacceptable total of 688,000 people at the end of March 1987, with more than 30,000 of them urgent cases who have been waiting more than a month for admission.

Infant mortality

Our record on infant mortality has indisputably improved, but by no means as fast as in other developed countries. Among countries with the lowest infant mortality, Britain ranked eighth in 1960, but had slipped to fifteenth by 1978. Britain now lies twelfth in the European league table; and one of the most comprehensive medical investigations ever carried out, the Court Report, which found that 'Infant mortality is a holocaust equal to all the deaths of the succeeding twenty-four years of life,' concluded that 'children still die in our lifetime of nineteenth century reasons.' Court drew attention to startling differences in infant and childhood mortality within regions and between social classes. Yet the report suffered the fate of many prophetic works, and its principal recommendation, an integrated child health service emphasising surveillance, is far from becoming reality.

Medical inequality

The Black Report, published with obvious embarrassment and in a deliberately inconvenient photostated form two months after the return of the Conservative Government in 1979, was a rigorous investigation by the chief Government scientist at the Department of Health and Social Security of the health experiences of different social classes. The question of class differentials in ill-health are many and complex, but after a comprehensive review of the scientific literature which has been called 'the most important single document on health since the war,' the report was quite emphatic that, thirty years on, the NHS has done very little to redress the dramatic variation of health according to social class. At the simplest level, this makes the child of parents in the profession-al middle class likely to live, on average, five years longer than the offspring of the unskilled, and means that twice as many babies of the unskilled die at birth or in the first month of life as do the offspring of Social Class I. The report judged that not only was poverty and deprivation itself a major cause of ill-health, but that there was also unequal access to NHS services. It concluded: 'present social inequalities in health in a country with substantial resources like Britain are unacceptable.'

Among its proposals were an increase in child benefit, the introduction of a child care allowance, free school meals for all children and urgent improvements in housing. Six years after its publication, in a period in which prolonged mass unemployment had sharply increased poverty and enlarged inequality between classes, the *British Medical Journal* could comment laconically: 'Like the Bible, the Black Report on inequalities in health is much quoted, occasionally read, and largely ignored when it comes to action. Virtually none of its thirty-seven recommendations have been implemented.'

Doctor–patient relations

On the less tangible question of doctor–patient relations, the health service is not as good as it likes to think. The Royal Commission on the NHS singled it out as a constant ground for lay complaint. And the burgeoning of 'alternative' or complementary medicine and the foundation of the College of Health as a consumer watchdog hardly suggested satisfaction with orthodox medicine. The Royal Commission had noted that 'patients are not given enough information about their treatment and despite constant complaints over the years they still might feel they are ignored when doctors discuss them with their colleagues.' A group of teachers of general practice at St Bart's noted recently that because of the difficulty of applying medicine as traditionally taught to the realities of life, 'many doctors become disillusioned with medicine and contemptuous of their patients.'

People may live longer, but the rate of improvement is now much slower than it was earlier in the century. And what kind of life do the old enjoy? Do they live or just survive? Is the increased volume of prescriptions, the antibiotics for virus infections which they do not cure, and tranquillisers for worries they do not solve, doing more good to the patient or to the companies that manufacture them? What kind of medicine do NHS doctors practise, and is it really what the patients want? How much does our enthusiasm for the principles of the NHS overshadow our candour about its faults? How much of the improvement in the health statistics can doctors honestly take credit for?

These questions are hard to answer with confidence. Statistics, even where they exist – and the NHS has been notoriously bad at evaluating its own performance – are only averages of arbitrary agglomerates. As one of the most penetrating investigators of the real conditions of the NHS, Dr A. H. Baker, noted in 1972, 'I am concerned at the very considerable gap between the generally accepted policies and the reality of the service as patients find it.' Health is about such intangible things as dignity, suffering and confidence, and it is here that a service which is not based on commercial considerations gives its most important but also most intangible value.

Early days

What can be said with certainty about the early days of the NHS is that proper specialist care, and with it the new technical equipment for X-ray and pathology laboratory investigation, arrived for the first time in areas of the country which had previously depended on the often shaky skills and apparatus of the local practitioner. Available medical skill no longer congregated in the big cities and around the teaching hospitals near the potential paying customer. Instead, central taxation provided specialists with a living more attractive than the fee rat-race, as well as the equipment needed to undertake modern medical practice. Local authorities also set about the provision of ambulance services, home helps, district nurses and day centres as an accepted part of their work rather than as an optional extra.

The most immediate gain was for surgical patients, especially married women who had been enduring known ailments until their condition became acute. A huge body of silently borne discomforts – fallen wombs, stress incontinence, heavy periods, the involuntary passing of water in old women and the reverse in men – was tackled. Like the pent-up demand for dentures and spectacles, this demonstrated not the patients' greed but the true extent of untreated illness; but patients' health improved because of better living standards and individual researchers in laboratories rather than through a better service from their general practitioners.

At the beginning of the century, arsenic for syphilis, alkalis for urinary infection and aspirin for fever were the most effective drugs, but the biochemical breakthroughs during the Second World War fundamentally altered the terms on which doctors faced serious illness. The sulphonamides were the first in an army of antibiotics which transformed treatment and mortality from infectious illness and began to make irrelevant the sanatoria and isolation hospitals of the past. Synthetic substitutes for body hormones enabled the replacement treatment of diabetes and thyroid diseases and prepared the ground for the Pill. Anaesthesia became much more reliable, with muscle relaxants and improved breathing and resuscitation equipment making surgery safer and making possible to deal with severe but temporary shock. Blood-matching and transfusion services had been greatly improved by the necessities of war. But the standards and conditions of general practice were not essentially altered; in some cases the workload increased and the medical basis remained the diagnostic snap judgement rather than scientific investigation. And, in addition, many of the general social assumptions upon which the NHS rested have proved unreliable.

The end of poverty?

Looking back to the 1950s, one senses the complacency of officials concerned with all aspects of welfare: the conviction that poverty was a thing of the past, that the affluent society had come to stay, that we had never had it so good and were going to have it even better in the future. In retrospect, this seems like deliberate self-deception, even though it was based on real, if not permanent changes in British society. One economist estimates that 'the system as a whole has never grown so fast for so long as since the war – twice as fast again between 1950 and 1964 as between 1913 and 1950, and nearly half as fast again as during the generation before that'.[1] Anthony Crosland, the leading theorist of the Labour Party, was convinced that this change was permanent: 'Capitalism,' he wrote, 'has been reformed almost out of recognition. Despite occasional minor recessions and balance-of-payments crises, full employment and at least a tolerable level of stability are likely to be maintained.'[2]

The poverty of the 1930s had been caused by lack of work; post-war full employment reversed this, the associated rise in wage rates protected it, and such wartime welfare measures as food subsidies and family allowances smoothed out hardship. The only remaining problem was to locate pockets of suffering and to bring them up to par; there was no problem which could not be solved by an allowance or a prescription. In health, Beveridge's assumption that spending would tend to fall as ill-health was identified, isolated and treated, was widely accepted. Deceived by the external appearance of affluence, social theory tended to attribute any lingering misfortune to poor adjustment, absent fathers or problem families, and conceptions wrenched from their psychoanalytic origins were presented as explanations of personal or family inadequacies. The unmarried woman who nursed her ill and demanding mother, the family which made ends meet on low wages, the old couple valiantly starving because welfare 'is for people who are really poor', the disabled, the mentally subnormal, the war widows, the old who never left their darkened homes, were excluded from the main source of improved living standards because they were unable to take part in the productive life of the economy. The welfare state took for granted the normality and desirability of the nuclear family: anyone outside it was, by definition, a problem.

Looking back at the fifties from the new depression of the eighties and facing the social and medical consequences of increased unemployment, it is all too easy to detect the naive optimism of the early days of the welfare state and the political consensus between corporatist Labour and reformist Tory. Economic growth was, in Rudolph Klein's shrewd phrase, 'the solvent of political conflict'. It is important nonetheless to emphasise that even at the height of the long post-war economic boom the allowances claimants received were smaller in real value than it is supposed – probably a smaller percentage of average wages than in 1938, or even 1912. And their universality was, from the outset, undercut by tests and charges which further lowered their real value. Not only did the poor lack the private insurance and taxation benefits with which the better-off could buttress themselves in times of need, but their entitlements were so complicated, so hard to track down and so surrounded with the aura of charity that many eligible people never claimed them. Baffled by forms or barred by pride, many of the most deserving soldiered on. It was, curiously, in the interests of both main political parties to exaggerate the extent of welfare and the equalisation of living standards brought about by progressive taxation. Labour was able to bolster its claims to social justice, and the Tories to substantiate their dislike of any form of universal welfare. So even at the height of affluence, what Tudor Hart christened in 1971 'the inverse care law', that 'the availability of good medical care tends to vary inversely with the need for it in the population served,' was operative.[3]

But the late seventies inaugurated a new era, in which unemployment and poverty were, as in the thirties, the fate not just of the single, the ill and the socially isolated but of the fit and previously well-employed working class and some middle class families.

It was after the 1979 Conservative election victory that unemployment began its quantum leap. Despite the enormous income generated by Scottish and North Sea oil, the eighties, at least outside London and the South-east, has not been a decade of genuine prosperity. Unemployment has risen by at least two million to a total which remains persistently above three million, and although inflation has been controlled, public spending cut and a consumer boom initiated, manufacturing output has fallen by 30 per cent.

Prolonged mass unemployment on this scale clearly exerts (and is intended to exert) restraint on those in work, by weakening their bargaining power. Trade union organisation, systematically eroded by legal restriction and financial penalty, has suffered the formal reverses of the 1983/4 defeat of the National Union of Mineworkers and the eventual rout of the Fleet Street print unions. A succession of Government decisions have affected lower-paid workers, whose inadequate wages are recognised as a principal cause of family poverty.

The overall effect has been, in a matter of years, to reverse a sixty-year trend towards more equal distribution of wealth. The *BMJ* has crisply summarised the statistical evidence of expanding poverty and its effects:

> In 1976 the poorest fifth of the population received 7.4% of national income while the richest fifth received 37.9%; by 1983 the poorest fifth received 6.9% and the richest fifth 39.3%. In 1984 4.6 million people were receiving supplementary benefit compared with 2.7 million in 1974, and if the amount received on supplementary benefit is taken as the poverty line, 7.7 million were living on or below the line in 1981 and 2.8 million were below it (the latest figures available). Because of the huge increase in unemployment since 1979 young families now make up a much higher percentage of the poor, and the number of children growing up in poverty doubled between 1979 and 1981. Homelessness is one of the worst consequences of poverty, and 140,000 heads of households were registered homeless in Britain in 1984 compared with 41,000 in 1979. Shelter estimates that 9,000 families in England are living in 'bed and breakfast' accommodation – 4,000 of them in London at an estimated cost of £26 million.[4]

Class and health: from birth to burial

It is often argued that to cavil about class inequality is to perpetuate a narrow-minded sectionalism. But class inequalities in health are matters of life and death, and to justify its existence one must cold-heartedly believe that unskilled workers deserve to die younger, be shorter of breath or lose more of their children in childbirth. The less well-off still suffer illness and make do with medical services which would be bitterly rejected by the wealthy. David Ennals summarised the evidence in a speech in March 1977:

> To take the extreme example, in 1971 the death rate for adult men in social class V [unskilled workers] was nearly twice that of adult men in social class I [professional workers] even when account had been taken of the different age structure of the two classes. When you look at death rates for specific diseases the gap is even wider. For example, for tuberculosis the death rate in social class V was ten times that for social class I; for bronchitis it was five times as high and for lung cancer and stomach cancer three times as high. Social class differences in mortality begin at birth. In 1971 neonatal death rates – deaths within the first

month of life – were twice as high for the children of fathers in social class V as they were in social class I. Death rates for the post-neonatal period – from one month up to one year – were nearly five times higher in social class V than in social class I.

Maternal mortality – down a long way from the figures of forty years ago – shows the same pattern; the death rate was twice as high for wives of men in social class V as for those in social class I.

The evidence in Ennals's speech was confirmed by the Report of the Working Group on Inequalities in Health (chaired by Sir Douglas Black, formerly the Chief Scientist at the DHSS and subsequently President of the Royal College of Physicians), published in April 1980. The Black Report reopened the debate on the effects on health of social inequalities which had been dormant since the thirties. The Report documented a gap in health experience according to class to the extent that, if unskilled manual workers and their families had had health prospects as good as professional workers between 1970 and 1972, 74,000 people now dead would still have been alive, including 10,000 children and 32,000 men aged 15 to 64. The Report noted that while over the last twenty years the premature deaths of social classes I and II had steadily fallen, those in classes IV and V had either remained unchanged or had actually increased. The Black Report concluded:

Present social inequalities in health in a country with substantial resources like Britain are unacceptable and deserve to be so declared by every section of public opinion . . . we have no doubt that greater equality in health must remain one of our foremost national objectives and that in the last two decades of the twentieth century a new attack on the forces of inequality has regrettably become necessary.

The Report pinpointed specific areas contributing to excessive ill-health and unnecessary deaths among the working class. There were very marked differences in the outcome of pregnancy according to social class, including late miscarriages, stillbirths and congenital deformities. Although infant mortality in all classes had improved, the improvement remains very relative: women of social class V have only now achieved the outcomes enjoyed by women of social class I in the thirties. The Report suggested that important factors here were the mother's general health and state of nutrition, levels of cigarette smoking, the quality of antenatal and intrapartum obstetric care and 'environmental' causes, especially industrial pollution, which would increase the rate of malformation and stillbirth and to which working class mothers suffered greater exposure because of the location of their housing.

Between the ages of one and four years, the class gradient remained very pronounced, and it was suggested that, since the principal causes of premature death were from accidents, respiratory disease and neoplasm, such class-varied factors as the degree of domestic overcrowding, the availability of safe public play space, car ownership, access to good medical care and levels of pollution and nutrition were determining factors.

To families on or below the poverty line, ill-health was a fact of life. The report quoted a study of family ill-health in Birmingham:

> The children in the process of growing up have many shared experiences. They live in overcrowded conditions, being members of large families; their homes are inadequate by current standards: the neighbourhoods are rough and disliked by most who have to live in them. They experience poverty, which means they go short of things considered essential or normal by others around them.

Ill-health in childhood rapidly affects education and can dog an individual for life. As the Court Report put it, inadequately treated and frequent bouts of childhood illness 'cast long shadows forward'.

At the other end of life, while the well-off can expect to enjoy a comfortable, healthy and active retirement, the working classes experience a decline in their income (which has itself remained relatively level throughout their working life). Housing, heating, quality of nutrition and access to private transport then become crucial in determining survival. They are areas in which the chronically sick, the disabled and those caring for them fare especially badly. The Black Report comments drily:

> What has to be remembered is that these outcomes are the end products of inequalities in the use of and demands upon the human body earlier in the lifetime, and the kind of environment in which human beings have been placed. At birth and at death, health is tied to the social division of labour and in this way inequalities in health are perpetuated 'from the cradle to the grave'.

Poverty, of course, is a very relative thing, and clearly today's poor have more purchasing power than the poor of the Distressed Areas and the Depression. The modern UB40 may just run a battered V registered Granada and will probably have a video and a 26-inch TV, but they lack what others take for granted: privacy, a garden, safe play-space, single bedrooms, regular holidays and access to leisure and entertainment facilities.

The British Medical Association's Board of Science and Education's Discussion Paper, 'Deprivation and Ill-Health', published in May 1987, updated the Black Report, noting that since Black's appearance 'the most striking social change has been the rise in the number of unemployed'. It looked especially at the problems associated with inner city areas, including 'economic decay leading to high unemployment, especially among the young; homelessness and poor housing; crime; lack of cohesion within the community and general environmental decline.' Although less comprehensive than Black, it reinforced its general findings and corrected several of its critics, noting that diseases of stress and affluence, like peptic ulcers and heart attacks, were more, not less, common among working class employees than executives, and that far from working class people being less likely to have mental breakdowns, there was evidence of extensive untreated mental illness, especially depression. The 1987 Report indicated the poor quality of even quite recent council-built housing, noting 'the problems of defective housing for which private landlords were once criticised are now most common in the public sector.' Many of the low-rise, high-density estates were still inconveniently designed, with little consideration for privacy and poor sound insulation, and prove prone to damp and expensive to heat properly. Likewise, 'the poor physical state of schools and limited availability' were bound to affect general morale.

On diet, the BMA Report concluded that 'while malnutrition due to inadequate energy intake remains rare in Britain, it is likely that lesser degrees of nutritional imbalance caused by poverty prevent a substantial proportion of children from achieving their full health and growth potential.' Nutritious food takes time, thought and money to organise; 'sweet foods are among the cheapest treats available and very heavily advertised.' The conclusion of the Report was uncompromising: 'Allowing deprivation to persist on the present scale is neither strategically nor morally justifiable.'

The National Health Service . . . on the cheap

It is perhaps the existence of these two quite different levels of expectation and demand which helped to sustain another myth about the NHS: that it was lavishly financed. It was quite possible for a metropolitan liberal to assume that the standard of care and the quality of equipment in the London teaching hospitals represented the normal rather than the exceptional. First, as regards financing, it is worth stating emphatically that the overwhelming proportion of NHS funding in the post-war period came from direct taxation. A survey in 1972 suggested that 80 per cent of those interviewed still thought that the health service was financed from their stamp, which in fact then produced only 8 per cent of the total. The NHS is not free in any real sense. It is paid for by direct taxation of wages and salaries. Although doctors sometimes contrive to give the impression that the health service is a magnificent act of personal generosity on their part, everything they prescribe or advise, as well as their own wages, is financed by the taxpayer.

The NHS has also meant health on the cheap. The most recent figures are worth dealing with in some detail. *Per capita* health spending appears to have increased a staggering sixfold between 1973 and 1985. But adjusted to allow for the general inflation rate, this rise is very much smaller, about 53 per cent. And as a figure for inflation which is specific to NHS pay and prices, the *per capita* spending has increased only 25 per cent, or 2 per cent per year. This figure is barely adequate to cope with the changing composition of the population, with a higher proportion of the old and the very old who are high users of medical services. And the budget also needs to be increased annually to keep up with the technical possibilities of medical innovation. So, since 1985, there has been an annual shortfall of about £400 million. The Government *has* produced record levels of NHS spending but it is still too low to prevent health districts running out of money for essential services.

The central point remains that the British, particularly the English, level of health spending is one of the lowest of all industrialised countries. In Switzerland, the USA and Sweden, average health spending exceeded the UK's by well over 100 per cent. Some of this disparity can be explained by the sheer inefficiency of marketplace health. The very high spending in the

United States reflects not a concern for good health, but the power of a health empire, where doctors and hospitals see making money as a legitimate aspect of their profession and are thus inevitably inclined to unnecessary referral, investigation and operation. But a more important cause has been the NHS's exploitation of the willingness of hospital workers, especially nurses, to put up with very low wages because of their vocational commitment to the service. 'Training grades' are used to provide cheap and uncomplaining labour, and receive in turn a rather perfunctory education. Both primary care and hospital service depend on an unseen workforce of low-paid and mainly female cooks, cleaners, clerks, technicians, nurses and health visitors who, in reality, do most of the comforting and caring. For the last decade their devotion has been rewarded by frozen vacancies, staffing cuts, increased workloads and the indignity of competitive tender for their own jobs.

This uncomplaining devotion also allowed an institutional meanness about buildings and resources to go unchallenged. The foundation of the National Health Service ushered in the slowest rate of hospital-building for two centuries. It is perhaps easier to appreciate quite how low average spending has been on the NHS by comparing it with the other social services: roughly half the nation's schools and nearly half of its houses have been built since 1948, but just a quarter of its hospitals. The majority of hospitals are pre-1914, whereas only one school in six dates back that far.

Supply and demand

If the staff and patients became acclimatised to penny-pinching, the suppliers of the service had access to a gigantic market. And where commercial principles came into conflict with the NHS, it was the former that appeared to triumph. I am not referring simply to the well-known cases of pharmaceuticals suppliers who milked the NHS by charging grotesquely inflated prices for drugs, but to a whole range of suppliers, from bedpans to tea bags, for which the NHS was a gigantic and none-too-inquiring corporate purchaser.

So, as a first approximation, and looking at overall targets, the NHS must be judged an honourable failure. Even at the height of the long economic boom of the fifties and sixties it was failing in its egalitarian objectives. Now, after a decade of depression, it can be seen quite clearly that the NHS has failed to improve health standards across the board. It has also failed to match the national commitment to health spending of comparable systems in industrialised countries. Indeed, to health economists, appalled by the potential explosion of medical costs, the NHS is most famous as a system of rationing. And despite the immense advantages of a national integrated system based on solid primary care, it has failed to exploit the potential for teamwork, planning or screening. The degree to which it has succeeded according to other criteria – public accountability, provision for women, the use of appropriate technology and its internal morale and ethos – is considered in the next chapter.

4

The NHS: 40 Years On – Part II

Democracy

Because of the sheer size and complexity of the NHS, internal structure and accountability to the public are of particular importance. A strong independent voice for those who use the health service is still more vital because of the fact that hospital and community health services are administered quite separately from the general practitioner service, and because elected local authorities have poor liaison with the NHS, although the planning decisions of each clearly have intimate consequences for the other. The lack of an organised and powerful voice for the users of the service has been a major weakness of the NHS.

Until the 1974 reorganisation the structure was, at best, paternalistic. Although there was some discussion with interested parties over appointments made by the DHSS to the Regional Health Authorities, District Health Authorities and Family Practitioner Committees, and certain places were reserved for the nominees of local authorities, medical professions and trade unions, the directly democratic element was insignificant. The curious myth that somehow the trade unions run the NHS could not be further from the truth. Studies of the social composition of the RHAs and DHAs show them to be heavily packed with social classes I and II. As John Patten, Under Secretary at the DHSS, put it in a letter to Labour MP Michael Meacher in June 1984, 'My impression is that by far the largest proportion of chairmen and members had some business background: there is also substantial representation of the medical, academic and legal professions as well as those with trade union interests.' (Sadly, the trade union representatives have a habit of being politically soft and frequent non-attenders, their appointment often the reward for a lifetime's conformity.) The general approach was, however, one of consensus, and this was reflected in the attempts to keep everyone happy at the local management level.

Consensus was one of the first victims of the cuts, and did not survive far into the eighties. Public cases of political appointment (and de-appointment) and the rejection of well-qualified but politically unsuitable members made it clear that the Government sought a still more centralised and streamlined system with even less room for audible dissent. The difficulties of appointed members who find themselves in disagreement with the Authority majority were described by Professor John Davis after his resignation from the Cambridge Health Authority in 1984:

> The major factor prompting my resignation was the realisation that with privatisation and other matters, the Government, through the DHSS, has been far from anxious to devolve decision-making to the appointed health authorities – as it professes to do. Instead, it has been only too ready in particular instances to dictate to authorities how they should act, very often motivated by purely political considerations, and making us responsible for decisions which we were in the event powerless to influence.[1]

Even this degree of central control was considered inadequate, however, and Roy Griffiths, Managing Director of the Sainsbury supermarket chain, was asked to investigate the 'management problems' of the NHS. The problem with Griffiths was not simply that he himself was a product of a retail giant exerting enormous influence over land use, food production and diet, but that the terms of his investigation dictated his recommendations, which were, entirely predictably, that the NHS 'undermanaged'. His solution was 'general management', to be executed by about 800 general managers. The new philosophy was sceptically received by the all-party Commons Select Committee on the Social Services, who commented: 'The NHS may suffer more in side-effects from the wonder drug of general managers than it gains from better management.'[2] The National Association of Local Government Officers, whose senior members were often under consideration for the new jobs, were concerned about the likely effect on NHS accountability, noting, 'Power will be concentrated in the hands of the Secretary of State, the tame chair-persons he appoints, and the obedient general managers they in turn appoint.' Indeed, despite the promises of new blood, of the first 219 general managers, 90 per cent came from within the NHS, most of them being merely promoted administrators. A handful of doctors were also appointed, and the majority of 'outsiders' were retired from the Army and the RAF and already enjoying a services pension. The first chairman of the new central NHS management board, Victor Paige, resigned in June 1986 after only eighteen months. Interestingly, a Government report of the decline in the status and efficiency of community medical officers, published in January 1988, which documents a 20 per cent shortage of specialists in this field, formally admitted that community physicians had been confused and compromised by the introduction of general management.

In fact, attempting to administer the NHS along the lines of a retail business is a nonsense. There is not, or ought not to be, a profit motive in the provision of health; yet it is, ultimately, the annual operating profit which is used to judge the efficiency of a commercial firm. Indeed, managers have very little data on patients treated, let alone on their satisfaction with their care, and seldom seem to have considered the other social factors which influence the demands made on the NHS. As the Charter for a Democratic Health Service noted:

> Local communities have little or no say regarding the services they use. Decisions about local health services, whether to close a ward or hospital, what equipment to purchase and whether to develop more responsive services are taken by Health Service managers, representatives of the medical profession, and appointed Health Authority members . . . within the constraints of national guidelines.

The Community Health Councils, set up to provide an institutional consumer voice, can only marginally offset this remorseless centralisation. While in some areas they have proposed alternatives to the managerial perspective of managed decline, and have been the focus of argument and campaigns against the cuts, more often they are mere safety valves, and in terms of the NHS's formal structure they can be of little more than nuisance value. And, as J. Dallas, a historian of the CHC movement has noted, 'Any group which is criticised by another group has sought to dull the critical edge by taking that group into membership.' Yet this consistent failure to listen carefully to what the users of the NHS have to say is not merely politically unhealthy but is also administratively unhelpful, depriving the service of precisely the information it needs to plan effectively.

The elements of popular control which had been so strong in the mining clubs have largely vanished. Now the public hardly has an adequate complaints mechanism, let alone a say in the direction of the health service they pay for and depend upon. This has protected the service from any severe criticism or assessment of its direction. The authorities often claim that the absence of complaints signifies general satisfaction with the system, but it is more likely to suggest indifference and passivity about even starting to ask for more or different health services. For doctors this presents the real danger that complaints about services could result in individual medico-legal law suits.

Hierarchies rule

Despite the NHS, hospitals are still governed by people whose attitudes deprive patients of rights and opinions and whose power seems to grow with each phase of the development of the health service. Ironically it is the doctors, and the more senior ones at that, bitter enemies of nationalisation, who have done best out of the NHS, and the patients who have forfeited their say in what is perhaps the most fundamental of the social services their taxes buy. The co-operation, potential goodwill and devotion which the service attracts from the public is unique.

By default, money has tended to follow the lines of the old medical establishment, towards the centres of teaching medicine, and to reflect their concerns. Heart surgery is more exciting medically than an occupational health service, although the latter would do more for overall health standards. And there is relatively little point in having specialised points of great expertise if the means of delivering it is neglected. Sudden advances in methods of treatment are deprived of their potential value if the means to make early diagnoses of the condition do not exist. This intensely hierarchical set-up is constantly refuelled by the male offspring of doctors who bring with them an inherited and unchanging set of assumptions about the doctor's role.

Inside the hospital, behind its neoclassical façade, lies an even more marked pyramid of power with the wealthy, white, male consultant at its pinnacle and Asian and Caribbean women cleaners, cooks and ward nurses toiling away, underpaid and under-appreciated, at the base. This highly developed hierarchy, with its intricate snobberies and subtle racial and sexual wars, corrodes the possibility of genuine co-operation upon which any effective healing depends and exaggerates the importance of medical actions made by doctors at the expense of nursing, diet and hygiene, in a way the classical physicians would have found bewildering. Such a system is not simply a comic anachronism suitable for *Doctor in the House* films, but creates problems which distort the patient care which everyone professes is the final aim.

The ultimate power is still possessed by the consultant as the head of the clinical team. The specialities themselves still tend to rank in prestige according to potential earnings in private practice rather than their overall social utility or medical challenge. The teaching hospitals produce a medical profession out of touch with reality: geographically located in the inner city, ideologically in the Home Counties. Medical schools have staunchly resisted educational democracy. A recent survey of Birmingham University Medical School confirms the over-representation of doctors' children and the disturbing fact that applicants connected to the hospital by birth appeared to require lower examination results. And a computer-assisted study of London medical schools demonstrated a clear structural bias in some against women and non-white applicants. The hospital consultants conducting the survey noted:

> There is a three- to fourfold difference between the numbers of Afro-Asian and Arabic doctors qualifying from the Westminster and those qualifying from the Royal Free. It would seem that the least progressive schools, those not prepared to move out of the centre of London and away from Harley Street and the lure of private practice, are also most conservative in their admissions policy.[3]

Race

In 1985, Greater London Action for Race Equality published *In a Critical Condition*, which documented racial inequality in detail and challenged health authorities, as large employers of black labour at all levels, to take decisive action against racism. Two years later its follow-up report, entitled *No Alibi, No Excuses*, found that, with some exceptions, there had been little overall progress, with a persistent lack of ethnic monitoring, widespread ignorance of the Commission for Racial Equality's code of practice and a general lack of regular assessment of the success or otherwise of equal opportunity policies. Several cases of discrimination against ethnic minority doctors have been taken to Industrial Tribunals, and in May 1985 a Sri Lankan microbiologist, Malila Noone, was awarded record damages of £5,000 for racial discrimination by an appointment committee which was described by the Tribunal as 'little more than a sham'. Senior staff and influential committee members in hospitals like St Bartholomew's, which now serves a population over 30 per cent black, remain lily-white. It is hardly surprising that the NHS only makes occasional and piecemeal attempts to make its services accessible to ethnic minorities.

Within nursing there is a similar caste system, with well-off white girls training at the London teaching hospitals, and few working class English girls attracted to a job which demands long hours for very poor money under antiquated discipline. Instead, in the low prestige big hospitals nursing staff have traditionally been women from Ireland and the West Indies, with Malaysian, Asian and African immigrants providing more and more of the womanpower. All training nurses have their labour exploited. They have to work harder than the full-time qualified staff, right up to their examinations, and are often too tired to study or to attend to the lectures properly.

The most elementary rights to privacy, telephones and an adult social life are forfeited; nurses can request evenings they want off but have to fall in with the ward sister's timetable. Unqualified staff are consistently landed with responsibility beyond their experience, particularly at night. The qualified night staff are forced to rotate through the wards hoping to be in the right place at the right time, and administrators nightly have to juggle their sparse forces according to the nursing needs of the patients. Sickness absence, which is higher than average among hospital staff because of the sheer pressure of their work, can destroy the best-planned night provision. For every hospital which frankly admits it has to close wards because of staff shortage, there must be several which are getting away with a calculated risk which would horrify the senior staff who do not see the hospital at night. A teaching hospital with staff falling over each other during the week can be a medical shell at weekends, with registrars living out, leaving junior doctors, agency casualty nurses and locum housemen holding the fort.

State-enrolled nurses are particularly exploited. They get a second-rate education for a qualification which is valid only in England. Yet as students they do the bulk of manual work on the wards with very little recognition, job security or prospects. And that work is demanding, both physically and emotionally, requiring concentration and precision as well as sheer brute strength and stamina. Dire punishment awaits the ward nurse if her tally of pain-killers is inaccurate or her observations are running behind, even though the drugs are harmless and non-addictive and the doctors do not always bother to read the charts. In medicine as in life it is the male sex which makes the decisions and the female which carries them out. The hospital hierarchy is one of sex as well as income and class. On ward rounds it is often still only the sister or staff nurse who speaks, and then only when spoken to. The cynicism with which the labour of women migrants has been used in British hospitals is signified by the Government's withdrawal of work permits to migrant nurses once they qualify, thus refusing them the only work for which their newly qualified status equips them. The contrast between the illusory glamour of Florence Nightingale and Dr Kildare and the reality of a ward of ill patients to nurse single-handed on a Saturday night is measured by the number of nurses who leave the profession, now a staggering 30 per cent per year.

Still further down the scale are those ancillary workers whose essential contribution to the well-being of the patient has only recently been acknowledged. Hospital porters, cleaners and cooks are the lowest paid of the low-paid, and only make ends meet by working levels of overtime which are unhealthy both for them and their patients. Yet without their toil, the most sophisticated surgeon and highest-powered clinician come to a stop.

Women

The emergence of the modern women's movement has had a particular importance for medicine, challenging some of its most hallowed assumptions. The early movement was uncompromisingly egalitarian. 'Women's Lib' insisted on talking openly about the social pressures on women which lie behind the stress, depression, 'minor ailments' and gynaecological problems which make women the most frequent users of doctors, hospitals and medicines. The struggle to combine bringing up children with working, the pressure of the two jobs women are expected to cope with when husbands refuse to do housework or to look after children when *they* come home from work, the loneliness of living in isolated homes in destroyed ugly developments, the ignorance of sexual anatomy which is considered proper to 'decent' women, the secret sense of disappointment and emptiness, all were invisible – considered normal – until large numbers of women began to protest and organise against them. This alone has altered the way doctors ought to think and has alerted them to the masculine bias and deep-rooted assumptions so powerful in clinical medicine. The women's health movement challenges doctors to ask fundamental questions about the kind of medicine we have hitherto taken for granted. All those casual hysterectomies, quick diagnoses of de-pression, induced and interfering deliveries and buckshot pre-scribing of tranquillisers, justified with some unspoken assump-tion about the inherent instability of the female intelligence, stood in need of review.

Specific issues where the NHS was failing badly have been identified. They ranged from the use, or rather misuse, of the injected contraceptive Depo-Provera through to less tangible mat-ters like doctors' insensitivity to miscarriage (more common than birth but often dismissed with the unfortunate euphemism of 'losing the baby') and the inadequacy of the services for the investigation of infertility and the organisation of artificial insemi-nation and *in vitro* fertilisation – these techniques very much suit the multi-disciplinary approach which is one of the strengths of the NHS hospital, but, too often, are only available privately.

And clearly an effective general Women's Liberation campaign would mean better health both for women and their children. Improvement in Britain's very poor provision of nursery education would assist the educational performance and social skills of the children as well as the mental health of their parents. Better child benefit would put funds directly into the hands of the parent most often responsible for child care and family expenditure. The Equal Pay Act promised to extricate working class women from the low-prestige, part-time sections of the labour market, generate job security and improve maternity rights. The return of mass unemployment and Conservative Government have, however, largely negated the advances made in the early seventies, and while the aspirations remain the material changes required are often further away than ever.

Obstetrics

Obviously the obstetric service provided by the NHS was also critical for women. Up to the late 1970s there was a long-standing complaint that the hospital maternity services were spoiling the most joyous moments of birth with production-line insensitivity. In 1973, 95 per cent of births took place in hospital, compared with 60 per cent a generation ago. Too often this involves being blasted with an enema, pubic hair razored, stunned with Pethidine and surrounded by nurses bellowing 'Just relax'. Childbirth takes place among scenes of pandemonium. The distraction, companionship and simple familiarities so normal at home suddenly become foreign. Childbirth becomes instead a dread event from which fathers, Englishmen anyway, have the decency to keep well away. Clearly in obstetrics, as in other branches of medicine, the technology and its usefulness and safety have not yet been properly evaluated.

It is also clear that midwives need to gain (or regain) more autonomy and better remuneration. But the main cause of perinatal mortality, which rose in 1986 for the first time in thirteen years, is not the success or failure of obstetric intervention so much as the vulnerability of low birth-weight babies associated with maternal poverty, smoking and alcohol abuse. And to remedy that, as the BMJ commented in April 1987, 'more money should be spent on improving the social status of women, ensuring that their housing, diet and general level of support before, during and after birth were adequate.' What has happened instead is the abolition of the maternity grant, the reduction of the number of women entitled to maternity pay and the freezing of child benefit.

Some of these controversies, particularly the increase of obstetric intervention, underlay the suspension of Wendy Savage, a progressive obstetrician in Tower Hamlets and lecturer at the London Hospital, and the subsequent public enquiry held into her alleged incompetence in 1986. The procedure the Tower Hamlets

Health Authority chose to adopt in the Savage case is designed to be evoked in emergency cases of severe ill-health or blatant incompetence of doctors who have *suddenly* become a danger to the public or to themselves. In this case, it was belatedly pressed into service to wage the battle of the high-tech, interventionist school of conventional obstetric care against Wendy Savage's woman-centred, community-based approach.

The enquiry was initiated not by public concern, but by professional colleagues. It reflected poorly on the intellectual climate within the College of the London Hospital that its medical debates, led by extremely expensive legal teams, took place in court. And for a health authority attempting to serve one of the most deprived districts in inner-city London, unable to pay its staff wages without service cuts and routinely offering its gynaecological outpatients long waits for appointments, this trial was a tragedy, a prodigious waste of medical time and public money. Even her opponents admitted Mrs Savage's diligence, thoroughness and accessibility. Review of her perinatal mortality figures revealed them as being as good as or better than her colleagues', despite her greater and more difficult caseload. In June 1985, she had been awarded one of the higher honours in her field 'for advancing the science and practice of obstetrics' when she was made a Fellow of the Royal College of Obstetricians and Gynaecologists.

She had been a valued source of clinical support and advice to beleaguered local GPs (sixty-eight of the eighty-four local GPs were among the 10,000 people who signed a petition calling for her reinstatement). She had pioneered joint work with paediatricians and child psychiatrists to try to unify the treatment of young children and their families. She was the first clinician of consultant status to seriously address the unsolved problems of Bangladeshi mothers. Indeed, one suspects that in some of her opponents' eyes, her worst crime was to have listened to the Bengali mothers, to the underpaid midwives, to the Community Health Council and to the local organisations who have tried to assert, in quite a modest way, their priorities against the accepted wisdom of the London Hospital and the tea-broking Chairman of the Tower Hamlets Health Authority.

In the event, the verdict not only vindicated Mrs Savage but represented a victory over the mystique of the teaching hospital establishment. Her accusers, so eloquent behind the scenes, were curiously muted in public. With the facts and opinions on record, the clandestine lobbying which secured Mrs Savage's suspension was revealed as biased and medically illogical, and a better-informed District Health Authority Chairman and District Medical Officer would have prevented rather than connived in it, and she was duly reinstated, although still cold-shouldered by her male obstetric colleagues.

But if the enquiry had not been held in public; if Mrs Savage had been represented by her original Defence Union-assigned solicitors; if her supporters had not taken her case to the streets, pubs and markets of East London and to the media; if doctors in primary care, in contrast to the deafening silence from her hospital colleagues, had not backed her clinically, then the original attempt might have succeeded, dealing a serious blow to progressive obstetrics.

Abortion

Abortion too has been a momentous battleground. The 1967 Act, generally supported by the exhaustive enquiry made in the Lane Report, has been subjected to considerable criticism and four major attempts, by the MPs James White, William Benyon, James Corrie and now David Alton, at restrictive amendment. The crux of their case, supported by the powerful anti-abortion lobby, is that the provision for legal abortion on social grounds has been abused by permissive or even immoral doctors and commercial nursing homes, resulting in excessive terminations and the lowering of sexual standards. Their opponents, led by the Abortion Law Reform Association and the more radical National Abortion Campaign, argue that the rise in the number of legal terminations represents the decline of the hazardous back-street abortion and the legitimate desire of women to exercise control over their own fertility. For them, and for me, abortion is an inevitable element in the medical spectrum of contraception and should be freely available, and early, at the request of women rather than at the behest of doctors. This does not mean one is 'pro-abortion' so much as in favour of allowing women themselves the choice of how to resolve the painful dilemma of unwanted pregnancy. Indeed, as the first socialist to campaign on a public platform for legal abortion, Stella Browne argued that women's control over their own bodies in reproduction is analogous to workers' control over production. Those of us in favour of choice also, and logically, oppose state control over women's reproductive rights as has occurred in government-funded contraception, abortion and sterilisation in the name of population control. As the slogan runs, 'Neither Church nor State should control women's reproductive fate.'

The campaign in 1979 against the Corrie Bill reached its climax in an 80,000-strong demonstration on 28 October 1979, called, remarkably, by the Trades Union Congress, a majority of whose members are male. Until the late seventies, the TUC had studiously avoided taking action on this 'divisive' issue, which had been seen as a matter of conscience. But Len Murray, the TUC General Secretary, and senior women trade unionists duly led off the march under a banner which stated, 'Abortion: TUC says Keep it Legal.' The huge size and energy of the march reflected not only years of steady argument and campaigning in the labour movement, but also the strength of the women's movement, the brio of organised gays and lesbians and a sizable, colourful and very noisy punk contingent.

The anti-abortion lobby, notably the Society for the Protection of the Unborn Child, which has twenty-one staff and a budget of £600,000 per year, has refused to allow women choice in this matter. The most recent attempt at restrictive legislation, two decades after David Steel's Bill, comes from the Liberal MP David Alton. His proposed bill is one of three which surfaced in 1987. Alton, who admits to being against abortion on principle, seized on genuine unease about a tiny number of late abortions (there were only some twenty-nine performed more than twenty-four weeks after conception in 1986) to propose an amendment which would reduce the time limit for abortion to eighteen weeks after conception. The probable result would be an effective limit of sixteen weeks or less because doctors would be obliged to leave a margin for error to avoid criminal prosecution. And given the delays, waiting lists and occasional outright hostility from anti-abortion doctors, this would force many women to continue with unwanted pregnancies. It would also render unworkable the sophisticated screening tests which are nowadays able to detect serious foetal abnormalities at the twenty-week margin. And it shows no understanding that the majority of those requesting late termination are under-age, psychiatrically ill or criminally assaulted women who have denied their pregnancy and simply haven't encountered appropriate medical help at an earlier stage of pregnancy.

As the veteran campaigner for women's health rights, Angela Phillips, put it:

> If David Alton really cares about reducing the number of late abortions, he could introduce a bill to abolish this red tape. He could also introduce legislation making it compulsory for every health district to establish a direct access, outpatient, abortion clinic. These changes would help women to get what they want: the earliest possible help. They would automatically reduce late abortions, without increasing the sum of human misery.[4]

The hospitals

'The NHS,' said Dr David Owen when Minister of Health, 'still has an appalling legacy of old buildings.' I can still remember the sense of shock when, after six years as a medical student, I arrived at a hospital which had *not* been built in the nineteenth century. It was quite unnerving to work without the familiar gaunt Victorian arches and corridors, blackened fire escapes, tea-coloured walls and cramped, viewless offices. As both patient and doctor, my idea of hospitals was automatically that they were outdated, unsuitable and depressing, and that a good deal of emotional effort had to be spent on overcoming their physical discomfort. Nearly a quarter of British hospitals are over one hundred years old; they were very often built as workhouses and contain in their stark architecture a deliberate gloominess. Within these shells hospital architects have exercised a great deal of ingenuity in adding on units, inserting façades and attempting to redesign ward spaces. But anyone who works in British hospitals will be familiar with pioneering research projects that take place in Nissen huts, venereal units stuck away in outhouses rather less comfortable than public lavatories, and maternity clinics in clanking halls that echo every word between doctor and patient to the entire waiting queue, staring, tealess and toyless, into space.

The sprawling maze-like structure accumulated from the various phases of improvement and uneasily amalgamated by the old corridor structure of the original hospital would fox the most ingenious laboratory rat. It is a major task simply to prevent patients, visitors and new staff from losing themselves. The point is not just that the hospitals are old and were designed for a type of medicine no longer practised, but that their rambling, inefficient and gloomy structures create a similar mentality in those who try to work in them. One becomes accustomed to cramped and dingy wards and accepts hospital medicine as being practised despite the buildings rather than with their aid. It becomes routine to see patients taken to and from operating theatres across open yards, food travelling large distances from where it is cooked to the ward where it is served, inevitably cold and dull, and outpatients' waiting areas cramped and uncomfortable. One forgets how to protest and becomes quite hurt if others do. Even some new hospitals are ageing prematurely because maintenance is being neglected in order to try and save money. In January 1987 the BMJ noted, 'Virtually every hospital is dirty and many are filthy . . . Many hospitals are unpainted, unrepaired and unmaintained. Privatisation has saved money but it has often made standards worse.'

Hospital morale

Both bad working conditions and increased 'patient turnover' affect staff morale and decrease the chance to build up friendly and human relationships with patients. Impersonality is inevitable when the object of the exercise becomes the speed with which a patient can safely be sent home. This is especially frustrating because of the fact that hospital work is always advertised as worthwhile and rewarding, even though it permits less and less involvement and reward. Nurses have often complained about this and the associated problem of understaffing (worse at night), and skimped training, rather than about the issue of cash. A Hackney doctor says:

> I wanted to become a doctor for all the usual sorts of reasons. Feeling that it was a worthwhile job, wanting to help people, professional status . . . What I found out when I started practising medicine was that the problems I was presented with as a doctor just couldn't be solved by me, however good I was. Say the people who get depressed because they live in really bad conditions, people who take overdoses. All I could do was pump their stomach, keep them in hospital for twenty-four hours, discharge them again as 'non-suicidal' and then wonder why they did it all over again in a week's time.

For the consultant who usually only sees the inpatient on two or three occasions, when all the preliminary groundwork has been done by the house staff, an increased turnover of patients probably increases job satisfaction. But to achieve it, the houseman has the unpleasant task of 'booting out' the least ill patients while the arrivals for the next list await their turn with a cup of tea in the sister's office. At the general practitioner's end there is an increase of problems with wound infections, post-operative pain and poor healing. Very often pressure on the wards delays even the notification of discharge dates and current drugs available, and a full summary of what has happened in hospital can often take several weeks to materialise. More patients, especially with abdominal pain, are discharged without diagnosis, and many patients whose home circumstances are not suitable for convalescence are deprived of a more gentle hospital recovery. Such is the tempo of investigation that many patients return home utterly exhausted. If the discharge is rushed, and this is more and more often the case, there is no time to warn relatives adequately, let alone the relevant social and nursing services.

'The patient is always wrong'

My first experience of hospital was during long childhood stays as a sufferer from first tuberculosis and then polio. Among my memories of the kindness of the nurses and the other patients, the presence of doctors seemed occasional and special, arriving in troupes to discuss the progress of one part of your body while you, rather embarrassed, stared at the ceiling, tried not to cry and pretended not to be getting in the way. After they had safely left the ward (doctors are always 'busy', if a life-or-death crisis requiring their presence lies around every corridor corner), patients would confer about what was decided, most importantly whether there was any chance of discharge. The junior nurses would join in the guesswork. I grew to understand that the patient was usually wrong about everything, that once you got your bedpan you would probably be stranded, perched on it for an hour, that the patients had only the dignity, status and rights they could squeeze from the system, and we all remained in ignorance about our progress because it was nobody's job to explain, except the houseman, who was half-asleep anyway. We were not people, we were a 'tib and fib', a 'Charnley', and 'two fractured necks of femurs'.

This kind of atmosphere was investigated and reported on by numerous campaigners and committees in the 1960s. It results not from personal malice or organisational incompetence, but from the whole system of acute hospital medicine as it has grown up. Even the measured official language of the time reveals quite how rigid and unsuitable the ward regimes had often become. In 1961 the Powell Report noted that 'Rest is an essential part of a patient's treatment, yet it is becoming progressively more difficult to rest in hospital . . . the patient is called upon to endure a marathon beginning far too early in the morning and ending late at night.' A parent and some enlightened paediatricians forced action on the unnecessary suffering of young children in hospital, crying, as I so clearly remember, ourselves to sleep at night with our nurses in tears at their inability to comfort us. Yet it took the campaigning work of James Robertson and the example of doctors like Dermod MacCarthy even to establish the desirability of parents staying with young children for more than the regulation visiting hour.

Florence Nightingale, who spent most of her life handling facts, figures and plans, still understood that their object was the comfort of the sick and suffering. In 1859 she wrote: 'Apprehension, uncertainty, waiting, expectation, fear of surprise, do a patient more harm than any exertion. Remember he is face-to-face with his enemy all the time, having long imaginary conversations with him.' Yet nowadays, when morale is mentioned, it is always the morale of the doctors, and it usually means they want more money. Staff have become more rather than less remote with the growing bureaucratisation of nursing. The increased division of medical labour means more and more medical experts extract blood, take pictures, inject dyes, measure, galvanise, manipulate. They all glance at the growing wad of notes to ascertain the case's name, smile fixedly and say, 'Now, just relax, Mrs So and So,' before beginning their work. Questions get only the vaguest answers, yet the patient who presses his enquiry further is regarded as something of a menace. Patients go from beginning to end of a prolonged investigation, told little more than 'a bit too much acid on the tummy,' or 'stones'. They would probably require more precision from the mechanic who overhauls their car: 'Departmentalism . . . is more given to silence than communication. Silence from those in authority, from doctor, sister, nurse, administrator, clerk, technician and so on often means a want of imagination; silence consents to fear among those who have great need for explanation and reassurance,' writes Richard Titmuss.[5]

Till death do us part

'It may seem a strange principle to enunciate as the very first requirement in a hospital that it should do the sick no harm,' wrote Florence Nightingale. But nowhere is the principle disregarded more callously than at the point of death itself, nowhere else are the interests of the patients so unregarded. Medicine exists to save life, not to prolong death. It has, however, created hospitals which are the hardest places in society in which to die with dignity. For my first year as a doctor, I sprinted half-dressed, half-asleep twice a week down a 600-yard corridor to attend to cardiac arrests. Dream-like, in front or behind, other doctors panted and bounced, the trolleys of equipment clanged, the buzzers squawked. Charging into darkened wards, we woke the patients, pummelled the dying one, jerked them inches off the bed with electric shocks, wrestled with their mouths to find a way down with an air-tube, cracked ribs, tried to interpret ECG squiggles and to titrate the right amount of drugs to elicit a response. Sometimes it was more like the experiments we had done with acetyl choline and frogs' muscles on stained physiology benches than medicine. Yet it was only on the night when a fairly fit patient had a heart attack just from watching what we were up to that it occurred to me to question the wisdom of what we were doing; for, while every effort can and should be devoted to monitoring and reviving patients in units equipped for intensive care, the kind of indiscriminate, ineffective invasion which we wholeheartedly conceived as solely for the patient's good, was in fact depriving the dying of their last shred of dignity in order to give us a little practice and a little false prestige. None of this is to argue that we should abandon or slacken our development of medical science, but we need to sharpen its focus, to take more seriously its implications and applications. We need to ask honest-ly, every time, whether its net result enhances the doctor's prestige or the patient's well-being, for these are not necessarily the same thing.

The challenge of AIDS

Many of these issues were brought into focus by the emergence in the early eighties of a new fatal illness, the Acquired Immune Deficiency Syndrome. AIDS is no more a gay disease than German Measles is German. Its clinical identification by physicians in San Francisco and New York in 1981 among young, previously fit homosexual men suddenly unable to resist the parasitic lung infection *Pneumocystis carinii* and the rare skin cancer Kaposi's Sarcoma, will probably eventually be seen as an accident of social history.

The figures on AIDS are always out of date by the time they are published, but by January 1988 the number of people known to have caught it passed 100,000, and the number of recorded deaths in the USA was 28,683, and in Britain 697. The proportion of those infected who will eventually die is unknown, especially since the introduction of a series of drug treatments which appear to mitigate the symptoms. But some researchers still feel that it will eventually prove fatal to all sufferers. What is also now clear is that blacks are suffering more from AIDS than whites and that Africa is both more affected and much less able to cope medically than is the USA, where the disease came to notice and prominence.

Any major epidemic reflects the state not just of medicine but of the body politic. Disease makes history as much as war: the Aztecs were defeated by smallpox, not Cortés, and yellow fever beat the French armies in Haiti as much as the slave rising. The international spread of AIDS reflects a world of persistent travel – migration, forced labour and air flight – and its incidence pattern reflects the widening gaps in health and nutritional standards between the rich West and the rest of the world. It also indicates moral prejudice, for it is clear that the initial low priority given to the disease was due to the social stigma still attached to homosexuality. Even the quarrelling between the French and the American researchers and the fights between the rival drug manufacturers are the product of a world which does not act collectively and internationally when faced with a global threat but seeks personal fame and financial advantage. If ever an international task force which could transcend national boundaries was needed it is in the case of AIDS: what we have seen so far is insignificant compared with what will happen in Africa if the disease is not controlled.

And one of the most distressing side effects of the epidemic is that anti-homosexuality has been given a tremendous fillip and that the period in which open gayness asked important questions about 'normality' may be over. Perhaps the most serious social consequences of AIDS would be to return us to the bad old days of not so long ago when homosexuality itself was a 'disease', non-procreative sex was 'immoral' and male chauvinist prejudice something men were proud of. So it needs to be said that we all owe much to the bravery of homosexuals now fighting the disease and that AIDS would have been infinitely more difficult to deal with if homosexuality was still concealed and closeted.

We in Britain are not yet facing a crisis of the kind which is being experienced in New York. But it will come, and the consequences for the NHS will be both fiscal and clinical. The cost of proper care for those suffering with the virus will be high and the work demanding. Every epidemic offers medicine a challenge, but the opportunities can only be taken if there is proper funding, especially into research. Charity balls and one-man shows are important but entirely inadequate for the task; one-off advertising campaigns are simply a gesture. The case for proper AIDS funding must reinforce the general campaign for proper resources for the NHS. It is also clear that caring adequately for the young, isolated and often very frightened people who contract the disease will require types of medical and nursing skill which were too readily discarded in the over-optimism of the antibiotic era. Doctors and nurses may have to learn, or perhaps remember, skills and ways of working we had thought redundant.

The missing dimension

However, to view the problems of the National Health Service simply in terms of unchallenged poverty, unequal access, skimped spending, out-of-date buildings, undemocratic operation and social inequality, although each of these factors has powerful effects, is to underestimate the problem. They add up to something more fundamental: a cheap but inefficient system which answers the needs of the individuals who stay in power and fails to tackle the major causes of ill-health. So although there has been a marked improvement in health care since the introduction of the National Health Service, it has been a piecemeal rather than a planned process. Those areas which have the most disease still have the fewest doctors and facilities, and better-off patients mysteriously manage to cream off the best standards of treatment. Far from evaporating, poverty and ill-health have persisted and worsened. The scientific advances are still isolated in the centres of excellence. Many of the medical opportunities opened up by a national service, especially in the fields of preventative medicine and health education, are not sufficiently explored. Many of the unattractive aspects of pre-NHS medicine – private practice with NHS facilities, the absolute power of consultants (which many do not themselves relish), the dominance of the teaching hospitals, the underdevelopment of general practice – have not been remedied.

None of this amounts to an argument against a national health service. The crisis in marketplace medicine in Italy or the persistently low standards of public health in North America should be a warning against any return to the old system. But we can now see that it was the wrong sort of nationalisation, its principles were not pursued consistently and it was leaking with the compromises built into its original structure. Most of all it has had to exist in a society whose central economic tenets are diametrically opposed to the values the NHS attempts to promulgate.

5
Primary Care

The family doctor is most people's first experience of the NHS. Nine out of ten patients who contact the NHS are seen by one of the country's 32,355 GPs, who make up under half the total medically qualified personnel. The GPs are the most myth-encrusted creatures in the service. They are supposed to practise in custom-built local authority health centres, according to Section 21 of the National Health Service Act, which states: 'It will be the duty of every local health authority to provide, equip and maintain and staff health centres.'

They are contracted to provide a twenty-four hour service to their flock, but over 10,000 use night answering services where, after a suitable delay for rerouting calls, a cruising night doctor attends to those who inconveniently fall sick out of hours. They are responsible for providing care all year round; a GP on a breathing machine after a heart attack is still technically responsible for his or her list! The GPs like to think that they provide continuous care, but in fact they mainly see patients at times of illness. GPs are unfairly attributed with mediocrity by many consultants, and with a specialised grasp of all aspects of medicine which they could never obtain by the public. Even the touch of personal intimacy with their patients is often obtained by an advanced sneak at the individual medical records kept for every person in Britain, a major achievement in itself. The BMA in its 1983 brochure *General Practice, a British Success*, was almost euphoric about 'the positive picture which emerges . . . of a professional group engaged in progressively improving the services it offers the public whilst maintaining worthwhile standards and traditions.' But, in reality, GPs are still a long way from achieving what Julian Tudor Hart describes as the 'open medicine' of general practice at its best, 'in which a consultation can become a productive relationship between experts: patients who know their own story, and doctors who can help organise it into a diagnosis and a plan for management.'[1]

Almost every survey of GPs is contradicted by the next one, and most definitions of their role are hopeless. At best the GP is a general physician with special skill in preventative and chronic medicine and experience of domiciliary practice, at worst a snap diagnostician with a telephone. He or she remains the first point of contact for primary health care and, with the exception of the accident and emergency departments, is the portal of entry, by referral, to the hospital system. Although the services they provide are largely financed by central government, they are independent professionals under contract to the ninety-eight Family Practitioner Committees in England and Wales and the nineteen Health Boards in Scotland and Northern Ireland. They thereby retain the right to practise privately. And supervision or inspection of their level of NHS service has, until recently, been remarkably unobtrusive, in view of the sums of taxpayers' funds they expend. Apart from the professional disciplines enforced by the General Medical Council – which still chiefly concern adultery, alcoholism and drug addiction – and a general responsibility to consider the price and efficacy of the drugs they prescribe, GPs have had remarkable autonomy with the FPC acting as paymasters rather than planners or supervisors.

Medicine's cottage industry

This crucial sector, whose organisation shapes people's access to and expectations of more specialised medicine, has changed slowly since 1949 and has benefited last from technical advances. 'The industrial revolution has passed general practice by; it remains a cottage industry, underorganised, undercapitalised and overworked,' said Professor Brotherton in 1963, and some of those cottages are still pretty ill-equipped. This is reflected financially. During 1986, the total cost of the Family Practitioner Services amounted to £4,484 million, equivalent to an average of £79 for every person in the country. Although this figure is thirty times larger than the total in 1949, when adjusted for inflation it amounts to only twice the sum expended then. So, in contrast with the fourfold increase recorded in the hospital sector and the threefold increase in overall NHS expenditure, the FPS's share of the cake has dwindled from over a third to less than a quarter. Although the number of GPs has risen (from thirty-nine per 100,000 in 1951 to fifty-two per 100,000 in 1985) this increase is far less than the rate of increase in hospital-based doctors.

1948

In 1948 the BMA's shortsighted concern was aimed at preserving private practice for those who could afford it, leaving the state to insure the doctor against poorer patients' inability to pay. Their insistence on the fictional independence conferred by the beloved capitation scheme allowed the specialists to steal the gravy and the hospitals, and left primary practice locked in its own, partly self-imposed backwardness.

The 'independent contractor' system of payment encouraged inefficiency and rewarded low standards. It was financially better to take on a big list and do the bare minimum from basic premises than to restrict the numbers, lengthen the time available for each patient and improve the facilities. Doctors in general practice became more rather than less separated from hospitals and each other. Practising alone, clinical standards almost inevitably sink and slumber, becoming accommodated to the realities of time and possibility rather than the organised thoroughness drummed into doctors at teaching hospital but plainly impossible in the trench war of general practice.

When the premium is on quantity not quality, why bother? Why examine a chest with all the intricate tapping and touching and listening you impressed the examiners with, when all the old boy is asking for is another bottle of 'the mixture'? 'A well-trained man will throw over the hard-won disciplines of clinical training and accept the limitations of general practice . . . such acceptance of bad conditions has a stultifying effect,' wrote J. S. Collings, a New Zealand doctor who was violently upbraided for his forthright survey of general practice standards in 1950.[2]

Collings found a jungle of premises, supervised by practitioners he divided into mercenaries and missionaries. He found small, cold and inhospitable surgeries, examination couches littered with records, instrument cupboards like museums of past interests, specula rich in dust, and the chemicals at the sink of purely ornamental value. Working single-handed was offered as the excuse, but he considered it little more than a convenient rationalisation of low standards. Examinations were usually confined to the offending organ and even then were cursory. 'With conditions as they are,' Collings wrote bluntly, 'refresher courses would do as much good as an injection of adrenaline does with a patient with terminal heart failure.'

Conditions of practice

Primary care did not in fact succumb, although it continued to operate from premises which dated from the days when GPs strode about waiting for the pneumonia crisis to be resolved. In an influential survey in 1965, Cartwright and Marshall found that in working class areas 80 per cent of doctors' surgeries had been built before 1900 and only 5 per cent since 1945.[3] Most were still converted shops with a bare waiting room containing tattered copies of *Woman's Own*, hard chairs and a few mouldering anti-smoking posters. Another survey of industrial practices found that one in three had no receptionist or lavatory. A majority of premises still lacked adequate changing rooms, which not only inconveniences the patient but effectively prevents methodical physical examination.

Concern persisted about the state of general practice in the inner cities, notably in the Royal Commission on the NHS set up in 1976 which reported, generally favourably, on general practice. The Commission noted, however, the familiar complaint that people experience difficulties in getting registered and in contacting their doctor once they are. It added:

> In some declining urban areas and in parts of London particularly, the NHS is failing dismally to provide an adequate primary care service to its patients . . . improving the quality of care in inner city areas is the most urgent problem which the NHS services in the community must tackle.[4]

Concern for the service in inner London was developed by the Study Group on Primary Health Care in Inner London (the Acheson Report), which heard extensive evidence in 1980 and was published with some 115 recommendations in May 1981. The problems of poor premises, low prestige and high workload and the sheer weight of the social problems of the inner city were noted, and a range of suggestions, including some which had been pioneered in Hackney by a Primary Care Planning Group led by Professor Salkind of St Bart's, were suggested. But, as a comprehensive follow-up report, *After Acheson*, by the Policy Studies Institute, noted in 1986, Acheson 'is the story of a Government promise which did not materialise.'[5]

Health centres

The health centres had been conceived to anticipate these problems, to sustain clinical standards by spreading the workload, linking other staff, and encouraging a degree of self-specialisation. Ten were opened in 1948, but by 1969 there were only eighty-seven, painfully slow progress for a service which was supposed to be a requirement for local authorities. In Tower Hamlets in East London, the first health centre was opened only in 1977. The amalgamation of individual principals into group practices has proceeded faster in the seventies and eighties. In 1952, 44 per cent of GPs were single-handed and only a handful were in partnerships of six or more. By 1985, the single-handed had fallen to 12 per cent, many close to retirement, and 17 per cent of GPs were in partnerships of six or more. Although this has lifted the inhuman pressure of single-handed night visiting, often it has been a merger of the bad elements as well as the good. In too many cases, the group practice partnership agreements were inequitable, with 'junior' or 'salaried' partners being exploited by seniors who could, for example, insist on registering patients in their own name while doing little of the work generated by them.

And, too often, the GP, by hanging on so grimly to fictitious independence and the status of a small shopkeeper, was in no position to adapt to change. Although the GP tended to attribute the low level of equipment, skill and morale to the public's abuses or the state encroachment, it really lay in the under-capitalisation of the primary sector, the limited access and liaison with the paramedical, nursing and health visiting professions, the lack of custom-built premises and the sheer absence of time for reflection and education. Nothing interferes with clear thought like the three minute cascade of patients whose demands are as various as their faces and whose complaints switch in moments from terminal cancer to the non-existent sore throat. Use of appointment systems instead of the first-come first-served scrum has increased until the GPs of three-quarters of patients were said to use them. But the Royal Commission on the NHS cited surveys which showed that waiting time had not appreciably altered, that 'overprotective' receptionists were a persistent subject of complaint, and suggested that 'continuity of care may simply not exist in many large cities.' And as the cuts started to bite into the hospital services, the rate of consultation has increased, with the average citizen seeing their GP 4.4 times a year in 1986, compared to the figure of 4.1 calculated in 1975. This despite the introduction of 'self-certifying' sick notes for the first week of illness.

And although the number of group practices has increased quite markedly, it is by no means clear whether the medicine in group practices has changed. Their aim was not just administrative convenience, but to alter the range of medicine and the roles of those who delivered it. The potential of a properly designed, modern and attractive centre which provides a working base for doctors, dentists, nurses, health visitors and social workers is that it could genuinely become a centre for health. There would be sufficient skills pooled to avoid unnecessary and long-delayed excursions to hospital consultants, and a large scale operation would allow the basic laboratory investigations to be carried out quickly and to high standards. The centre could be staffed at night to offer emergency callers personal advice and, if necessary, immediate access to relevant personal medical records. It could become a community centre which local people felt they had a right to attend and where they were welcome when they were well for screening and advice that went further than what is narrowly defined as 'medical'. It could be the basis for services which patients themselves could help arrange: playschools, nurseries, physiotherapy, help during convalescence, and specialist lay groups of fellow sufferers, such as people trying to lose weight or to stop smoking, who could support each other. Naturally, almost imperceptibly, attitudes to health could be altered and health education and medical self-knowledge become a reality.

With these centres well established, hospitals could indeed insist on stricter referrals, better case summaries from GPs which conveyed their full social knowledge, and patients could be discharged earlier with safety. Hospitals and health centres could perhaps exchange personnel fruitfully instead of just as a stopgap, with a hospital specialist taking an occasional health centre clinic and a GP working a session or two in his or her special interest at a hospital. Health centres could have unclogged the hospitals of the cases which were otherwise drawn to them by default, and could have really developed their unique expertise. A GP referral for 'an opinion' could be just that, not the transfer of a patient to a never-ending career as a hospital outpatient. Patients could recover a voice and some measure of sovereignty over their own health care.

Domestic midwifery could begin a genuine revival, not with GPs whose knowledge of abnormal midwifery is so sketchy that their best contribution to averting catastrophe was to arrive late, but with obstetrically experienced GPs committed to decent antenatal care, proper care of the newborn and democratic co-operation with a midwife sharing the premises. And, more important than all that, the GP could turn the tables on the deluge of demands and crises which threaten to swamp him or her, and could start to plan screening and preventative work. The GP's local population could offer tremendous potential for local epidemiology and relevant health promotion.

As John Robson argues,

General practice in the 1960s/70s was largely concerned with the queue outside the door. It dealt with a sequence of largely unstructured presented problems and responses were transactions in the shopkeeping tradition, with no attempt to either anticipate and modify risks, or to involve local populations in any way. There have been important developments since then. Intervention for whole populations has been shown to be effective in reducing serious ill-health or death. Primary care has been shown to be an effective vehicle for such intervention. Anticipatory care – using routine patient contacts for case finding and risk discrimination, combined with follow-up has been shown to be an appropriate way of working. Populations here and abroad, locally and nationally, have begun to take up the question of involvement in health care and prevention. Patients' Committees, the Patients' Association, women's organisations, trade unions, patient-held records, and so on, are now on the agenda for anyone seriously proposing strategies for the 1990s.[6]

In fact, because well-located, properly staffed and serviced health centres did not exist in the early life of the service, hospitals and GPs pulled apart. By the mid-sixties, practical problems of pay structure and status reached a crisis. This was partly about pay, but as the *General Practitioner* rightly observed in 1965, 'the sooner the Ministry of Health and the BMA realise that what the vast majority of general practitioners is interested in is service, and the means whereby they can give this service to their patients, the sooner the citizens of this country will receive the medical care to which they are entitled.' And the BMA stated:

> The public at large and the Minister of Health should realise that this discontent lies deep. The medical profession too should realise, in fact does realise, that this discontent is only in part due to the mechanics of the health service. It is caused as much by the rapidly changing position that the general practitioner faces today with medical science far outstripping in its discoveries and application what he was taught at his medical school ten or even five years ago . . . The GP has to get back into the mainstream of clinical life.[7]

The crisis was really about the failure to find the means to deliver medical care at the speed at which its potential was expanding. While great things were happening in the furnaces of the teaching hospitals, the GPs attempted to keep up to date with back-issues of the *Lancet* and teach-yourself guides to electrocardiography.

The Government produced the 'GPs' Charter', a collection of reforms. More capital funds were made available and practice improvement and surgery expenses were better compensated. Links with hospitals were formally established through a programme of postgraduate teaching centres. The rate of health centre building was speeded up – that is, until the country ploughed into the next trough of economic crisis. There were now training courses; the Royal College of General Practitioners, brainchild of a handful of pioneers, took on real authority.

These measures staved off the crisis, but did not solve it. For some doctors they meant that for the first time in their professional lives they were reasonably well off. For keener young doctors there was now a route to general practice that took training seriously, not just as the second-best option when you gave up hope on the hospital career ladder. In some centres and groups a new spirit of co-operation between staff was established. But all too often the substance did not alter. Pioneer health centres merely confirmed the backwardness of the rest. Some of the trainee schemes were merely a way of ensuring that unpopular junior posts were filled rather than a means of providing the future GPs with education. Some doctors in groups still did not even talk to each other, let alone to the social worker.

Teaching GPs

The teaching of general practice in medical schools has grown from virtually nothing to become the subject of specialised university departments. Indeed, the growth of academic general practice departments recorded in the 1986 Mackenzie Report, and the general improvement of postgraduate education, has been one of the most heartening aspects of postwar general practice and has undoubtedly done much to contribute to the growing popularity of general practice as a career choice.

Less than thirty years ago, the first independent department of general practice was created in the University of Edinburgh; now there are twenty-four such departments. Since the pioneer 1961 Christ Church Conference, the GP Postgraduate Centres have become a national movement. But even the best teaching cannot prepare one for the sheer variety of demands. As two GP academics at Leicester put it:

> General practice is a setting in which undifferentiated problems present at early stages of development, where there is a complex mixture of clinical, psychological and social components and where the many symptoms presented may be accompanied by few clinical signs.

This puts greater demand on clinical reasoning: the good GP is as much a medical intellectual as the good researcher. The method of teaching future GPs must be further improved and altered in its location.

Hospital teaching is based on uncommon but interesting diseases and the mastery of an immense body of scientific fact. Yet, however sophisticated the newly qualified doctor is in dealing with computerised quizzes, he or she is a novice in the maze of hunches, background information, social insights and medical suspicion through which the GP has learnt to find a way.

More and more, what start as strictly medical questions go beyond medicine itself. Many common problems of tension, over-eating, addictions of various sorts, have their roots in how people live and work. To tackle them with pills alone may seem scientific, but it violates the deeper canons of serious medicine. Many of the questions patients now ask do not require a simple 'yes' or 'no' answer, backed by some unexplained authority; they require the doctor to present information so that the patient can make the decision.

What are the risks inherent in the hospitalisation of older patients and how do they compare with the disadvantages of home care? Is the use of new and energetically promoted preparations (for example, to ease the menopause by hormone therapy, or to increase blood flow to the brains of the elderly) justified? What are the patients' rights over their own bodies – especially when, as in the case of abortion, the patient's wishes conflict with medical and religious established wisdom?

These questions, and others like them, once had a simple answer: the doctor was a 'God with a bedside manner'. Part of his informal training was learning to tell convincing lies and to answer difficult enquiries with a blast of long medical words or a brief bit of soothing.

As long as patients could be seen as simpletons, the doctor had a vested interest in maintaining their ignorance. There was more stress on fitting in socially with senior colleagues than on being able to talk openly and clearly to people who were sick; and in fact many patients wanted GPs to keep up this almost religious but very comforting image. As for their own diagnosis, treatment and anatomy, ignorance *was* bliss.

But now, for most doctors and most patients, the era of medical infallibility is over. Most newly qualified doctors, at last educated more widely in sociology and psychiatry and drawn from a less narrow class background, start in practice aiming at an honest, democratic relationship with their patients, based on the skills they actually possess rather than on mysterious powers or social authority. They appreciate rather than disdain the 'lay' knowledge of their patients. There is a commitment to screening and prevention and a determination to *apply* a scientific approach rather than simply to regurgitate it. Primary care is better organised, better financed, better informed, better paid and potentially strengthened by the shift of emphasis towards community care.

Primary care in the eighties

But it is also clear that both the Health Ministers of the Thatcher era and the DHSS aim to narrow the 'clinical freedom' to which GPs have been accustomed and, through the long-postponed White Paper on Primary Care, to begin a revision of the terms of the GP's contract. 1946 had brought the security of the NHS, the new deal of

1966 gave reimbursement of rent and rates, 70 per cent staff reimbursement, the Basic Practice and Group Practice allowances. But the 1987 White Paper, larded with good intentions, was less palatable medicine. A preliminary sortie, which provoked some of the fieriest protest meetings in the postwar history of GP politics, was a largely unsuccessful attempt by Kenneth Clarke to introduce tighter regulations over GP use of the deputising services. A number of informal surveys, persistent complaints, and the occasional tragedy through failures of communication or reluctance to visit, had focused attention on the use or abuse of these services, which in most cases are commercially run. In their defence, it must be said that the quality varies widely and the better deputising set-ups are modern and highly efficient. In fact, without the back-up of the commercial services, it may well be the case that GP home visiting (which, like doorstep milk delivery, is a British peculiarity) might have begun to go out of existence in British cities.

So what are the objections? Some of the services, undercutting and overextending at the same time, have made a fortune for the entrepreneurs who own them. The conditions of work for the doctors, often between jobs or taking exams and usually qualified overseas, are poor, with low, piecework-based wages and without either security or any career structure. And the fact that the service must respond to every call (and makes its money per visit, regardless of its merits) encourages pill-oriented flying visits when telephone advice and a proper examination in the surgery would be more appropriate. High speed, late night, one-off consultations – fast food medicine – are a parody of the well-recorded continuity on which primary care ought to base itself.

And in certain categories of home visits – for the dying, the very young, the pregnant and all those other medical occasions, such as an asthma attack, where prompt, informed medical care is important but hospital admission is not necessarily required – a patient is entitled to the attention of a reasonably familiar doctor who has personal access to their records and their own GP. After all, more than half the GPs in Britain manage to do their own cover already, if only because deputising services hardly exist outside the big cities.

But why all the sound and fury? It is because the deputising service has become, for both sides, a symbol. To the traditional GPs who rend the air at protest meetings, the right to switch over to the answering service pretty much when they fancy (the supervision of use of the service had been derisory) is a part of 'clinical freedom'.

For those of us critical of traditional general practice's ability to really get to grips with the health problems of the modern city, the unrestricted use of the answering service is also symbolic: of 'bare minimum' general practice, of deliberate inaccessibility, of rationing of medical care to suit doctors' convenience. It is the practical mechanism by which GPs get away with working long past a sensible retirement age, living miles away from the community they serve, and refusing to collaborate in group practices. And it is a pioneer example of the perils of privatisation: inconsistent standards, low pay, profiteering out of needs which could be remedied from within the NHS.

It is not progressive to work long hours for peanuts. And the medical left is not keener than the traditionalists to increase direct state control over general practice. But many GPs would support the Medical Practitioners' Union's recommendation that doctors who do provide their own out-of-hours care should be eligible for better payment, reimbursement for modern communication equipment, and a lower list size (the simplest, single reform would be to increase the man- and woman-power in primary care so that night work can be properly carried out).

Beneath all these symbolic interactions in which it has become embroiled, deputising continues, and both the deputies' wages and the supervision of the service have already improved. At its best, it is good and, judging from Kenneth Clarke's almost complete climbdown, is here to stay. Certainly the monitoring of relief services, now conducted by 50 per cent lay FPC sub-committees, *has* improved.

The Limited List

A similar standoff, whose importance is symbolic rather than actual, occurred over the introduction by the DHSS, in November 1984, of a 'Limited List' of preparations it would allow chemists to issue on NHS prescriptions. As I argue in Chapter 7, the issues here are complex, and the 'Limited List' initiative proved an unsuccessful half-measure. It is undoubtedly the case that many of the blacklisted preparations are, in the considered view of the clinical pharmacologists, illogical, ineffective and possibly dangerous. There is also a strong case for generic prescribing, that is, the writing of doctors' prescriptions using the pharmacological title of the drug required rather than the brand name adopted by a particular manufacturer. Quite apart from the considerable economic savings, it encourages doctors to think about the contents of what they are prescribing. 28 per cent of prescriptions are already generic. But the 'Limited List' produced little genuine saving and a great deal of confusion and resentment with products moving confusingly between black and white list. And although the keen young GP vocational trainee may be able to recite the literature which proves that cough mixtures were no good anyway, the bronchitic patient simply registered the fact that he was now charged for his bottle of linctus as another act of petty meanness.

In assessing British general practice, it is only fair to give due weight to the pressures GPs themselves experience. GPs are only human. They are under very considerable direct pressure from the drug companies. The GP is the middle-man between them and their market; each one prescribes, on average, over £14,000 worth of drugs per year. There is not only direct sales contact to pamper such big spenders, but sponsorship of give-away medical publications which mix academic medicine with wine know-how, stock market tips and hard-sell advertisements. Pity not only the GP but also the GP's postman. General practitioners themselves have become responsible for a great deal of administrative and clerical work. They are facing, with the cuts, the shrinking of the very services which were promised as an essential part of a new deal for primary care. The fact that a Ministry computer has come to the decision, on economic grounds, that a local hospital must be closed or a group practice building postponed yet again does not make it a medically sound decision.

The GP's traditional role has been undermined, and yet nothing more tangible seems about to replace it. Many doctors are in a quandary: on the one hand, they genuinely want more medical teamwork and a better-educated public; on the other, they are reluctant to relinquish their old authority and unique responsibility. GPs are, in this respect, victims of their own reputation of omniscience. They are still expected to have influence over the housing authorities and the law courts who, nowadays, disregard their carefully penned pleas. And they are still expected to deal with medical and social crises long after the social workers have packed up office. I have found it sobering to see how often the GP and the police officer, targets of so much radical social criticism, end up doling out the common humanity that Family Units and community activists accuse them of lacking. Indeed, read carefully, the current complaints of the police and the general practitioners are quite radical in their implications: they are saying they can no longer cope with the degree of social unrest that has become their responsibility; that they want to return to chasing criminals and healing the sick instead of providing a complaints bureau for a disgruntled and divided society.

Indeed, for city doctors this problem is worsening. The era of 'community care', by coinciding with the epoch of 'the cuts', has turned out as something of a confidence trick. The traditional support of hospitals is becoming more partial and harder to obtain, while the expansion of community-based facilities, the necessary counterbalance to any hospital closure, is proving elusive. Many essential and long-promised community facilities, in particular day care centres for the old and sheltered dwelling for the newly discharged psychiatric patient, are shelved and the services are operated at such a level of chronic understaffing that only emergencies are tackled, and then often with reluctance. Especially in mental health, the old set-up has been abolished and the new, born into a financial vacuum, is in disarray. And it is the GP who is expected, by the relatives at least, to carry the can, just as in the family the mother is once again expected to act as amateur nurse, psychiatrist, ward orderly and therapist as well as to carry out her domestic work, and often a job into the bargain.

The White Paper

Despite all the talk of a computer on every surgery desk and the rhetoric about consumer sovereignty, the White Paper introduced by John Moore in December 1987 was notable for what it omitted rather than what is specified. Indeed, there were elements of a pre-1966 perspective in the increased freedom for patients to change doctors and the bonuses for GPs providing screening. The theory, imported by analogy from the battle in the High Street between chain store and corner shop, was that 'good' doctors will drive out 'bad'. In fact nothing of the kind will happen. The bonuses, like the 'Good Practice Allowance' piloted by the Royal College of General Practitioners and rightly rejected by the profession, would buy the silence of the advanced sectors of the profession (by putting money in the pocket of the individual GP rather than into resources). But even they will soon close their lists by restricting them geographically. Doctor-hopping will often be impossible and anyway leaves the 'bad' doctors unchanged except for a slightly lower income. Instead of proper resources and tangible rewards for services which make a real impact on ill-health (systematic screening, child health clinics, community-based obstetrics), there is an illusory choice for the patient with no rights. There is world of difference between combing the High Street for the best price on a video and choosing the best-buy doctor . . . and getting on the chosen doctor's list.

The White Paper was a resounding anticlimax. Perhaps most notable was the removal of free eye testing by opticians. Apart from their other virtues, these tests provided the basis for national screening for the early detection of glaucoma, a major, preventable cause of blindness.

The general drift of the document and its philosophy for the improvement of general practice was equally depressing. Where there are laudable ideas, they are largely old chestnuts which should have been introduced years ago (like retirement at 70 for GPs . . . why not 65?) or part of an administrative process already under way. A good deal of lip service was paid to the virtues of preventive medicine. Although the prospect of more dietary asides from Edwina Currie astride an expensive exercise bicycle is appalling, it should be recognised that this emphasis picks up on decades of argument from medical and political progressives and, in the case of cervical screening, active campaigning by the women's movement.

For the inner urban GP, the problems are clear-cut and well documented. The service is now more heavily used, with both consultation rates and house calls up. This is becoming more pronounced as the bankrupted hospitals seek to decant outpatients and their medication, while discharging inpatients into something called 'the community'.

The challenges for inner city medicine – young, single mothers, recent migrants, itinerant patients and the raised incidence of psychiatric problems – mean a steady stream of crisis work which thwarts the systematic, doctor-initiated health education we all want to practise. Certainly, since the demise of the GLC and the collapse of the Labour-led councils' anti-cuts stand, the social and community services with which good primary care needs to be allied are themselves in crisis. So when one is called out at 3 a.m. to put a demented old lady to bed, or to traipse up back stairs strewn with faeces and graffiti to reassure an anxious, isolated mother, one can always 'comfort' oneself with the knowledge that it is all part of a larger social crisis in which medicine itself is a minor factor.

Inner city GPs are not short of ideas: many were aired in the discussion of the White Paper and the preceding, largely unimplemented, Acheson Report. We think shorter, not longer, lists are essential, and that the primary care team, properly staffed and housed, is the only way to deliver continuing multi-disciplinary care in which the doctor is not always the key figure.

We understand the importance of screening only too well. But we know from bitter experience how much harder it is to achieve high rates of immunisation, cervical cytology and cardiovascular risk assessment in the turmoil of the inner city than in, say, Oxford, where the use of the health promotion nurses was pioneered. Satisfactorily explaining the point of a smear test and performing it for a non-English-speaking Bengali mother, who probably has her kids with her, simply needs more time and resources (including a translator and probably a female doctor). It is significantly harder for a health visitor to get the inhabitants of Limehouse to take up their measles jabs than it would be in leafy Surrey.

We know from the experience of Site Hill, Edinburgh, that antenatal care based in a properly organised general practice achieves earlier and more convenient booking and better outcomes. But that needs attached community midwives, consultant support and premises capable of holding them in comfort. Practice-based immunisation and child development surveillance improves both uptake of vaccine and early detection of problems, especially deafness. It is probable that long term medical problems like diabetes, hypertension and asthma can be managed better in GP clinics than by endless hospital outpatient waits, with a different doctor each time. But setting up these facilities needs more space and more clerical and reception staff. And most of us still practise in shoe boxes.

Reforms which would have brought resources to the areas of greatest stress include the long-overdue London, or inner urban, weighting (Acheson's Proposition 12), retirement of 65, a registration fee (which would also assist high turnover lists in retirement areas and is Acheson's Proposition 7), extension of fees and funding for doctors doing their own out-of-hours visits, and an increase in the 'Red Book' allowances in the cost rent schemes to compensate for the real cost of land and building in the inner cities. Serious screening needs special funds for staff and software which could, on the ancillary staff principle, be 70 per cent reimbursable. What would lend weight to the lip service paid to screening would be some understanding of how anticipatory care, using routine patient contact for case finding and risk discrimination, can be used systematically to reduce ill-health. This, as has been shown in Finland, must work hand in hand with 'primary prevention', that is a sustained national food and pricing policy and consistent health education.

But in reality, if primary care is to improve, so the Treasury argues, it can only do so at the expense of the hospitals. And we get the usual grocer-shop mentality, the language not of populations and social classes, but of consumers and rival professionals. We risk moving still further away from a national system to two- or three-tier provision according to social geography. Yet again, those with greatest need for good primary care will be served by poorer doctors, unable to afford more staff, practising in hopeless premises with bare minimum standards. And lurking behind the whole White Paper is the intention to extend 'cost limits' to primary care. The spectre is that the GP will become the rationer rather than the spender of resources, with the cash-limited FPCs unable to pay for staff or new buildings because the allocated monies for the year have already been used up. Underneath the high-sounding aims, the Medicines Act which accompanied the White Paper was a clear attempt to put the same fiscal thumbscrews on primary care which have caused the hospitals such public agony.

New roles

The real equivalent to the GP's Charter of 1966 would be an alternative to the competitive market-based vision of unplanned care put forward in the White Paper. The proposals put forward by the Medical Practitioners' Union and widely discussed by younger inner city doctors in particular included:

i *New roles for the general practitioner* – priority given to promoting health and preventing illness; community general practitioners as part of a move towards greater teamwork and away from doctor-centred teams; closer relationships with hospital doctors; smaller lists (1700 patients for each principal); and changes in working conditions.

ii *Revised organisational structure* – a new primary care and community unit, incorporating the present Family Practitioner Committee and the community unit of the District Health Authority, which would plan primary and community care at district level. Neighbourhood health units would be formed to co-ordinate the work and account-ability of primary care services, and the public would participate in the planning and monitoring of both these units.

iii *Revised system of remuneration* – a new independent contract and a salaried option offered to all general practitioners.

iv *Innovations in health centre practice and organisation* – 'experimenal' health centres to pioneer new models of primary health care.

v *Medical education* – changes in the selection of medical students to overcome its present race, gender and social class bias, and greater emphasis on the community in the medical curriculum.[8]

These in turn require more representation for inner city GPs in the professional bodies which have for so long given lip service to the problems.

Wanted: resources

The problem of resources was demonstrated by the Government response to the Acheson Report, the recommendations of which were left with little financial backing (especially on the potentially expensive items like enforcing retirement). And on the question of new money, the Conservative Government was unequivocal: 'Additional spending on the scale that would result from the Report's recommendations,' said Secretary of State Kenneth Baker, 'is quite unrealistic in the present or any foreseeable circumstances.' As Brian Abel-Smith notes, the problem is politi-cal: 'The dissatisfied customers were not politically mobilised, however, or readily mobilisable: they were disproportionately the poorer sections of society, the ethnic minorities, the unsettled and mobile without a community base.'

The key to change in general practice is general criticism. Julian Tudor Hart, late of the Glyncorrwg Health Centre in Glamorgan, is one of the GPs who argue that the new primary-care doctor must be exposed to criticism by medical peers and patients and must operate as part of a genuinely democratic team. This process would depend on the participation of a much more active, informed public. He says that 'The most evangelistic of health promotion and anticipatory care cannot be effective if the mass of people have a fatalistic approach to their own health.'

David Ryde, a South London GP and a member of the Royal College of General Practitioners, has recently described how his own illness forced him to think carefully about traditional reliance on pills and ignorance, and inclined him towards the idea of the doctor as 'a purveyor of ideas, an interpreter and an educationalist in health.' His drug prescriptions now amount to only a third of the national average prescribed by GPs. He feels that 'a doctor's prescribing costs are inversely related to his grasp of the problem and his understanding of the patient, and to achieve this, the doctor must listen. The doctor who looks at his watch instead of his patient should take a long look at himself.'

Here again the most influential criticism of medical mystery-mongering has come from the women's liberation movement, in the form of their demands for health care which starts with an acceptance of the patient's absolute right over his or her own body. Peter Huntingford, a Maidstone obstetrician, has argued that this kind of challenge is not a nuisance but an inspiration to doctors who really want to practise medicine which answers the real needs of the patients rather than the convenience of the doctor. 'I have been forced,' he has said, 'to question my own attitudes because I was fortunate enough to be involved with a group of consumers who have questioned the attitudes of myself and others like me who wished to care for them.'

Perhaps it will only be when other sections of the community also have the confidence to want control over their bodies that medical professionalism will back down. For that confidence to develop, the greatest possible amount of well-informed lay debate is desirable, even if it does dent doctors' self-esteem. To assert more control over the medical institutions they pay for, the lay public needs the knowledge to challenge medical secrecy on informed terms. Medicine is much too important to be left to doctors alone. Populations, locally and nationally, need to become involved in health care and prevention.

6
Mental Health

Madness is no longer taboo; but it is still talked about in a special tone of voice as something that happens to other people. Yet the normality of family life is a carefully achieved invention. The neighbours might believe it but doctors do not. Five million people consult them each year about mental health problems, over 30 million working days were lost in 1986 because of mental and emotional problems, and one in six of us, more in the case of doctors, can expect to spend some time as a mental patient. Over 80,000 school-age children are emotionally disturbed enough to need professional help every year, while two in every hundred people are mentally handicapped. We all know someone who has been or will be mentally ill. It might well be ourselves.

Yet, until recently, mental treatment seemed designed to illustrate the precept 'out of sight, out of mind'. Patients were either given pills and left to work their own way through the turmoil of their fears, tears and desperation, or they were imprisoned in overcrowded asylums. A third of all people in hospital are mental patients, but only a ninth of our hospital doctors and a fifth of our nurses are available to attend to them. Although one in three hospital inpatients is mentally ill or handicapped, only one seventh of total hospital revenue is spent on their care. Until twenty years ago no one even seemed to care about this state of affairs. Now it is a subject for concern, but in many ways the plight of the mentally ill is worsening again.

The problem of reform without resources is illustrated most strikingly in mental health, where the movement towards community psychiatry and the ending of the anti-therapeutic and increasingly expensive asylum system has landed some patients with the worst of both worlds, without the protection of hospital and with very sketchy support outside it.

Victorian psychiatry

Despite previous eras of reform, often reflecting a radical political upsurge in society, at the beginning of this century therapeutic gloom still confined the majority of mental patients in remote asylums where they were imprisoned at low cost. Since treatment was non-existent and madness was thought to be hereditary, the vigorous prevention of sexual intercourse was the main aim of doctors, isolated within their own profession and suspected by the public. Growing interest in possible organic causes led to a few doctors with biological training accumulating much descriptive information, but these systems of classification were not to be the basis of active treatment until the discovery of biochemical and physical methods. Psychoanalysis unlocked the key to the neuroses and was an active treatment method *par excellence*, but, for practical as well as political reasons, it has never made real inroads into British psychiatry, which for much of the twentieth century has been dominated by a doctor-centred orthodoxy which was biologically reductionist, obsessed with diagnostic pigeon-holing and over-reliant on pills and electricity. Pioneer treatment methods were as pragmatic as they were barbaric. Wagner-Jauregg injected bacteria to cause an artificial fever in Vienna in the hope that, through the haze of nightmarish pyrexia, sanity might come stalking back. The discovery of insulin coma (by Sakel in Hungary), of electro-shock (by Cerletta in Italy), of leucotomy (by Moniz in Portugal) and, most importantly, the synthesis of the major tranquillisers, did not offer an alternative to purely custodial methods.

Institutional neurosis

A postwar group of American sociologists and British psychiatrists independently developed an analysis suggesting that at least part of the disturbance of the patients undergoing long-term asylum treatment was actually due to the functioning of the institution.

At about the same time the population of British mental hospitals had reached a point of such overcrowding that 'treatment is handicapped, the hospital atmosphere is disrupted and patient attitudes are adversely affected,' according to the consultants themselves.[1] The practical pressures reinforced the theoretical points made by the reformers. In fact, the reality behind the ornate mullions and spacious but always empty lawns was even worse than the psychiatrists dared admit. Patients had, by and large, surrendered to the rules of the institution, lacking even the rudimentary possessions with which to assemble an identity. Rehabilitation was designed with the economic efficiency of the hospital as its first concern. Staff were distant, hidden behind their roles and were quite often themselves unstable as well. Routine use of sedatives and major tranquillisers, demoralising ward atmosphere and the concentration of medical effort on only a couple of wards left the rest of the backward patients at the mercy of the nurses. Dr Rees, Medical Superintendent at the Warlingham Psychiatric Hospital, described the pyramid of power: 'The ordinary nurses had a key that could single-lock any door. The junior doctors and the sisters had keys which could double-lock patients and nurses in wards, and with my master key I could go round and lock the whole lot of them in.'[2]

The permanent tremors, social withdrawal, flatness of affect, lack of speech and endless repetition of single phrases and movements shared by the faded figures who edged down corridors or argued with themselves in a ward corner chair were in part products of the hospital regime, acquired long after the original cause for admission had disappeared. Contact from 'outside' was completely closed off; across the park was another world. If they could not get out within the first year they were there for life. In 1977, 30,000 people had been in mental hospitals for twenty years or more. As a student I worked in a unit attempting to ease long-stay patients back into shared, sheltered dwellings in the towns they had grown up in. I had to visit relatives to sound them out about the possibility of their loved ones leaving hospital. One old lady had been in the hospital thirty-two years and her sister told me the only reason she ever went in was because she had 'a breakdown' in the church when her fiancé jilted her. Yet when we mentioned the possibility of her returning home, her family's faces fell in collective horror and they fell over each other with excuses why they could not have anything to do with the process. In the 1950s asylums were about as easy to leave as dungeons.

Nevertheless, the combination of drugs and skilled rehabilitation methods was utilised in an attempt to develop what remained positive in the patient and to support it with what resources could be mobilised among relatives, the community and 'half-way' institutions. Although the effort started with the oldest institutionalised patients, it suggested new methods to prevent the same cycle getting a grip on new patients. Pioneer work at Henderson, Dingleton and Shenley used the ideas of the therapeutic community which had originated in the treatment of young, largely male patients suffering from war neuroses to alter and democratise hospital inpatient life. Relationships with fellow patients and the nursing staff were seen as a valuable part of therapy. The psychiatric and political implications of this approach were developed most fully by Ronald Laing and the late David Cooper in that dazzling burst of British 'anti-psychiatry' in the 1960s. Although both were turned into gurus and went on to produce enigmatic collections of epigrams for the troubled middle classes, their formative and most interesting work was done with working class patients in National Health Service hospitals. Work in their tradition, however, continues through the Arbours Association, who run, on a charitable basis, both long-term communities and a crisis centre.

In the late seventies, these themes were taken up in Trieste under the impetus of the Professor of Psychiatry Franco Basaglia and the working group Critica delle Istituzioni. In 1978, a new Italian law was passed which forbade admission of any new patients to mental hospitals and proposed the creation of 'alternative structures' in the community. Fifteen-bed crisis and diagnosis units were to be set up in general hospitals but compulsory admission was to last only for forty-eight hours in the first instance. What has become known as the 'Italian experience' is complex and not without its ironies, including a resurgence of private psychiatric care. Indeed, it tends to confirm the view expressed by the medical historian Roy Porter that 'Decarceration may in turn solve the problems created by the asylum: but that in itself cannot be a final solution to the problems of mental illness but only the beginnings of a new search.'

Subnormality

The case for taking people out of institutions was even stronger in the subnormality service, which accounted for half of the patients receiving local authority funds: 38,000 mentally handicapped people still live in hospital, 5,000 of them children. The 'colonies' or long-stay institutions for the defective assumed that improvement or useful treatment was not possible and that what remained was custodial care, undertaken with various degrees of humanity. But mental handicap is not an illness, it is a permanent disability which can be helped by education and training. Closer study by a Medical Research Council unit has shown that, while the severely subnormal, usually suffering from clear-cut brain pathology, tend to improve little and to be bed-fast and incontinent, many of the less severely subnormal children suffer from a more temporary incapacity and are able to make dramatic improvements if they get positive treatment instead of the barrack ward. Inflexible, regimented treatment, depersonalisation, especially lack of possessions and clothes, the social distance of the staff, with their uniforms, separate canteens, dislike of physical contact and tendency to give orders instead of just talking, all characteristic of the older, poorly staffed hospitals, were the worst possible treatment. Migrant children, particularly West Indians, suffer especially in this kind of home, to which they are more often sent than their white equivalents.

On arrival at a newer style of home, the subnormal children at first reacted to their new freedom with frightening, inexplicable tantrums in which anger and grief mingled with bewilderment at the sudden lack of punishment and restraint. The longer they had been in institutional care, the more painful was their arrival:

> Very often a child would fly into uncontrollable storms of anger and grief in which he would beat his head against a wall or bite an arm hard enough to draw blood . . . [But after two years there was a marked improvement in mental age and, more importantly] the old pathological behaviour had largely gone, nearly all the children were able to enjoy simple group play with other children for long periods, they talked quite a lot among themselves and they are affectionate and happy children, usually busy and interested in what they are doing.[3]

The National Association for Mental Health (MIND) estimates that 35,000 more places are needed in occupation and training centres than are now available. As things are, the majority of subnormal children will simply never get the chance to discover their own human potential. Instead they will be made more subnormal by a process of victimisation so routine it is hard to perceive.

The 1961 hospital plan

On the basis of the postwar evidence, together with the ever-mounting costs of the Victorian asylums, a plan of closures was announced in 1961. It forecast that 'the acute population of mental hospitals was to drop by half in the next ten years and the long-term population was ultimately to dwindle to zero.' In its place was to be a new era of co-operation between local authority services and psychiatrists based in mental wards of the new district general hospitals, united in an attempt to prevent chronicity and to treat most patients in their homes or in their local areas. Tooth and Brookes's famous curve, which showed the entire long-stay population of mental hospitals disappearing completely by 1975, through death or discharge, and a much lower ratio of beds (1.8 per 1000 people rather than 3.3) was uncritically incorporated into the plan.

In fact, the number of hospital places for the mentally ill fell by 24,000 (from 90,000 to 66,000) between 1974 and 1984. In England and Wales in 1986, sixty of the remaining mental hospitals were approved or provisionally approved for closure. But only half of the bargain was kept. There was a forced decline in the number of hospital beds, which plummeted from 152,000 in 1954 to 66,000 in 1984, but there was also a very slow and uneven provision of the local authority services on which patients were now to rely. Furthermore, there was a decline in morale and conditions for both patients and doctors stranded by the run-down and a very slow development of district general hospital wards, which consequently came under heavy pressure. After the initial burst of success with the rehabilitation of dischargeable chronics, a more intractable and unresponsive group was revealed, most of whom now had no contact whatsoever with the outside world, and often deteriorated rapidly and in anti-social ways on discharge. The rate of admission, far from dropping from the 1959 level, increased by 30 per cent, and epidemiological studies showed a frightening degree of undisclosed and untreated serious psychiatric illness. A field study in Anglesey unearthed 1104 ill patients who had never seen a psychiatrist, including forty-five schizophrenics and forty-eight sufferers from organic mental illness. A similar study of GPs showed that, although 14 per cent of their consultations were on purely psychiatric grounds, only three in a hundred of their patients were referred to psychiatrists. The rate of re-admission for those who went to hospital also stayed high.[4] For many the open door turned out to be a revolving door.

In some areas, the health authorities have responded to the closures of the traditional asylums in constructive and imaginative ways. The closure of the Digby Hospital near Exeter, built in 1877, and itself a fine example of Victorian institutional architecture, was met in Devon with an ambitious plan for genuine community-based mental health centres. But Banstead Hospital, whose 200-acre green belt site has proved extremely attractive to commercial developers, has been principally replaced by an expansion of the smaller Horton Mental Hospital in Surrey, said to be the prototype of a new 'super-bin'. But Horton is inadequate and badly located for psychiatric problems presenting in inner London. The Chairman of the CHC in the Riverside DHA, Frank Honigsbaugh, has put the problem graphically:

> We only accepted the closure of Banstead on the basis that sufficient funds were made available to provide adequate care in the community, and there are still huge gaps. Homeless, mentally ill people appear in increasing numbers on the streets of London, and we need housing and day care for them. The proportion of mentally ill people among residents of voluntary hostels has nearly doubled from 17.6 per cent in 1985 to 33.3 per cent in the first half of 1986.
>
> Westminster Council reports a 59 per cent increase in the number of homeless mentally ill people over the past year. Who is responsible for meeting this problem? We believe that the health service must accept part of it and use the capital to provide housing rather than evade responsibility.

Clearly, class and social geography has been insufficiently considered by partisans of community psychiatry. What works in Trieste or Sydney or Madison might be a catastrophe in Milan, Staten Island or Tower Hamlets, especially in an era of mass unemployment and acute housing shortage.

Community care?

Not only was the tempo of new building pitifully slow, reflecting the low prestige the mental health service still had, but the quality of many of the facilities was poor and tended towards the very institutionalisation they attempted to avert. For every futurist general hospital psychiatric ward with armchairs and original acrylic paintings, there were inactive day centres, authoritarian hostels and unvisited sitting rooms. The difficulties for everyone, let alone someone emerging painfully from hospital treatment, to find a home and a job, prevented the final critical step of re-entry into normal life. Although families did their best to support ex-patients despite low income, overcrowded homes and their own poor health, there was often evidence that the mental health of the patients and the relatives got worse rather than better.

One survey of the hostel accommodation which professed the aim of rehabilitation found that 60 per cent were less permissive than the hospital wards themselves, and some were staffed by people who had left the hospital service in protest against relaxation of disciplinarian methods! The day hospitals too, usually in old Victorian houses in residential areas rather than custom-built, increased the number of their patients fourfold in the 1960s but provided little more than social supervision, acting more as a long-stay day ward for chronic patients whose illness had stabilised, and, apart from some rather arbitrary ECT, provided little active treatment.

Industrial therapy, once the cornerstone of rehabilitation, proved less than triumphant. In one of the best centres, at Bristol, after seven years and 678 patients only 174 were established in open employment. In many schemes, the industrial work provided is simply used to give chronic patients 'something to do', has no therapeutic value and is very badly paid into the bargain. The slow development of group and health centre practices has slowed the GPs' involvement in community care. Instead of co-ordinating clinical and social services, the GPs were sometimes indifferent to both, and tended to treat minor psychiatric illnesses with tranquillisers. Even today there is relatively little evidence of awareness of how changes in the care of the mentally ill will alter the future role of the GP.

A positive trend has been the growth of community psychiatric nursing. The Community Psychiatric Nurses vary widely in experience and duties, but all are nurses with a specialist psychiatric training, working outside the hospitals. Seen by some doctors as little more than the enforcers of depot medication and pills, they have the potential to make clinical assessments and to act more like the old Community Welfare Officers. More than anyone, they can become links between hospital, GP and patient. When working in conjunction with GP group practices, they can significantly improve the psychiatric service offered.

Another product of decarceration has been the Crisis Intervention Unit, multi-disciplinary, psychiatrist-led teams, available at short notice to assess, assist and monitor families in psychiatric crisis. Here timely allocation of intensive resources at a time when they can be of greatest use may prevent problems becoming intractable and insoluble.

Psychiatry and civil rights

Concern over the abuse of psychiatric power, initially directed against Soviet mental hospitals, has broadened its scope. As Christopher Heginbotham, Director of MIND, wrote in 1986:

> The Soviet Union is not alone. Japan is there with a vengeance. South Africa treats mentally ill black people shamefully, often discharging those with acute illnesses back to their 'homelands' where no psychiatric facilities exist. The deliberate neglect of institutionalised ex-patients dumped into city streets in the USA borders on criminality.

In Britain, rank and file organisations campaigning for the rights of mental patients, like the Mental Patients' Union, People Not Psychiatry, COPE and PROMPT, have tended to start with enthusiasm, all too often short lived. But at the 1985 meeting in Brighton of the World Congress on Mental Health, an alliance of consumer groups including the Dutch Gekkenbeweging and ex-patients from Scandinavia and North America pushed through a strong declaration in defence of mental patients' civil rights. And MIND, the Congress organiser, has had a powerful influence on British mental health policy and on the three postwar Mental Health Acts. Most recent concern in Britain has been focused on the apparently high application of Section 136 (which granted the police additional powers of detention) to Afro-Caribbeans in London and Birmingham and the related, but complex, issue of the over-representation of blacks in mental hospitals in general. The explanation may well be a genuinely high incidence of mental illness among second-generation British blacks, with racism often a principal factor, rather than misdiagnosis by monocultural psychiatry. There is also controversy over the ethics of the proposed Community Treatment

Order, which would give psychiatric doctors and nurses the legal right to administer medication in the community.

But, in general, the danger of being confined and forgotten in mental hospitals in the UK is now gone. The local authorities have a duty to re-integrate rather than a power to apprehend. The quality of psychiatric social work has improved out of recognition. The 1983 Mental Health Act has undoubtedly extended the civil rights of patients, formalised a review procedure and thereby sharpened up mental hospitals' admission procedures and diagnostic precision. Nonetheless, lack of resources for training specialist social workers gave the Act a bad start, and the Tribunals are proving spectacular consumers of time and paper, not least in the Forensic Units and in repeated ill-advised applications by patients with clear paranoid and manic depressive disease.

New dangers

But a new set of dangers now prevails. The community psychiatry movement was a child of economic necessity. 'Finance is still the best crude criterion of our commitment to community care,' states Richard Titmuss, and, judged on that basis, the authorities care very little. All the faults of the asylums can be reproduced in community settings. Instead of a fear of permanent unwilling admission, there is now concern about regaining admission when it is desperately needed, so hard-pressed are the existing psychiatric beds. If psychiatrists were once over-anxious to admit, nowadays inpatient mental care is often hard to get, discharge is early, and appointments, even for emergencies, long put off. This is most apparent in the field of psychogeriatrics, where those suffering from Alzheimer's Disease and other forms of senile dementia are becoming one of the biggest and least well-served single patient groups. For a GP in a health district with a growing population of the very old, often left behind by family and friends who have moved up and out, the physical safety of the mildly demented elderly is a constant problem, with tremendous pressure on in-adequate warden-controlled accommodation. But the facilities for the acutely demented are still more scarce, and too often admission is via a policeman who apprehends the wandering, distressed and often violent patient, rather than by a GP or psychogeriatrician. Acute admission, especially of mobile or homeless patients, is made still more difficult for the GP by the mental hospitals' rigid geographical zoning policies.

The warnings about 'community care' sounded in the seventies were justified by events as the closure of the large asylums remorselessly continued. In 1985, a statement by the National Schizophrenia Fellowship and the Richmond Society unequivocally pointed out that, in the experience of its members, the services for mentally ill patients outside hospital were 'totally inadequate'. The hostels and group homes, insufficient in number anyway, were being under-utilised through spending cuts. So community care meant, in reality, back to the family, and probably to the female members of it: 'Relatives,' the statement pointed out, 'then try to cope with sometimes bizarre, violent or potentially suicidal situations with little or no support. Many former patients without families or whose families reach breaking point, get no care at all and end up in prison, as vagrants, or commit suicide.' Indeed, they asked specifically for the improvement of hospital service, imploring the Government 'to give shelter and care to those most mentally disturbed in the only places properly equipped to provide it – our psychiatric hospitals – unless or until other adequate alternatives actually exist.'[5]

In a famous article, 'So-called Care in the So-called Community', Dr Malcolm Weller of Friern Barnet Hospital cited detailed statistical evidence which suggested that premature and inappropriate discharge would lead not just to difficulties in resettlement and obtaining continuing medical care, but to suicide, destitution and crime. These 'unpalatable facts', argued Weller, 'indict "community care" policies that advocate the shift of precious, barely adequate NHS resources to discretionally funded social workers, with ill-defined and unenforced statutory responsibilities.'[6] In 1986, a very detailed report by the Audit Commission, called *Making a Reality of Community Care*, revealed a frankly chaotic situation, with joint planning and community care in disarray, causing both the waste of funds and unnecessary suffering. The chair of the BMA's Doctors' and Social Work Committee, Arnold Elliott, commented that the report vindicated the BMA view that it was necessary to maintain existing services while funding transfer into the community, a process which can take years.

Indeed, as the housing crisis deepened in the eighties, it became increasingly difficult for psychiatric social workers to provide the first essential of community care, suitable housing. Instead, the chronically mentally ill, especially single men, have gravitated towards ill-run and overcrowded commercial hostels, often claiming to provide 'bed and breakfast', whose inflated bills are paid directly by the DHSS. Even the worst wards in the old asylums were less depressing than the sight of a pair of chronic chain-smoking schizophrenics sharing an ex-bathroom and single bar fire in a cheaply converted house whose absentee landlord gets £75 a week per person for the room and for posting a greasy egg on toast through the door every morning.

As the 1986 Audit Commission explained,

> If people can be accommodated in facilities where they qualify for social security, then the cost to the health and local authority is correspondingly reduced. The bridging finance is effectively provided by supplementary benefits. The danger is that it can distort policies since [these] options may be preferred over other more suitable options [which may be cheaper] for which there is no money.

Once in private lodgings, patients lose any right to local authority housing, should it exist. And the whole vile business ends up costing the tax payer an estimated £200 million a year, most of which ends up in the pockets of the private landlords.

With the old reception centres and common lodging houses closing too, many dischargees end up sleeping rough or in prison. The co-ordinator of the Manchester Night Shelter noted in 1987 that his staff were 'daily amazed at the attempted referrals made by hospital staff who are trying to discharge patients to our totally unsuitable common lodging house, accommodation which is being closed down in twelve months as unfit.' For as a veteran psychiatrist of the Maudsley Hospital and Brixton Prison, Dr Peter Scott, commented, 'When the mental hospitals are full, prisons are relatively empty, and the present-day scene suggests that the converse is equally true.' I would defy a humane adult to spend a day in Prince's Lodge, Commercial Road or Ward C1 in Holloway Prison and not emerge angry and ashamed at the mistreatment the psychologically ill are made to endure, as a result of well-intentioned but ill-executed and grossly underfinanced Government policies.

And even those mentally ill and handicapped who are looked

after in the home impose a tremendous strain on those who care for them. At least those who live in residential establishments have a Health Authority budget heading, paltry as it usually is. But practical support for those looking after the mentally ill or handicapped at home – nursing care, respite care and CPN involvement – is suffering badly under the cuts. As Judith Oliver of the Association of Carers puts it,

> What family carers need is a community nursing service available round the clock – at 6.30 a.m. as well as during 'office' hours. Many are themselves ill; they need the assurance of immediate and total replacement at times of high crisis. Many seek congenial residential surroundings for their relatives which do not categorise people with handicaps into the mentally ill, mentally handicapped, disabled or elderly and then sub-divide them into continent, incontinent, confused, and so on. Families find it hard to believe that they, untrained and unsupported, are expected to cope with any and all of these conditions, whilst trained and paid workers reel back in horror at the thought of providing care for any but the most straightforward and acquiescent cases.

For in the end it is the volunteers, of all types, who prevent open collapse. In the words of Harry Reid of MIND:

> The voluntary sector is being forced to plug the gaps in provision that should be filled by statutory services. It is a disgrace, a very sad and depressing situation.

It is, however, a situation which suits the Government very well, where a mixture of cuts and privatisation force volunteers to attempt individually to cope with a problem which needs organised, planned and expensive resources, whether in hospitals or in the community.

7
The Drug Industry

Profiteering, price-fixing, promotion of ineffective and dangerous goods, questionable advertising, high-pressure sales techniques, suppression of information, ferocious rivalry leading to monopoly trading – it sounds like Chicago in the era of Prohibition, but it describes the painstakingly documented growth of the pharmaceuticals industry, whose business is not illegal hooch but life-saving chemistry. It is ironic that the industry with the most honourable of purposes, the relief of suffering, exhibits the most piratical features of modern big business.

Drugs, until recently dispensed from common ingredients in a backroom of the surgery, have become the biggest of big business, whose power is such that it can render the NHS, in theory a monopoly purchaser, pathetically vulnerable, can defy Royal Commissions and laugh in the face of attempts to reform it. The companies' influence is no longer merely financial. They do much to mould research, therapy, education and the whole ethos of contemporary medicine. Their growth and their still unchecked power are dramatic examples of how the idealism of the NHS has been exploited by commercial interests and how doctors' insistence on their professional freedoms – in this case the freedom to prescribe – has in fact meant their dependence on the firms' definitions. Here is the reversal of Paracelsus's honourable maxim, 'I seek not to enrich the apothecaries, but to cure the sick.'

Put simply, there are now too many drugs produced. They are overpriced and misleadingly promoted. Their overconsumption is itself a cause of illness, their overprescription a substitute for clinical skill, and their overpricing a crucial cause of the poverty of the NHS. In our profligate use of prescribed drugs as well as chemist-shop remedies, we are squandering precious medical resources and generating unnecessary risks in a way which will shock succeeding generations. Mood-altering drugs, prescribed by mainly male, always middle class doctors as a substitute for altering the conditions which give rise to depression, sleeplessness and unhappiness, increase the mainly female, mainly working-class patients' sense of passivity and self-reproach. They try to enforce a chemical solution on what is more often a social or sexual, and therefore a political, problem. And we inflict a system which is a scandal in the industrialised West on the undeveloped world, where it is nothing less than a crime. Yet attempts to reform the system rebound ineffectively from the protective exteriors of the companies.

Origins

How has this situation arisen? The major discoveries in organic chemistry were made in the nineteenth century, but large-scale pharmacology had to await the expansion of the chemical and oil-related industries during the First and Second World Wars respectively for their crucial leaps in scale. War was the bloody midwife of medical innovation, and the pharmaceuticals industry emerged, no longer as purveyors of laxative pills and tonics with the inventor's bewhiskered profile on the bottle, but as a major chemical industry. In the ten years to 1972, the British industry expanded at an annual rate of 10 per cent, three times the rate of manufacturing industry. A year after the NHS began, the total cost of GP NHS prescriptions was £35 million. In 1968 it had risen to £177 million; by 1986 it was £2,031 million. The cost of pharmaceutical services as a percentage of the total cost of the NHS increased from 8.4 per cent in 1950 to 9.8 per cent in 1986. For most of the last four decades, the growth rate in the hospital drug bill has been higher than that of any other single sector.[1]

The total NHS expenditure on pharmaceuticals issued in hospitals, community clinics and by GPs who dispense their own medicines increased between 1968 and 1986 from £139 million to £1,947 million. And even when this apparent fourteenfold increase is corrected by the GNP deflator, it still represents, in 'real' spending, a 100 per cent increase. The number of prescription items issued increased too: from 306.3 million in 1968 to 397.4 million in 1986, an average of seven items per head of population per year. However, expenditure on medicines and drugs in the UK as a proportion of GNP has remained reasonably stable (at about 0.6 per cent) compared with more pill-conscious nations like West

Germany and France, where the average *per capita* outlay exceeded that of the UK by more than three-quarters.

It is impossible to say what proportion of this growth represents therapeutic progress, and what is simply the product of more effective marketing. Interestingly, the proportion of prescriptions for drugs affecting the central nervous system, in which sedative tranquillisers and hypnotics were the major items, has fallen between 1975 and 1985. The growth has been in the gastro-intestinal, rheumatological and cardiovascular areas, such as the new H2 receptor blockers, which have revolutionised the management of stomach ulcers, the non-steroid anti-inflammatories (some of which have now been withdrawn), and greater identification and treatment of 'silent' hypertension by improved screening.

From the original free prescriptions in 1948, the price per item has risen to the present £2.60. The increase has been most rapid under the Thatcher administration, who by 1987 had made a total of seven increases, taking the price from 20p per item when they came to office to its present level, a twelvefold increase. However, the majority of prescriptions are still issued without charge since the high user groups tend to be exempt from payment.

For the potential investor, pharmaceutical shares offer a high return on capital with the added virtue of morally legitimate aims. Small wonder that competition within this exceptionally lucrative market is so bloodthirsty. The industry quickly became highly centralised, and saw a rapid sequence of mergers and takeovers in the 1960s which mopped up most of the smaller companies and transformed the bigger national companies into multinational giants. The absence of either genuine market competition or effective enforcement of machinery for price controls means that there is an inbuilt tendency to overprice. This, and the extraordinary profit levels, are justified by the costs of research and development, which the drug companies claim are uniquely high and involve undue risk. The profit-seeking of many of the most ethical suppliers has been for some time masked by the 'transfer pricing mechanism', a device whereby a subsidiary processes ingredients which it then 'sells' to the parent at greatly inflated cost, and which the 'manufacturing stage' (often not a great deal more than the putting of goods into capsules) further increases.

Research

Undoubtedly the fundamental research, which involves following blind hunches but is necessary for real innovation, *is* expensive, and so is the methodical and exhaustive safety testing which must precede the mass marketing of new drugs. But the apparently impressive resources devoted to research need to be looked at on a comparative basis. On average, research and development expenditure comprises only 10 per cent of costs, while advertising and promotion take up nearly 20 per cent. The industry's contribution to total medical research has fallen over ten years from about a third to less than a quarter of the budget. The drug companies' research bill included investigations into the acceptability of package colour, prestige conference expenses, 'me-too' investigations into subtle alterations to rival formulations to get round patent laws, and money simply squandered in the early stages of new drugs, only one in 5000 of which will ever reach the market. Such is the investment in that one successful product that, once launched, research thereafter *must* be favourable. However *bona fide* its financing and scientific pedigree, this research becomes a species of advertising, shaded paragraphs of which will be flashed under doctors' noses in the course of a sales talk, between the embossed desk-pad and the free samples.

It is certainly clear that commercial research has not prevented the steady increase of drug interactions and of death and illness caused by prescribed medicines. Adverse reactions to medicines account for 5 per cent of the admissions to hospital medical wards, and between 10 and 15 per cent of patients suffer an adverse reaction of one type or another during their admission. A growing list of disease syndromes are known to be the legacy of the over-enthusiastic prescribing of a previous generation of physicians. Even such commonplace medicines as the 'white medicine' for gastric acidity can affect the performance of other drugs taken simultaneously.

When drug side-effects are discovered, there has so far been little in doctors' or manufacturers' behaviour to justify great confidence. The Distillers Company did their best to avoid paying adequate compensation to the limbless victims of Thalidomide; that Eraldin induced eye damage came to light through a letter to a medical journal rather than the formal 'yellow card' early-warning system, although following the appearance of that report some 200 cases were notified. But a full twelve months after the drug was withdrawn, in July 1975, it was still being prescribed. Most doctors simply assume that only safe drugs are marketed. Most manufacturers take safety seriously, but within the overall framework of aggressive 'safemanship'. A letter I received recently contained a warning about the hazards of tricyclic anti-depressant overdosage, but it turned out to be from the marketing director of a firm producing a rival tetracyclic preparation! In March 1984 a drug company headed by the president of the Association of the British Pharmaceutical Industry, Mr Ron Wing, was censured for breaking the Association's code of conduct on advertisements to doctors. The Association's own (notoriously lax) Code of Practice Committee ruled that the advertisements for Cordaronex cited out-of-date research and minimised side-effects. But the advertisement was typical of the type of promotion which uses high-impact commercial graphics and virtually unreadable citations to published research to which few GPs have direct access anyway. A large number of the free medical magazines and newspapers sent to doctors are effectively financed by drug company advertising.

Although it is fashionable to be 'in research', the value of much of it seems questionable, and needs to be firmly measured against existing need. Research into ways of making more money or making people consume more is downright harmful. So is the overwhelming concentration of research resources in pharmaceuticals when we know so little about more fundamental factors, such as our patients' diets, the effects of different physical treatments and the identification of pollution and health hazards. It serves once again to distort, almost without our noticing it, the nature of illness, turning it into a sort of commodity which can only be dealt with by another, rival, commodity. It is absurd that sheaves of material are on hand about the effect of a chest inhaler on lung volume while it is impossible to measure or assay the lead levels of the air the patient will breathe into his newly expanded lungs in the fume-choked streets outside the surgery window.

Attempts to undertake independent testing of the efficacy of drugs are considered highly unsuitable by the industry. In 1965 a panel of British experts assessing the therapeutic effectiveness of 2241 of the 3000 products then available judged 35 per cent of them to be ineffective, obsolete or irrational combinations, and in 1971 a similar investigation of 2000 products by a panel of the American Food and Drug Administration found that 60 per cent lacked any evidence for their therapeutic claims. It is now well known that up to 50 per cent of patients do not take their drugs as prescribed, a syndrome known as 'poor treatment adherence', which not only lowers the beneficial effect of treatment but wastes money and stockpiles unwanted but potentially dangerous drugs. In September 1986, the watchdog body Social Audit said that hospitals could meet all their patients' needs with less than a third of the thousands of drugs now on the market. But why should the companies worry if patients don't take the medicine? Their business is to sell it.

Product testing

Further, not all research is as scrupulous as it should be. Particularly in North America there is evidence that poor, black or desperate subjects have been used as guinea-pigs in tests where risks were very great. The women of Puerto Rico were selected as a suitable and docile control group for the first testing of the birth-control pill before it was used in the United States. During this period the Puerto Ricans were 'tried out' on doses both lower and higher than the effective amount. Similarly, long-stay prisoners have been tempted with remission of sentence in exchange for volunteering for high-risk drug experiments. The CIA are known to have tested psychedelic drugs on unknowing victims.

This lack of scruple has also been apparent in the recent chemical-plant disasters. The Seveso explosion in July 1976 hurled the contents of a reactor containing dioxin, a chemical by-product hard to degrade and extremely dangerous even in small doses, over many acres in a poison cloud. It was several days before Roche, the responsible company, undertook proper analysis. In that time the poison spread, crops wilted, dogs died and unborn children were deformed in the womb. The full toll is still unknown. Similar tragedies in Amsterdam, at Flixborough, the Coalite works in Bolsover, and, most devastatingly, at Bhopal in India, suggest that the chemical giants are not prepared to spend the necessary money on safety or to carry out sufficient research on production and waste-product risks until it is too late. Although the companies complain bitterly about the scale of product testing now required before marketing, this will provide little consolation for those who died from Hoechst's anti-depressant Merital or Eli Lilly's anti-rheumatic Opren.

It is also inevitable that drug companies are reluctant to undertake commercial research into rare diseases, where there is no prospect of general application and consequent high returns. Nor is much attention paid to the widespread illness in areas and among people too poor to make the grade as potential purchasers. Indeed, only a small percentage of the total spent by industry, governments and charities on medical research is devoted to the major disease problems of the developing world. There is little interest in natural as opposed to petrochemical sources. Yet it is surely lack of confidence in modern commercial medicines which is leading to a revival of interest in this country in traditional homeopathic and folk remedies which, even if not particularly successful, at least do not harm the patient.

Promotion

If research costs are inflated, promotional expenses are grotesque. Doctors have about £3,200 each spent on them per year, including over a hundredweight of literature and gifts. The biggest single expense is paying the representatives, often scientifically trained, who lurk in hospital canteens and wait in surgery queues in order to see doctors. At present rates, the average doctor can expect to have £50,000 spent on 'education' by the drug companies during his professional lifetime, nearly the cost of the real thing at medical school. The drug companies provide the most insistent form of postgraduate education most GPs receive, and can spend 10 per cent of their annual turnover on promotion.

It is of course the drugs of dubious merit which require the most lavish promotion. As Professor M. D. Rawlins, the Newcastle-upon-Tyne clinical pharmacologist, has put it: 'The promotional budget for a new drug is inversely proportional to its therapeutic novelty.' The treatments for diabetes, for example, are standard and of proven value, so the manufacturing companies only need to spend a small percentage of the total cost of the drug on advertising. But for cough and cold remedies, whose real clinical value is dubious but for which the potential market is immense, the amount spent on television advertising alone is enormous.

Another worrying factor is the degree to which drug companies have direct links with medical faculties. In the *Lancet* one consultant wrote:

> Very few in our profession and practically none of the general public realise that some of the holders of professorial chairs and important positions in the medical world also act as paid advisers to industrial concerns. This may not affect their judgement, but they may reasonably be asked to declare their interests.[2]

There is an obvious conflict of interest when leading researchers are conducting trials, sponsoring conferences and editing publications for the drug companies themselves, problems acknowledged but not solved by the Royal College of Physicians' 1986 report *The Relationship Between Physicians and the Pharmaceutical Industry*. Although composed in marvellously emollient prose, the College's report made it clear that doctors themselves were by no means blameless. Many, it suggested, write to drug companies asking for funds to pay for foreign trips, and 'one doctor even stated that unless his request was granted he would stop prescribing the company's products.' Another group of doctors refused to attend a film unless it was 'shown with a meal organised at a restaurant of their choice.' On another occasion 'physicians who all live in one NHS region' went to a drug company meeting on a 'Mediterranean island,' which, as the College laconically observed, 'could not have the advantage of convenience.' As the *BMJ* noted, 'A tougher and more specific code – even one with teeth – will eventually be needed.'

The scale of the problem was further indicated by the resignation from the Medical Research Council of a distinguished hypertension expert, Dr Ian Robertson, in December 1986, after it was discovered that he had been involved in extensive private consultancy work for the drug companies without official approval. A spokesman for one of Dr Robertson's employers, Janssen, said succinctly, 'He did a considerable amount of work on our behalf and was remunerated accordingly.' But the implications of his resignation were considerable, since the treatment of hypertension provides a huge potential market, in which the therapeutic recommendations of senior researchers could have considerable influence on prescribing patterns and thus sales and profits.

This interpenetration extends into government. In July 1984, Dr John Griffin, the civil servant in charge of drugs for the

NHS, resigned at the age of 46 to become . . . the Director of the Association of the British Pharmaceutical Industry. Unsurprisingly, he promptly began to attack the introduction of a 'Limited List' based, in part, on the advice of the British National Formulary which, in government office, he had previously promoted.[3]

In 1984, the television reporter Tom Mangold devoted a programme to the type of clinical symposia where 'the signing of the hotel register was the most intellectually demanding chore of the week.' 'We caught,' he went on, 'one Italian drug company, Farmitalia Carlo Erba, through its British subsidiary, loading the Orient Express with rheumatologists for a couple of nice free days in Venice . . . [We found] doctors tucking into smoked salmon buffets and champagne after their arduous "symposium". The drug that was being promoted – Flosint, yet another anti-arthritis pill – has since been withdrawn following alarming side-reaction reports.'[4]

It is a mockery of the years of training in organic chemistry and the inculcation of meticulous habits of observation that one should end up leafing through the trade gazette of drugs, MIMS, head reeling with the fanciful trade names devised for items differing only in the degree of overpricing, no longer able to recall the dosage of the basic treatment taught at medical school. We prescribe under a bombardment of brand-named calendars, stencilled biros and embossed tongue depressors: advertising of a lower standard than that used to promote aftershave lotion. It positively encourages doctors to avoid tackling factors like industrial pollution, smoking, diet, stress, lack of exercise, excessive alcohol intake and other environmental factors in illness, and instead binds us to the chariot of the latest chemical innovation, whose impetus might be medical but whose final motive will be commercial.

This rampant commercialism is particularly objectionable when it is directed towards problems which are themselves products of the competitive, profit-motivated system.

The most offensive case of making profits out of unhappiness is in the field of minor tranquillisers. In financial terms, the NHS has been subjected to what amounts to daylight robbery, although no one is impolite enough to use that term. The Monopolies Commission Report shows conclusively that Roche netted £24 million from sales in Britain alone in the period 1966–72 by selling drug ingredients to a subsidiary at vastly inflated prices, which bore no resemblance to real costs.[5] By this means, real profits were safely siphoned away to the parent company and discreetly buried in inaccessible accounts. In 1970, Roche Products (UK) was purchasing the ingredients for Librium and Valium at £370 and £922 per kilo respectively from the parent company in Switzerland when the same ingredients could be bought for £9 and £20 per kilo respectively in Italy. The Commission modestly calculated that the real profits to the company on sales of Librium and Valium were 55 per cent and 60 per cent respectively, implying a return on capital employed of over 70 per cent. At the height of their patent life, the two drugs' worldwide profit levels were US $2000 million. In the United States at one time, one person in ten was taking benzodiazepines for at least one week a year; and the consumption of these drugs doubled in a decade. In 1974, US doctors wrote twenty million prescriptions for one thousand million tablets of chlordiazepoxide (Librium) and sixty million prescriptions for three billion tables of diazepam (Valium).

In February 1984, BBC Television's *That's Life* conducted a survey of 2,000 viewers with experience of tranquillisers and found that:

- Most patients saw their doctor for less than ten minutes on the first visit when the drugs were prescribed.
- Half the patients were not even told they were on tranquillisers.
- Nine out of ten were not told that they are only effective for a short time, nor warned about side-effects.
- Nine out of ten were given repeat prescriptions, enough to cover a period of longer than four months.
- 62 per cent had been taking them longer than five years.
- 40 per cent, nearly 1,000 people, had taken them longer than ten years.
- 93 per cent of the people who took part in the survey had tried to give up tranquillisers.
- Only just over half – 57 per cent – succeeded.[6]

'Valium for the prisoners of a society of stress,' said the advertisements which skilfully picked out the pressures of commuters, locked into wordless boredom and vacant faces, and housewives, imprisoned by tower blocks, overpriced supermarkets, demanding children and an unsympathetic and exhausted spouse: 'Valium helps your patient enjoy his work. Formerly nervous and tense, he takes a greater interest in his job and is better able to meet and solve his daily problems.' If marriage is loveless, the streets without beauty and nights without peace, take a pill. Valium filled the space between the patient's desperation, the doctor's incompetence and the health service's disintegration. It provides the appearance of a solution satisfactory to all, but in reality it undermines patients' ability to help themselves and debases doctors' clinical skill. It confirms the (mainly women) patients' sense of themselves as failures, confirms an inner suspicion that they are mad and, in the process, makes a very great deal more money for the drug multinationals.

The failure of reform

Drug companies are fond of conjuring up pictures of the chaos that would ensue if any limitation on their freedom to operate like this was taken. However, even the straightforward step of insisting that all NHS prescriptions were made by the chemical title (which is insisted on during training but usually discarded under the pressure of practice), would lead to enormous savings. It is irresponsibility rather than clinical freedom to insist on prescribing, say, branded rather than formulary ibuprofen, when the former costs so much more than the latter. A logical step would be to make drug manufacture a public venture in the same way the NHS is. The drug industry is effectively state-financed, since most of the prescriptions signed by doctors are paid for out of public taxation, so it ought to be in public ownership and to concentrate on the cheap, safe production of standardised drugs of proven value, and on an increased and genuine research effort aimed at dealing with real medical problems. Doctors would be the first to benefit from much simpler, medically sounder prescribing, instead of constantly attempting to evaluate new preparations on very sketchy and partial evidence. They would also benefit from the gigantic increase in resources available for staff and facilities.

The veteran radical Sir Richard Acland recently suggested the following proposals 'to mount a massive attack on the ever-increasing cost of drugs prescribed by doctors':

    i. Establish a public service to give doctors – say once a month – concise, objective, and unglamourised reports showing possible benefits and side-effects of new drugs; and making comparisons with cheaper drugs dealing with corresponding ailments. It might cost £25 million a year.

ii. Strike off the register any doctor proved to have taken a free holiday at the cost of a drug company. If the companies had not found that medical jamborees in places like Venice increase their drug sales, they would not pay.

iii. Impose fines of up to £100,000 on any company communicating directly with doctors, and pay the proceeds to the NHS.

Ideas by no means as crazy as they might at first seem, and which could no doubt be elaborated by the many doctors, especially clinical pharmacologists, who are genuinely anxious to rationalise prescription. But their implementation is extremely unlikely because, as Acland also noted, 'The country is run by a cabinet whose members adore any privately owned money-making corporation, even when its dividends are mainly paid by all of us in taxation, and loathe the idea of any public service being offered to all of us and financed by all of us.'

The consumer group Social Audit, in their observations on the UK Government's *Study of the Control of Medicines*, also argued for much tighter controls on manufacturers:

> Responsible behaviour can be secured only if the individuals concerned can be called to account for the conclusions they reach and for the recommendations they make as a result. Moreover, unless the individuals concerned are bound by such a discipline, they will never have sufficient power within their organisations to do what the public might reasonably expect of them.

Among younger doctors there would probably be considerable support for the introduction of a generic list (not to be confused with the 'Limited List' of 1984 which banned some cheap, well-established and safe generic formulations). However, many doctors remain wedded to the notion of freedom advocated by the drug companies. This notion is only an extreme example of the commercial values which surround and profit from the NHS. The companies are quite literally a law unto themselves, and even quite determined efforts to impose some kind of responsibility on them have been unsuccessful. Since the Sainsbury Commission was set up in 1965, progress in controlling the industry has been tiny, and the Labour Party's 1976 proposals failed to restate some of the points made by Sainsbury, even though the intervening years had seen repeated conference, Labour Party and trade union declarations. The Greenfield Report on generic substitution has been ignored and 'price freezes' have been pathetically ineffective. In August 1983, in response to the highly critical Public Accounts Committee's investigation into drug prices, Kenneth Clarke ordered a price standstill. But prices soon began to soar again, and by January 1984 they were up by 9 per cent on the previous year. The complex attempts by the DHSS to assess and moderate drug company profits under the Pharmaceutical Price Regulation Scheme were easily evaded by the drug company accountants.[7] Indeed, drugs, as a proportion of health spending, and the total number of prescriptions, continue to grow. We are certainly prisoners: not of a society of stress, but of one which profits from it.

8

Private Practice and Privatisation

Private practice facilities shrank somewhat after the introduction of the NHS. Nevertheless, the contract on which most hospital consultants were employed was usually tailored to allow part-time sessional attendance, so doctors could see paying customers in non-NHS time. A few doctors remained wholly in private practice, but most had a few private patients who provided the financial jam on the NHS bread and butter. In neither case did the patient receive better medical care. A good doctor is a good doctor wherever he or she practises, and Harley Street has had perhaps more than its fair share of charlatans. But private practice *did* allow more time and personal attention than is usually possible in NHS conditions, including immediate appointments and surgery at convenient times.

When on the NHS wards, the consultant would rely heavily on his resident team and would be only too pleased to delegate to them, but in private practice this would simply divide up the proceeds. There was relatively little private practice in fields with low prestige, like geriatrics or mental handicap, or in those which require expensive ancillary facilities. Apart from that hard core of doctors who convinced themselves that a healthy doctor-patient relationship can only really be established if cash changes hands, many, while unwilling to take action against private practice, probably hoped that the NHS would steadily improve to such a point that private practice would become anachronistic.

The rise of health insurance

Two separate developments had altered the terms on which private practice was carried out. First, a growing proportion of consultants, including the most scientifically eminent and those working in the professorial units in the teaching hospitals, which had become the centres of the best hospital medicine, worked full-time. This, essential to a serious execution of clinical, academic and administrative duties, effectively redirected much of the enthusiasm which a previous generation had put into developing their private clientele into raising NHS standards. Where the full-time consultants were so eminent that private or overseas patients insisted on seeing them, fees, if charged, were paid into a department research or travelling fund rather than directly to the individual.

Second, some of the deficiencies in the NHS detailed in previous chapters enabled the survival of private medical insurance in the 1960s. The British United Provident Association became the largest of the organisations offering private medical care. Although itself non-profitmaking, it is closely linked to supply companies which certainly are. Its schemes offered the best of both worlds: the full benefits of the NHS but none of its disadvantages. If surgery was needed, it could be taken in privacy, at an arranged time, executed by a surgeon of your choice. BUPA also provided access to commercial preventative medicine: screening and 'check-ups' designed for early detection of health hazards, which if detected were referred back to the NHS GP! But as, in general, waiting lists became longer and harassed consultants was glimpsed rather than consulted, BUPA schemes, often arranged as part of managerial salary perks, became more attractive. In this situation, the part-time consultants who in 1948 had wrung the right to admit their private patients to beds in the hospital to which they had been appointed were in a commanding position. Bevan had choked the profession's mouth with pay-beds as well as gold, and the former had turned out to be more valuable.

The NHS pay-beds

The 1946 Act bound the Minister to provide, to such an extent as he considered necessary to meet all reasonable requirements, hospital accommodation for private work. The Health Service and Public Health Act of 1968 reasserted that, at the Minister's discretion, this should continue. By 1970, about 122,000 private patients were seen annually in just under 5000 beds inside the NHS, with the thirteen London teaching hospitals providing 15 per cent of the total beds. The proportion of pay-beds has kept fairly constant, at one in a hundred of total beds, but such is the nature of the instant service they offer that they lie empty for over half the year. The private beds in the NHS at this time totalled only a quarter of the number existing outside in independent nursing homes and private hospitals. But their particular relationship to NHS facilities enabled them to tap resources in a number of subtle but important ways, all stemming from the part-time consultants' dual role, with their ability both to practise privately and to maintain their positions in the NHS.

The most obvious abuse resulting from the double position does not even require a pay-bed. It is the practice of seeing a private patient on a free-paid consultation and then expediting that patient's NHS admission for routine surgery. More unsavoury is the use of NHS facilities and personnel for private work. My first direct experience of this was overhearing a fellow houseman delightedly telling his successor that there was a chance once a month to go and hold the chief's retractor in the London Clinic; such was the man's sense of loyalty and careerism that he considered this unpaid duty as a positive privilege. The House of Commons Committee that investigated private practice in the NHS heard evidence from a junior doctor about the eye department, where 'The consultant operated on the private patients in the Ophthalmic Department operating theatre after the afternoon's NHS list had been finished. The regular nursing staff were in attendance at the private operations for which extra duty they received an occasional box of confectionery.' The consultant probably got £400 for his work. The nurses got sweets, but the people who cleaned the theatre, washed and packed the linen and cleared up the mess got nothing. A senior laboratory technician reported that 'The arrival of a single "private" specimen, which must invariably be done "straight away", throws the whole routine into chaos.' When he questioned this, he received the reply that private practice work was 'pure profit' and should not therefore be interrupted. Until recently, the rate charged for private NHS work was below cost and certainly made no allowance for capital costs. Even then, a surprising proportion of NHS pay-bed patients defaulted on their bills!

On occasions, the abuse of the NHS was simple theft. NHS equipment, such as sterile instrument packs and specialised technical devices (private theatres are often badly equipped) are commonly borrowed, and I have several times seen anaesthetists vanishing with a handful of syringes, drugs and, occasionally, anaesthetic fluids.

In a 1985 survey for the GLC Industry and Employment branch, the following cases, culled over a two-year period, were cited:

- In February 1982, Reg Bird of the Association of Scientific, Technical and Managerial Staffs, representing laboratory workers, claimed, 'Cheating takes place on a wide scale . . . Reports giving us most concern are coming from within twenty-five miles of London . . . The most widespread reports concern the misuse of NHS laboratory facilities – tests are being made for which payment should be made but isn't.'

- In February 1982, Leeds Area Health Authority wrote off £21,000 – lost because a consultant had been collecting NHS charges from his private patients and was not told when the charges were increased in 1977.

- In March 1982, a Government auditor found that private patients in Medway had been occupying more than their allowed quota of beds; that they had been supplied cut-price drugs; and that hospitals had relied on incomplete information supplied by consultants.

- In August 1982, it was reported that the Director of Public Prosecutions had demanded further fraud squad inquiries following investigations into ninety-eight consultants, mostly related to private practice in NHS hospitals. One Grimsby consultant had been arrested and released on police bail. Twenty names had been forwarded to the DPP.

- In March 1984, it was reported that police were investigating alleged malpractice at the Prince Charles Hospital in Merthyr Tydfil. Allegations concerned private practice specimens being sent to NHS laboratories; private patients admitted to NHS beds; doctors seeing outpatients on NHS premises without paying rent; and patients being charged for facilities they should have received for free.

- In May 1984, the Social Services Secretary announced, 'Alleged irregularities in the handling of private patients' charges at Good Hospital, Sutton Coldfield, are being investigated by the police, the Inland Revenue and my department. The Director of Public Prosecutions is being kept informed.'[1]

As a result, the Secretary of State, Norman Fowler had to send auditors into thirty-seven District Health Authorities. The *Lancet* commented: 'Mr Fowler's response so far has given some credibility to the claim from other quarters that this kind of dishonesty is now endemic at the interface between the NHS and private practice.'[2] Now, most employees of big institutions 'borrow' odd bits and pieces and regard it as part of the perks. But it seems somewhat unfair that a hungry nurse can be reprimanded for finishing off a patient's meal and a domestic fired for taking home a sliced loaf which would otherwise go mouldy, but when consultants help themselves to NHS facilities they are somehow defending clinical freedom. In reality, the best way to abolish private practice altogether would be to improve the NHS so that the Hackney General was raised to the level of Addenbrookes or Edinburgh Royal. Of course, private medicine flourishes because precisely the reverse is happening, and most people realise it.

Direct action in the 1970s

The pay-bed issue seemed likely to simmer quietly on without anything very much being done, a token to be volleyed back and forth across the ideological fence. The 1974 Labour Party manifesto included a promise to phase out pay-beds, and a prolonged and inconclusive committee under David Owen's chairmanship was to discuss the matter. Meanwhile, hospital workers, in the course of their first national strike in 1972, had discovered that refusing to do the extra chores for private patients produced an unprecedented response from management. Whereas most previous union action had inconvenienced only the ill public and put pressure on the employers (the Government) very indirectly, the ban on private patients hit the pockets of the most influential consultants, who made their feelings felt in no uncertain terms to local and national management.

This tactic continued after the strike was defeated, more as a way of exerting selective industrial pressure than as a campaign against private practice itself. At the Brook Hospital in South London it was carried on after the strike, which, despite a poor settlement, had greatly enhanced the organisation and morale of the ancillary workers.

The entire Wessex region began operating a ban, based in Portsmouth, from March 1973. Although there were only thirty private beds in the city, they catered for over 2000 patients per year – over half the city's waiting list. There, and at the Hammersmith Hospital soon after, the ban proved a considerable success. The hospital management, who had previously scoffed at union claims that the extra attention for private patients was affecting service to the rest, found out for itself just what was involved. Most important, the private beds were cleared for NHS patients.

But these initiatives remained local and unofficial, despite attempts to spread the word, until a crisis suddenly blew up on the fifteenth floor of the new Charing Cross Hospital in July 1976, a crisis which suddenly plummeted the pay-bed anomaly back into the national headlines. Once again, NUPE members had begun to put pressure on the private section, particularly in view of the slowness in introducing the 'consolidated' waiting lists which had been promised since 1 January to guarantee that queue-jumping unrelated to medical urgency was curtailed. At Charing Cross, the consultants, already in dispute with Barbara Castle (the then Minister of Health) over the renewal of their contracts, were organised and ready to make an issue of it.

The doctors reacted by introducing 'sanctions' which increased ill-feeling in the hospitals and had little wider impact. Hospital workers in turn stepped up unofficial action and non-co-operation with private patients in NHS facilities to force the Government's hand.

Direct action of this kind, whose implications go further than the money-militancy of traditional trade union action, expresses a political questioning that goes beyond the cross on the ballot paper at the general election. As the hospital workers pointed out gleefully, the pay-bed business had been through all the democratic motions, was duly offered in the Labour Party's manifesto on which they had won the election, and *still* nothing happened. As *The Times* put it, 'Labour Party policy is that private beds should be phased out, but as recently as last February, all appearances were that there was no great urgency about starting. All that was changed, by the bans on private patients by non-medical staff.'

Barbara Castle was at least honest about the importance of the hospital trade unionists, noting in her diary, 'I begin to feel that the only way we will get phasing-out at the end will be by the direct action of the unions.' But it was also a rank and file rocket aimed at the Labour Party and the union officials. For, in truth, it was an ideal issue on which to seem radical in the Bevan idiom, to give the appearance of challenging the medical establishment without spending a farthing. In retrospect, it enabled the Labour Party to introduce the first cutbacks in the NHS unnoticed, indeed radiant in the reflected glow of the beds.

Ultimately, the pay-beds *are* a side issue, albeit an important one, in the overall crisis in the National Health Service. They enabled union presidents to make radical-sounding orations at the seaside instead of really tackling the issue of raising basic wage rates. They gave the Labour Party a veneer of egalitarianism on health, enabling them to crow about the NHS's vanishing virtues while depriving it of the resources which might make them possible. It gave the BMA the chance to bang the drum of clinical freedom. It *was* true that many poor and middle class people had saved for health insurance, not out of any sense of élitism but because of first-hand experience of the NHS's decline in quality and low respect for patient convenience, which the Labour Party, in power for fourteen of the first thirty years of the service's existence, had allowed.

The solution?

In the eventual compromise negotiated by Lord Goodman, private practice emerged considerably strengthened. Rather than stating a case on principle against private medicine, the compromise suggested it was perfectly acceptable as long as it took place outside NHS premises, an ostrich-like attitude which has given the go-ahead for the biggest burst of speculative commercial hospital building since the Victorian age. Castle was probably right that 'we need never have accepted this fudged and dangerous compromise, if only Harold hadn't panicked and played into Goodman's hands.'

It was commerce and concessions which finished off what the hospital workers' honest indignation started. Lord Goodman, who was appointed by Harold Wilson to act as a go-between with the BMA, wrote to *The Times* on 27 April 1976, boasting about the extent to which the Castle Bill had been watered down:

> The Bill is hardly recognisable as the offspring of the Consultative Document of August 1975. It reflects massive concessions, may I say achieved by the tenacity of the leaders of the profession principally in the establishment of an Independent Health Service Board . . . It is I think common knowledge that the figure of 1,000 beds was determined as one based on a very large measure of agreement that they were redundant and many of them already in NHS use . . . If this Bill

is approved by Parliament I believe it provides a secure base for private medicine and a springboard for its continuation and I hope enlargement.

Once the pressure of direct action on the wards was removed, and the issue itself removed to the rarefied air of 'committeedom', its meaning was reversed. An instinctive move towards fairness ended by strengthening privilege. Barbara Castle ended by stating that her measures were 'an expression of the Government's commitment to the maintenance of private practice in this country.'

In the eighties

The pay-beds furore was highly convenient for the 1979 Tory election campaign. The Conservative manifesto promised to halt their removal and to abolish the Health Service Board, which had the duty to supervise the closure of pay-beds and, to a strictly limited degree, control the growth of the private sector. After winning an election campaign which exploited the 'Winter of Discontent', Mrs Thatcher's Government took several immediate steps to facilitate the expansion of private medicine. The contract hospital consultants sign with the NHS was redrafted to expedite the 'maximum part-time' option, where a consultant is paid ten elevenths of the full-time salary but is allowed to practise privately, and to permit 'full-times' to practise privately if their earnings are kept below 10 per cent of their NHS salary.

These were small but significant changes, and the number of 'maximum part-timers' rose by 28 per cent in 1979–80. The maximum part-timer was also encouraged to take a planning and financial role in new private hospitals. According to Dr David Bolt, the former Chair of the BMA's Central Committee for Hospital Medical Services, which negotiates for Britain's 16,000 consultants, 'We put a fair amount of pressure on consultants to move towards facilities outside the NHS. Even after the change of Government in 1979, we used to impress on consultants that they now had a five-year "breathing space" that they should use since, if at the end of that time the opposition were to come to power, there would be very little notice before all NHS facilities were closed to private patients. As a result there has been a very striking development in terms of provision of private facilities.'[3] Consultants were even able to utilise the Business Start-Up Scheme to obtain finance for their private clinics. The result was a rapid burst of hospital building. In 1979 there were 153 private hospitals with operating theatres in the UK, containing 6,736 beds. At the end of 1984 there were 202 such hospitals, with 10,126 beds.

Many of the new hospitals were owned by American multinationals, and the majority were in London, often in close proximity to teaching hospitals in the part of Westminster now known as bedpan alley. The Cromwell Hospital, owned by Medical Services International, well placed on the route to Heathrow Airport, has 490 consultants accredited to its facilities (all but ten mainly NHS doctors); the Portland Hospital for Women and Children, which opened in 1983 and was owned by Hospital Capital Corporation until its purchase by American Medical International, cost £7.5 million, which included direct investment by thirty-eight consultants. Kuwaiti financial backing is involved in the sixty-three bed Churchill Clinic in Southwark, opposite the Imperial War Museum and within one mile of St Thomas's Hospital. From 1941, the building served as the Hospital of Our Lady of Consolation, but the religious order abandoned it due to rising costs. £6 million were spent on converting the building. It reopened in May 1981, and in its first two years had 5,550 admissions and carried out 4,800 surgical procedures. About one third of its patients are foreign. The hospital has 170 staff and 80–100 consultants use the hospital regularly.

The expansion of medical insurance was even more rapid, and was the motor for the hospital expansion, since only a small and declining group of those seeking private treatment pay out of pocket. Because of the NHS, the insurance market has historically been relatively small, and has had the character of middle class subscription associations allowing 'genteel' clients to avoid the lower orders. But the three major companies, who provide 90 per cent of the private medical insurance, BUPA, Private Patients Plan (PPP) and Western Provident Association (WPA), all expanded rapidly in the late seventies, principally through company schemes. The total number of subscribers (many policies also cover the spouse and children) was only 50,000 in 1950, and still only 616,000 in 1964.

The surge came in the late seventies, with the number of subscribers rising from 1,058 million people in 1977 to 1,917 million in 1982, and over 4.9 million, around one in eleven of the population, by 1985. The typical subscriber would be an affluent Southerner: the General Household Survey of 1982 revealed that 23 per cent of 'professionals' are covered by private medical insurance, while only 2 per cent of the semi-skilled and unskilled manual groups are covered. However, the right wing leaderships of the electricians' unions in particular pursued private medical insurance as part of wage negotiation. And the private insurers were keenly aware of the political utility of encouraging working class subscribers. Dr David Gullick, executive medical adviser to BUPA, said 'The more the rank and file union members are transferred into potential private patients, the more difficult it will be for their leaders to pursue their vendetta against the private practice of medicine.'[4]

The character of the insurance firms was further changed by their adoption of high-profile advertising and marketing techniques on television and in the glossies, which contrasted 'the BUPA Health Service' with the queues and waits of the real NHS. One PPP advertisement which stated 'your son could wait up to sixteen weeks with appendicitis' was defended by the company to the Advertising Standards Board because it also included the words 'The NHS is fine if you're desperately ill'! In fact, the cover that the private subscribers were buying had many limitations, and could hardly be described as comprehensive, since it fails to cover GP consultation, accidents, childbirth, chronic, geriatric or psychiatric care. And renewal rates, unlike other forms of insurance, increased each year, quite sharply in the retired age group. In reality, the cover is for acute surgical illness in otherwise well people with the odd 'multi-phasic' health checks of dubious utility.

Failing to cope

It was not only the subscribers who stood to get their fingers burnt. The big three companies were unable to cope with their sudden expansion and found themselves squeezed by rising costs and even more severe problems of budget control than those experienced by the NHS. In 1981, BUPA actually made an underwriting loss, partly through rising medical costs, partly through pitching its premiums too low in an attempt to attract new trade, some of it in less healthy occupations. And the all-important impression of 'luxury care' was proving hideously expensive to deliver. Prices were hiked, with BUPA introducing in 1982 a mid-year subscription rise of 20 per cent and a further year-end rise of 15 per cent. They were also forced to introduce a 'banding' scheme to grade the status of the hospital to which the subscriber was eligible, and to attempt to enforce fee schedules on the consultants. The decision of the American firms to enter the business suggests that there will be further attempts to exercise cost controls over the doctors working in the private sector and that there will tend to be a merger of the insurance and hospital ownership and management (along the lines of North American 'health maintenance organisations') to do this. Private medicine is still a numerically small area of medicine in the UK, but it is rapidly expanding with the active encouragement of the present Government and the consultants who, it is calculated, earned an average of £19,000 in 1987 from private work on top of their sizable NHS incomes.

Privatisation

As it became clear that the expansion of private medical care was neither potentially infinite nor particularly efficient, many of the other health care wheezes dreamed up by the new right were viewed with less enthusiasm by the Thatcher Government. Not only did the NHS remain an electorally popular institution, but the various Think Tank reports and missions by DHSS investigators tended to confirm that the NHS was good at doing exactly what every health care administrator wants to do, that is control costs (particularly doctor-initiated expenditure) and ration public access. Thus, after 1981, a DHSS working party had visited the USA, Australia, France, West Germany, Holland and Scandinavia to explore ways in which NHS finances could be reorganised along insurance lines. Norman Fowler somewhat ruefully announced in 1982: 'The Government has no plans to change the present system of financing largely through taxation.' Similarly, in September 1982, the Central Policy Review Staff (the Think Tank) Report which explored 'partial change' (charges for visits to GPs and hospital admissions) or 'comprehensive change' (a national insurance based scheme) was disowned by the Cabinet and forced Mrs Thatcher's famous pledge: 'The NHS is safe with us. The principle that adequate health care should be provided to all, regardless of ability to pay, must be the foundation of any arrangements for financing the NHS.'

What actually happened in Thatcher's second term was a shift away from the expansion of private medicine towards the privatisation of the NHS. It was easy to see the political attractions for the Government. Stuck with the stubborn fact that the NHS remained popular and that people, probably self-deludingly, felt they had some sort of stake in it, they sought to subdivide that loyalty. There was the 'good' NHS: the doctors and nurses who didn't go on strike and worked all the hours God gave. Then there was the 'bad' NHS: bureaucrats, porters and domestics who were always on strike, whose work was incidental and could easily and more efficiently be taken over by more competitive outside contractors. 'Privatisation' was clearly a way of weakening hospital trade unionism. It also made good sense within the Conservative Party itself, where the 'wet' tradition of *noblesse oblige* Toryism, which still took some pride in public service, was being overtaken by the fast-food franchisers and contract cleaning elements who saw the NHS very differently: as a large and none-too-discerning potential customer. The links were sometimes direct: Michael Forsyth, for example, who became an MP in 1983 and was one of the best known back bench advocates of privatisation, had previously been a leading member of the public relations firm consulted by the contract giant Pritchards.

Contracting out

'Contract out' was the parrot cry, and the push began in April 1981 with a letter from the then Health Minister, Dr Gerard Vaughan, to the chairs of the AHAS and DHAS, chiding those who had not 'responded constructively to approaches from commercial companies, notably from the cleaning industry.' Model contracts were outlined in a May 1982 draft circular, and a second draft circular in February 1983 turned the screw still further. By this time, the 1982 hospital workers' strike had been beaten, the DHAS had been further weeded of dissent and the Government, as an extra sweetener, had undertaken to refund the VAT which hospitals would have to pay if introducing outside contractors. Finally, the 1946 Fair Wage Resolution was repealed to enable the outside contractor to undercut the minimum NHS wage levels and thereby undermine union organisation. The final circular made it compulsory for various services to be put out to tender. The only alternative was a competitive 'in-house' tender which led to the shameful situation of already low-paid workers co-operating with their managers to reduce their own wages and increase their workload, in a contest in which, as the catering magazine *Hospitality* put it, 'the in-house caterer enters the boxing ring with one hand tied behind his back.' Whether the external or the in-house tender succeeded, any real saving was made not by increased efficiency (it often visibly deteriorated), but by increased exploitation of the workforce. This provoked long and bitter union disputes involving the Medway Health Authority, the Littlemore Psychiatric Hospital in Oxford, Hammersmith Hospital, Addenbrookes Hospital in Cambridge and Barking Hospital in East London, where sacked cleaners picketed for over ten months against non-union labour introduced by Crothalls, the biggest subsidiary of the Pritchard Services Group. When, in 1988, the Scottish Health Boards were finally forced to begin privatisation, there was strike action too, with one gigantic Edinburgh banner reading: 'Fight for the Right to Care . . . Without Profit.'

Low standards

In Cambridge, the paediatrician Professor John Davis resigned from the Health Authority in protest over the privatisation of domestic services at Addenbrookes. In a letter to the authority explaining his resignation, he said:

> You will know that my attitudes are essentially conservative, but there comes a time when one must be seen to live up to one's professed principles and true conservatism means recognising that the economy is made for man and not vice versa, given the necessary recognition that resources are not infinite.
>
> If we are not prepared to pay the economic price for acting morally, we may end up by paying the moral price for acting economically.[5]

A less elevated sounding but more plausible motive for privatisation was suggested by a contract cleaning employee writing to the *Guardian*:

> Each week we were issued with a definite supply of disinfectant, bleach, etc., which had been diluted to a minimal potency. If this ran

out on the fifth or the sixth day, then the job had to be done with water only; not very hygienic in a household of four, let alone a ward of twenty.

It was not only this, however, that transformed what might have been a rewarding (albeit unpleasant) task into sheer frustration and drudgery, for we were explicitly instructed by the management not to talk to the patients in the firm's time. So that, for example, cheering up sick and distressed persons, even for a couple of minutes, was disapprovingly categorised as 'wasting time'.

Perhaps the key to the Government's strategy is this. The NHS unions are vociferous in their defence of that organisation; the workers of contract cleaning companies are conspicuously lacking in unions. Substitute the latter for the former, and the NHS is one step nearer to being like putty in its hands.[6]

In some cases the contractors were simply inefficient, sometimes dangerously so. A hip operation in Addenbrookes had to be cancelled when blood and bone was found on the operating theatre floor. Doctors and nurses were reported to have found 'the mess when they arrived on Friday morning to perform the hip replacement operation.' They subsequently found dust on a clean-air vent. The surgeon, Mr David Marsh, said, 'We were furious. We called in our consultant bacteriologist, Dr Roderic Warren, and he advised that we should not go ahead with the operation. Hip replacements are very susceptible to infection.' Skimped work was common, for, as a leaflet issued by Hackney Health Emergency put it, 'You cannot cut costs of cleaning without more dirt. You cannot make profits out of hospital food without cutting quality.' In at least one case, that of the Cornish Health Authority, Ministers acted to force acceptance of a private cleaner of hospital linen's tender, even though it was £47,320 *more* than the in-house tender.[7]

And in a further attempt to remove the barriers between the NHS and the private sector in 1987, hospital general managers were exhorted, with little recorded success, to consider cutting their waiting lists not by improving their own service but by farming their patients out to private hospitals and footing the bills themselves. Since the private hospitals' operating time is always underused (essential if they are to offer immediate treatment), it suits them extremely well to take in NHS patients, and the financial deals appear attractive. But, because of the concentration of private hospitals in the South, it is not a viable national strategy, and is no substitute for appropriate NHS provision. And, if the NHS were to come to depend on farming patients out in this way, the present 'loss leader' pricing would promptly increase. There is also a renewed drive to site private clinics within NHS hospitals, as at the Radcliffe Day Clinic in Oxford. Thus, too, Ronald McDonald of the hamburger chain was to be found raising funds for a Ronald McDonald House for the parents of children admitted to Guy's Hospital, and a fluoride toothpaste manufacturer's charity scheme used the logo of Great Ormond Street Hospital for Sick Children to identify their product with the NHS at its most heartrending.

In another triumph for commerce, a national conference sponsored by the accountants Touche Ross suggested the sale of fast-food franchises, petrol stations in the outpatient carparks and advertising videos in the waiting areas. The era of the voluntary worker with the tea urn and the digestive biscuits has been replaced by the commercial transplant surgeon who removes kidneys from 'a donor' who has in fact been paid with a free airline ticket and £2,000. It may be sad for the 3,000 NHS scrapers-up of faeces, launderers of urine- and blood-sodden sheets and cooks for the sick that they got the sack for all their pains, but it has made a lot of accountants and company directors happy. Hawley's Mediclean, for example, who picked up ten major hospital cleaning contracts, were able to announce pre-tax profits of £31.5 million in 1984, a 121 per cent increase on 1983.

Walking on two feet

It is sometimes difficult to evaluate the real importance of private practice and privatisation to the Government. Clearly they dislike the NHS on principle, don't make use of it themselves and regard the expansion of commercial medicine as worthwhile in itself, because it enlarges 'consumer choice' and 'self-reliance'. On the other hand, the expansion of commercial medicine beyond a certain point brings problems of its own, and is blatantly aimed at increasing the wealth of a small percentage of private consultants who work full-time in the acute specialities, and the mainly American investors. The first private general practice, in Harrow, failed to pay its way. Privatisation, announced with such fanfare, has caused a great deal of demoralisation and dissent for little tangible political gain. And, while some of the income maximisation schemes which Health Authorities have been forced into involve significant asset-stripping (notably in having to sell hospital land to the highest bidder, usually property developers), projects like opening shopping arcades in hospitals, selling souvenir mugs and other business-orientated new developments are little more than window dressing.

But while Government gimmicks sometimes seem almost comically irrelevant to the central problems of NHS financing, they should be taken seriously. The task for the British Government in the eighties is to make Britain's careworn industry capable of holding its own in the intensely competitive world markets. Part of that, so far not very successful, drive is said to require the weakening of the 'wage-push' of trade unionism (wrongly identified in the seventies as the main cause of inflation) and the reduction of spending on welfare (in the NHS, because health care provision is so labour-intensive, the two go together). But, in the real world, it has not proved possible for even Mrs Thatcher's abrasive *diktats* to achieve the scale of cuts in NHS staff costs and services which her strategy demands.

The hospital unions have been duly bashed, the NHS budget annually squeezed nearer to the point of breakdown and the private health sector bribed and preened – but with a great deal of difficulty and some very noisy resistance, much of it from dangerously near traditional centres of support. And all with nothing like the reduction in welfare costs or the shift in the mix of public-private health care which had been anticipated in the early years of the first Thatcher term. In 1982, for example, I was told by Gerard Vaughan in a moment of candour that the intended relationship between the private and public sector would be 'like that of the commercial TV and the BBC,' (i.e. 50:50, with the former having, of course, acquired 'a licence to print money').

This kind of mix is still the Thatcher administration's aim, but progress towards it has proved idiosyncratic and inconsistent. One foot is the hospital cuts and remorseless restriction of NHS spending which each year works further and deeper down the budgets. The other foot is the expansion of the commercial and private sector. Both elements are essential and closely interrelated: although at times one or the other seem to dominate Government thinking. But slowly decreasing real NHS spending and 'weathering the storm' acts to force-feed the private sector, while the new commercial hospitals to which NHS consultants devote such zeal in turn indict the long waits and low morale in the NHS. When evidence of hospital cuts in December 1987, centring on the repeated postponement of cardiac surgery to a Birmingham baby, brought an unprecedented wave of pressure from senior consultants, Thatcher stonewalled. But, lo and behold, Tory MP Tony Newton let drop that the old chestnut, tax relief for private health insurance, was being considered 'to take the pressure off the health service.' And Norman Tebbit, right on cue, began publicly musing on 'alternative funding', i.e. the introduction of commercial health insurance.

It is in this process that consultants' attitudes to private practice and their NHS work can play a crucial role in tipping the balance, either way. Although unnecessary with a properly financed health service, in the present situation it is hard to raise objections to an NHS consultant wishing to see patients privately, if there is no abuse of the 'NHS/private interface' and if the doctor's NHS commitments are not neglected. But when a senior consultant becomes extensively committed to work in private hospitals, especially in ones in which he or she has a financial stake, there is a real threat to NHS morale and services. However skilful the doctor, he or she is unlikely to be able to be in two places at the same time, and it is virtually inevitable that such a consultant's commitment to teaching, administration and service planning, let alone routine work, will suffer.

And, of course, new human resources are not created, but rather transferred. The private sector, despite repeated promises, has undertaken no significant doctor or nurse education, and Dr Paul MacLoughlin's repeated promises to open a new private school of medicine, first on the site of the old Royal Free Hospital and then on the old Bedford College site, have not materialised. The example set by the consultant is influential: if he or she is giving a greater commitment to private work and can offer 'his' intensive care nurse an enhanced salary, well, why not? A generation of consultants whose medical education was publicly financed and whose training and experience was wholly within the NHS are now being put under considerable pressure to jump ship, pressure which comes at least as much from their genuine frustration with working conditions in an underfinanced NHS as from any great ideological enthusiasm for private medicine.

9
Health Trade Unionism

In the early seventies, hospital trade unions emerged from their shadowy existence somewhere in the wings of the NHS to the centre of the political stage. From a situation in which industrial action was virtually unknown, even on wage issues, by 1977 every grade of hospital staff had taken some sort of national strike action, including direct action for and against the retention of private pay-beds within NHS hospital wards, strike protest against Government welfare policy, pickets of hospital workers against proposed stiffening of the abortion laws, a multitude of disputes over hours, conditions and discipline, and, finally, action against 'the cuts' in defence of the service itself. This has reflected the general postwar growth of trade unionism among the predominantly female employees of the welfare state, whose effective boss is the Treasury, and whose work, in schools, hospitals, nurseries and welfare centres, has been, almost because it was concerned with caring rather than with producing profit, very lowly paid. Like a surfboard rider, the expansion of welfare jobs hurtled forward even as the economic wave that carried it crumpled within. The NHS continued to gobble up labour long after the size of the industrial workforce had been forcibly restricted, giving hospital trade unionism a new weight and political importance within the labour movement.

This growth was not an orderly, automatic and respectable expansion, but had been punctuated by strikes, marches and battles, with management experiencing more of the militancy of the mines and workshops than the obedient, even pleading, tones they had been accustomed to. From the unofficial strikes of the 1972–3 wage dispute, which gave birth to the modern hospital trade union movement through the massive, ebullient demonstrations against the first Labour-initiated round of health cuts in 1976, to the tumultuous year of 1982 which saw the biggest ever wage dispute and national TUC-led stoppages in support of the NHS, a new sort of trade unionism seemed to be being born.

But the late eighties have seen a reverse in the general fortunes of the union movement, from which health workers have not been exempt. Since the Clegg Report which ended the 1982 dispute, the basic wage settlements in the NHS have been kept relatively low, and health service wages have fallen back again, not only in comparison with the private sector, but also compared with other public sector workers like the police and the fire service. Union membership has not slumped, and the main hospital unions remain left of centre. But the high turnover of staff, especially in nursing, the low morale engendered by the cuts, and the apparent indifference of the Government to the scale of the NHS's problems, have proved demoralising. The health unions may have better-designed stationery or even better-designed policies, but the rhetoric has had increasingly little to do with the realities of working for the NHS. The union leaderships, and even more curiously the Labour Party, were, until forced into action by their rank and file in 1988, conspicuous by their lack of protest against cuts and closures in Thatcher's third term.

'Whitleyism'

The establishment of the NHS brought automatic recognition of the right of all hospital workers to join a union of their choice. The unions, very roughly represented according to membership, meet nationally to negotiate over conditions of service in bodies known as Whitley Councils, ten separate but linked bodies covering the different grades of hospital worker. This method of wage bargaining applies generally in the public sector in Britain and was consciously introduced as a check to the vigorous local bargaining which was the backbone of the syndicalist movement earlier in the century. Whitley himself was a Halifax cotton-spinner, and although the terms of the Commission he headed in 1916 were mildly intended to 'make and consider suggestions for securing a permanent improvement in the relations between employers and workmen,' they reflected an urgent need for securing industrial peace by some compulsory system of negotiation which would regain the initiative from the shop-floor. Not only had strike levels risen to record heights in the years immediately before 1914, but workers, animated by the syndicalist idea of workers' control, regarding nationalisation as the employers' last ditch and suspicious of their own leaders' respectability, were looking more to the revolutionary advocates of soviets than the top-hatted leaders of craft unionism. J. T. Murphy, one of the most forceful advocates of the soviet conception, saw the aim of Whitley's Committee as being 'to kill the workshop movement as an independent movement.'

But while Whitley cut little ice with industrial workers, it was a godsend to weaker unions like NUPE and NALGO who clung to the coat tails of its legal recognition of a joint bargaining structure to spread trade unionism peacefully.

While Whitleyism guarantees the right to union membership, it is stamped with a very restricted notion of union activity. Rights granted rather than won often remain nominal. Although the Whitley Council handbook rules cover hospital workers' conditions in extraordinary complexity, hospital workers would often have to undertake great battles to extract rights which were supposed to exist anyway. Until recently, union life centred on an infrequent area-wide evening branch meeting. Sometimes the officials were retired, and in some cases were in receipt of a personal bounty according to the size of the membership – which positively encouraged them to maintain large and unwieldy branches. The rank and file members' subscriptions to the union were just another deduction from the wage packet, a possible source of cheap insurance or travel, or a useful counterthreat in disciplinary cases. Once a year 'their' leader would be on television, either making dire threats of disruption or exaggerated claims for recently negotiated settlements.

NUPE

The consequences of Whitleyism, trade unionism from above, are clearly seen in the National Union of Public Employees, the biggest hospital union, which organises manual workers in four main sections: local authorities, hospitals, universities and water authorities. It has about 250,000 hospital members (including porters, domestic workers, ward cleaners, chefs, cooks, kitchen workers, telephonists, gardeners, laundry workers, and workers in many other manual trades, as well as a growing number of nurses) and grew out of a union for all London municipal employees founded by a London socialist sewage worker in 1888. By and large its hospital members simply tagged behind the settlements negotiated with the local authority manual workers. Although the union grew enormously with the foundation of the NHS, the only major industrial action it took was in 1956, when mass meetings of women domestics in London forced the union to take up the struggle for the 44-hour working week which had been granted to every other industry and service in 1953. In most hospitals, union dues were checked off automatically by management, union meetings were infrequent, and the officers of the local branch tended to be re-elected without change or challenge, often simply because of the status of their hospital job rather than their commitment to unionism. The unelected full-time officers of the union seemed to see their role as almost philanthropic, looking after 'their' hospital workers. Its national leaders have traditionally been drawn from outside the union: Jack Wills, a building worker; Bryn Roberts, a miner; Sydney Hill, an engineer. Alan Fisher was appointed to the union staff at the age of 16 and, apart from war service, has worked for the union all his life. His successor Rodney Bickerstaffe, the current General Secretary, has a similar background.

The union's national membership was 105,000 at the end of the Second World War. By 1955 it had 200,000 members and was the ninth largest in the TUC. Twenty years later it had expanded to 508,000, and it is now 663,776. As a proportion of the membership women rose even more rapidly, from half in 1968 to two thirds in 1975. In 1985, 42 per cent of stewards were women, two thirds of the members. There were six female area officers out of 127 and five reserved seats on the 26-strong National Committee.

But, until the union's first national strike in 1972–3, most members had only the most passive connection with and vague understanding of their own union, which was run for them by professionals. The results were exceptionally low basic wages for a demoralised membership, forced to work enormous amounts of overtime to earn a living wage. Equal pay existed: it was equally low for men and women.

COHSE

The Confederation of Health Service Employees is in theory the industrial union for the NHS, but in practice its real base is among the predominantly male mental hospital nurses and some of the more senior nurses in the general hospitals. It has 212,980 members and is descended from the old Asylum Attendants' Union and the Poor Law Nurses' Union, and capitalised on the Royal College of Nursing's exclusion of men up to 1960. A militant campaigner among the nurses after the establishment of the NHS, COHSE was disaffiliated from the TUC during the battle against the Conservative Government's Industrial Relations Act for registering itself on the official Government roll which the majority of trade unions were boycotting. In terms of its local weakness, COHSE suffered from all the defects of NUPE in more acute form. Nonetheless, the conditions of its members were so terrible that there were still occasional muffled COHSE explosions.

In some ways COHSE is the more typical union, with a good deal of craft pride, respect for the book and solid class consciousness. A COHSE branch secretary is unlikely to subscribe to *Marxism Today* or to want to emulate the aspirant chic of the university-educated NUPE full-timer. He or she might, on the other hand, prove a very effective fund-raiser for a Miners' Support Committee. About 55 per cent of COHSE's members are nurses, and nowadays three out of four members are female. In the 1988 nurses' strikes, the lead, at least outside London, was taken by COHSE members.

Other unions

The Transport and General Workers' Union (1,434,005 members), the general workers' union, organises some hospitals, notably in Scotland and the North, but this seems to be a matter of chance. The General, Municipal, Boilermakers' and Allied Trades' Union (839,920 members) also has a base in some hospitals. Curiously these, plus NUPE and COHSE, with widely differing memberships, have equal votes on the Whitley Council covering ancillary workers. It consists of sixteen trade union representatives and nineteen management representatives, of whom sixteen are from various NHS governing bodies and three are appointed by the DHSS. The management and the DHSS have a permanent majority, but this is scarcely needed since all decisions on money matters rest with the Treasury official in attendance, and most decisions are arrived at by consensus anyway.

Nurses

Nurses were undoubtedly the most exploited section of NHS workers, especially student nurses, who account for over half of nurses working on the wards. Current weekly take-home pay for a newly qualified nurse is about £70, which means they have problems simply paying for their accommodation and transport, and 'moonlighting' is essential and widespread. Nurses are also required to do shift work, much of it in unsocial hours, without a regular pattern and rotated at short notice. Their earnings are made up of a basic rate and special duty payments (SDPs) for hours worked at unsocial times, which the DHSS figures suggest is some 30 per cent of the total time worked. Unlike other workers who have compulsory night and weekend work (like television, airport and essential service workers, who get a percentage premium of total salary), the nurses are only paid a higher rate for those hours which are designated 'unsocial': if a staff nurse were to achieve the sort of antisocial hours premium that an airline worker for British Caledonian enjoys, her wages would be increased by 28 per cent at a stroke. The Government attempted to abolish SDPs, which caused successful nurses' strike action in Manchester and London in January 1988.

Work hours are often informally extended for hand-over or because it is customary to do extra time if ward work is not finished, and they often include a shift split into two – which manages to ruin the whole day. Student nurses will often listen to lectures, even sit examinations, after a full night on duty. Leisure time is spent within the nursing home, slumped in front of the common room television.

Much ward work is still swamped in unexplained routine. Indeed, there is often one routine for the tutor sister and quite another to please the sister on the ward. The combined effect of a heavy and difficult workload, petty discipline and lack of qualified staff makes the job very wearing. A student nurse wrote in despair:

A student nurse with only a single month's training finds herself alone at night with pretty well full responsibility for a whole ward of patients. She is frightened – but not just of making mistakes. She is frightened of calling her superior, engaged elsewhere, even in an emergency. So the student does make some mistakes. The next day she is severely reprimanded – as if a young girl learning about nursing doesn't punish

herself enough for not doing all she might have done for her patients.
The next night she is back on the same ward, in the same situation, with
the same fears. She makes further mistakes. She goes away. No one
knows what has happened to her or where she has gone. She's just
another statistic in the wastage rates.

Until recently nurses have only rarely joined the industrial
unions, preferring membership in professional bodies like the
Royal College of Nursing and the Royal College of Midwives which
combine educational and professional functions with wage negotiation. These bodies are dominated by senior nurses and there is
no effective and democratic control by student and ward nurses.
Thus, when the rank and file pressure inside the RCN at the 1969
conference led to the setting up of the 'Raise the Roof' campaign
for higher pay, a 38-hour week and proper student status for
trainee nurses, the campaign was carried out along strictly controlled and respectable lines by the senior RCN members who had
themselves imposed some of the petty restrictions. One nurse
wrote:

> The whole campaign was controlled from the top. The slogans and
> demands were already prepared. The meetings were dominated by
> speakers from the platform – the establishment – and any independent
> militant spirit was crushed wherever possible. The nurses were told
> they could not strike; we were not left to think about this and decide for
> ourselves – even though many possibly would not anyway. Eventually
> most nurses stopped attending the meetings – they could not be
> bothered to be talked at yet again.

A similar approach dogged the RCN's anti-cuts effort 'Nurse
Alert', and led to many problems in the 1982 disputes, since
the RCN leadership clearly feel that any association with trade
unionism will jeopardise their relationship with other professional
bodies like the BMA, not to mention their 'Royal' status.

The RCN branches, called centres, tend to concentrate on
educational or social activities: the members are consulted, if at all,
by postal vote (twice rejecting government pay offers in 1982). It
holds annual conferences but is run by a council which is elected
every four years and tends to be dominated by nurses in management positions in the NHS. The College often recruits on the basis
of its no-strike Constitution, although there have been repeated
attempts by rank and file members to abolish Rule 12, which

effectively rules out industrial action. This high-minded position enables the RCN to take a lot of excellent policy positions (most recently on AIDS) and to bask in Mrs Thatcher's praise, but it has not rewarded working (as opposed to managerial) nurses with any tangible financial benefits. It debars nursing assistants and auxiliaries, a large section of the nursing workforce, from membership. During the 1988 strikes, Trevor Clay made further progress towards his knighthood with systematic and repeated attacks on the motives, professionalism and size of the nurses' strike, which had made the crisis in the health service front page news. To the horror and shame of many RCN members, he was the only trade unionist in the country to take the Government's part.

Clerical workers

Hospital clerical workers and administrators also join a mixture of professional and trade union bodies, but the National Association of Local Government Officers (752,131 members), the militant Town Hall union, has become increasingly dominant. NALGO's origins were conservative. It was founded in 1905 as a frankly Tory association of Town Hall clerks. Its founder, Herbert Bain, later became national agent for the Conservative Party, and its first paid national secretary stated that 'anything savouring of trade unionism is nausea to the Local Government Officer and his Association.' It only really began to grow after the House of Lords found in favour of the Whitley System in Town Halls as late as 1942, which enabled the establishment of suitable national salary scales for local government officers. A rank and file revolt began in protest at the 1969 local government settlement, and this affected the NHS membership, and became embodied in the successful rank and file body, the Nalgo Action Group. Although NALGO branches have been prominent and sometimes effective in opposing cuts in the local government field, their NHS members have been less active.

A scattering of industrial and craft unions cover the skilled manual tradesmen such as electricians, plumbers, builders, and the silver and gold trades workers inside hospitals. These craft unions, which have been increasingly attempting to negotiate wages directly with the DHSS, have often provided a core of trade union experience within hospitals.

Doctors

Doctors have traditionally had a different negotiating procedure, the Review Body system. At periodic intervals, when professional discontent reaches a certain level, an independent group of members of the establishment, usually chaired by a retired managing director, takes evidence from all interested bodies and submits an award to the Prime Minister of the day who can accept, modify, postpone or reject it. The Review Body system resulted from the Pilkington Commission in 1960. It was to be that most elusive of beasts, the 'independent' body whose recommendations could be rejected by the Government of the day 'only very reluctantly and for the most compelling reasons.' Nevertheless, the seventh Kindersley Review Body Report and recommendations were deferred and then not paid in full, and in 1970 the whole Review Body resigned when its recommendations were halved. It has served as an indirect instrument of Government incomes policy and has produced the lowest-paid doctors in Western Europe and a steady fall in doctors' incomes relative to other British professions.

Despite regular uprisings and splits, the effectively dominant representative body remains the British Medical Association. The Junior Hospital Doctors' Association emerged in the mid-1960s to dramatise the conditions of house officers undertaking their compulsory pre-registration jobs. They drew public attention to this almost medieval apprenticeship and to the long hours, poor residential conditions, and bad educational facilities for registrars, who were still undergoing hospital-based postgraduate specialist education but were more often used as cheap medical labour. More recently the provincial consultants (the heads of the hospital clinical teams) have attempted, unsuccessfully, to break away from what they see as an unrepresentative and London teaching hospital biased BMA élite.

The Medical Practitioners' Union, the only genuine doctors' trade union, has traditionally been based among general practitioners, but it has recently expanded among more radically-minded hospital juniors as part of the general spread of trade unionism among white-collar workers in Britain. MPU members were prominent in the 1975 junior doctors' dispute, and were active, and better organised than the BMA, in pressing home local negotiation after the settlement. The union has significant support in hospitals in London, the West Midlands and the North-west, and some strength among younger GPs and consultants in the inner cities. It has been active in the campaign against excessive hours for juniors and for a new GP contract. In response, the BMA has set up its own system of Industrial Relations Officers, some from trade union backgrounds.

The MPU was formed in 1914 from an organisation of doctors supporting a state medical service. Its members were mainly drawn from 'panel' doctors who considered that the BMA did not represent their interests. After the First World War it affiliated to the TUC and remained perdominantly a GP organisation until it joined the Association of Scientific, Technical and Managerial Staffs in 1971. It is now a subsection of ASTMS, the fastest growing of the white-collar unions, which organises in insurance, research and technical laboratories, but whose membership includes airline pilots, executives, and office workers as well, and has a total of 390,000 members. Its base in the hospitals is among medical technicians, pharmacists, biochemists, physiological-measurement technicians and junior doctors. It has traditionally campaigned for reform of Whitleyism, more spending on the NHS and a proper occupational health service in view of the particularly high health risks in hospitals. ASTMS itself merged with the Technical and Supervisory Staffs union into the MFS, a new federation with a projected membership of 700,000.

Industrial action

Before 1970, despite a fair amount of muttering and grumbling, none of these unions seriously attempted to use industrial action to improve wages or conditions. The emphasis was still on the quality of the negotiations rather than the potential power of the membership. In this respect there was not much difference between those unions which adopted left wing resolutions at their annual conferences and those which passed right wing pronouncements. The lack of effective hospital organisation has fostered a measure of importance for the national leadership, which in some cases borders on megalomania. Trade unions became servants of their machines. Women workers, migrant workers and most male workers who lacked previous trade union experience were outsiders in their own union, whose wage bargaining was conducted in almost incomprehensible complexity by professional management, professional union full-timers and civil servants, who had more in common with each other than with hospital workers.

When hospital managers and union full-timers meet, it is obvious how similar they are, in sex, in clothes, in that particular managerial habit or skill of making things sound more complicated than they really are. On the other hand, what is remarkable about the health workers the union leaders represent is their diversity. Everything that links the professionals is different: colour, size, shape, nationality, personality and temperament. Scuffed suits and patterned ties trying to deal with a sea of differences; wiry gay telephonists, gigantic cooks from Barbados, disabled X-ray porters, sardonic Catholic staff nurses, effusive impatient Spanish ward maids, graceful giggling Thai ward nurses, Home Counties house doctors busily flapping their white coats, and pathology technicians in grubbier coats figuring out their overtime and quick routes to the local.

A hospital has a single aim which is carried out in a multitude of different but interdependent labour processes, each with its own species of grievance: the student nurse wants another gas-ring in the sitting room, the night porters are worried about their overtime, the assistant orthopaedic appliance maker wants upgrading. It has only been as the rank and file hospital unions have taken up day to day issues that they have dented the rigid classifications of skills and jobs that keep all health workers compartmentalised, and that the union has taken on a real meaning in the hospital. And to do this members have had to fashion their own informal union structures.

Ancillary workers' strikes 1970–3

The first sign of a different mood came from the underpaid and under-appreciated ancillary workers. In 1970 an unofficial strike broke out in the Royal Free Hospital in London, an establishment founded by women suffragette doctors. The Cinderellas of the hospital service, the porters, theatre technicians, domestics, telephonists and boilermen, went on a one-day strike, joined by union members in St Mary's and Bethnal Green Hospitals. The mixture of caution and desperate impatience can be seen in one of the leaflets distributed at the Royal Free Hospital:

We apologise for any inconvenience this may cause you, but as you know our basic wage in the hospital service is scandalous considering today's cost of living, and our conditions of service leave much to be desired, like the fact that we have to work seven years before we get three weeks' annual holiday.

The basic rates for married hospital workers were still £14 per week, £2.50 less than the national minimum wage suggested by the TUC.

An informal and unofficial rank and file body, the London Alliance of Stewards for Health Workers, called for a one-day stoppage on 27 November 1972, and was frankly amazed at the support it received, especially from black women workers, who had previously been largely excluded from union activity.

The unions were forced to act if they were to retain any hold over the situation, and called an official national one-day strike on 17 December 1972 which had a massive response. An estimated 180,000 went on strike, many for the full twenty-four hours.

By February 1973, after a complex and long-winded balloting procedure, national action was announced. But in contrast to the ballot's emphatic call for an all-out strike by over half the members, the unions called for a series of half-measures: selective strikes, to be co-ordinated from the head office, an overtime ban, and 'withdrawal of co-operation'. The strategy, if it existed, was to allow strong branches to take the brunt of the attack while allowing the less militant areas to choose their own tactics according to their level of confidence.

In those two weeks of March, British hospitals were shaken. Before the strike, the vital work done by the ancillary workers had largely been out of sight; in the boiler-house, the sewing rooms, the kitchens, and the record files. The general public just did not see the porter wrestling with an oxygen cylinder, the ward maid replacing blood- and urine-sodden sheets, or the hospital telephonist trying frantically to rouse doctors for a sudden case of heart seizure.

The first national strike surprised everyone, the Tories, the hospital administrators, the consultants, and many hospital workers themselves, with its determination and spirit. The picket-like posters put it plainly with the slogans 'We are against the Government, not the patients' and 'Hospital workers stick together'.

Women workers, scarcely represented in the union hierarchy and always blamed by male union officials for lack of militancy, led many of the strikes and marches. At one Birmingham hospital, women pickets at one gate succeeded in turning away lorry drivers who promptly drove down the road and talked their way in through the male picket line. Workers of all languages, colours and nationalities were joined together, and signs on picket lines were in Italian, Greek, Spanish, even Gaelic. Over 400 hospitals saw industrial action, ranging from one-day strikes to all-out stoppages. A cluster of sit-ins took place in response to management attempts to bring in volunteers. Selective action in laundries and sterilising depots began to put direct pressure on the ability of many hospitals to keep even an emergency service open, and nine hospital boards wrote to Sir Keith Joseph, the responsible Minister, asking him to pay the wage increases at once. The eventual settlement was financially dismal, a face-saving formula between the Tories and the union leaders.

But out of the technical defeat of the strike, a new mood of determination surfaced in the branches. It was here, and in the detailed hospital activities, not in the self-important but craven declarations of the union leaders, that the huge expansion of membership was achieved. It grew in little unsung battles against bonus schemes, increased canteen prices, understaffing and the use of agency and contract labour, management attempts to rationalise work and the first of the hospital closures and NHS cuts.

The nurses act

The mood had altered. Within weeks the Nurses' Action Group was leafleting nurses' homes with the message: 'Professionalism means nothing when we are used as cheap labour. We are doing a hard skilled job and we do it because we care. We also care when we are unable to do it properly because of lack of manpower and inevitable falling standards in a crumbling Health Service.' In the autumn of 1973 the 1500 ambulancemen followed the defiant Scottish firemen in challenging Phase 3 of the Tory pay code, and, using their traditions of militancy and high mobility, they achieved a substantial increase. Rank and file nurses rejected the March 1973 offer, and in April and May the situation exploded, to the amazement of the Royal College and unions alike.

All over Britain nurses were holding spontaneous meetings and setting up informal action groups. The biggest single female workforce arose from its servile state with exuberance and utter disrespect for the 'right way to do things'. Birmingham nurses defied the regional NUPE secretary and his police advisers and, two-thousand strong, forced their own route through the centre of the city: 'We are finished with the old image of the nurse and as such we demand a new brand of leader, not people who are too busy with their slide rules to act on our behalf.' 900 nurses packed a NUPE meeting in Houldsworth Hall, Manchester, with even more unable to get in.

The setting up of the Halsbury Inquiry did much to damp down action, as it was intended, but not without protest. When the inquiry finally reported, a total of £170 million was raised, which, as usual, was reported as '30 per cent average increases for nurses', although the increase varied from 58 per cent for the higher minority staff grades to as little as 5.6 per cent for first-year students over 21 years of age.

Medical technicians

In the meantime, medical technicians in the Association of Scientific, Technical and Management Staffs struck and were shortly joined by hospital radiographers. Over 3000, out of the country's 8000, marched in uniform through central London on 6 July 1974, demanding an interim settlement with slogans like 'No Raise, No Rays', '30 per cent or Bust' (illustrated by an enormous bosom), 'X-Ray Pay Up Now' and 'Your Genes in our Hands'. Radiographers in the Royal Free Hospital became the first ever to strike – 'a last desperate measure to save our profession' – and they were joined by an all-region stoppage in the North-east. This led to an interim settlement averaging 22 per cent being made in the autumn, and the first full review of paramedical wages for twenty-five years by Lord Halsbury, which eventually awarded rather larger sums.

By the summer of 1974, most sections of the NHS had taken action, including 50,000 doctors, 11,000 dentists, 370,000 nurses (who succeeded in Wales and Manchester in bringing out miners and engineers in sympathy strikes under the slogan 'Strike a blow for the nurses'), 4700 radiographers, 4500 physiotherapists, 1600 occupational therapists, 350 dieticians, 200 speech therapists, 250 remedial gymnasts, 270 orthopaedists, and 150 chiropodists. It was a strike wave which would have seemed impossible only four years earlier, and for a time it was difficult to open a newspaper without seeing a striking hospital worker in uniform striding across it. When the junior hospital doctors went on strike in 1975 (making sure that medically qualified pickets were always on hand for real emergencies), the last taboo was broken.

Nothing, least of all hospital trade unionism, takes place in a vacuum. The period from 1969–74 was a watershed for the whole of British trade unionism, with the widespread adoption of new tactics like factory occupations and flying pickets, 'political' strikes and widespread sympathy and solidarity strikes. These actions were underpinned by the rapid spread of trade union organisation, especially in the public sector. The advances made in the hospitals sheltered under this general umbrella and perhaps appeared more substantial than they were to prove.

The Labour Government which came into power on the strength of this popular feeling generated a virtual mountain of legislation on workers' rights, equal pay and industrial democracy, but its price was a 'Social Contract' which introduced state-imposed annual minimum rises. Real wages fell sharply, and when workers like the firemen took action anyway, in November 1977, the Labour Government did not hesitate to use troops to strike-break. Workers with low basic rates, such as health workers, do especially badly during state control of wage rises: a percentage of nothing is still nothing. And the real impact of cuts in health spending was really beginning to bite, especially in London. Everyone's job was getting harder.

And the hospital managements had, in the period of passivity engendered by the Social Contract, regained command. Old scores were settled, with the victimisation of many who had been prominent in 1973. There was a rash of occupations to block the closure of smaller hospitals, and the London Division of NUPE called one of the biggest and best demonstrations against health cuts in October 1976. But the union leaderships refused to sanction effective, open-ended strike action: it was, after all, still 'our' Labour Government. The dilemma was sharply posed by the clumsy management attack on the occupied Hounslow Hospital on 6 October 1977, with furniture broken and patients ferried away by private ambulance. If this outrage didn't merit a really forceful response from the national hospital unions, nothing would. But the protest was unofficial and bound to be short-winded, and while the union chiefs were very eloquent about the Gestapo-style tactics, they were not prepared to call any official action.

It was action over pay that exploded in the hospitals in 1978–9. Wage restraint was very publicly defeated by the Ford workers in the autumn of 1978, but the Callaghan Government was still trying to make it stick in the public sector. But hospital workers were simply not prepared to settle for less than the going rate just to save what was left of the Labour Government's face. And this time their leaders knew it. The 'Winter of Discontent' was the result. NUPE members joined it in a more bitter and depressed mood, quite unlike the exhilaration and spontaneity of the 1972 strikes, although in statistical terms it was the largest ever NHS strike. Unprepared to lead an all-out strike, the union head offices advocated a piecemeal strategy with people doing their own thing: sectional strikes, working to rule, overtime bans and one-day strikes here and there.

But even if it was a desultory campaign, it was largely successful. The Government bowed to pressure and set up the Clegg Commission into low pay, which eventually led to increases substantially more than 5 per cent. It also led to a change in the annual settlement date for hospital ancillaries from October, which was close to the local authority manual workers, to 1 April, which would coincide with the settlements of workers thought to be more docile, like the nurses and the clericals. The unforeseen result of this was to bring nurses, porters and clerks together in 1982 in the longest wave of strikes British hospitals have seen.

The Tory response and the 1982 dispute

The other result of the Winter of Discontent is said to be Margaret Thatcher. And the new harshness of Thatcher's Toryism, with its outspoken élitism, its disdain for trade unionism, and its old fashioned anti-communism, possessed a certain icy logic. The axe had been honed and swung already under Healey. But now the paralysis and indecisiveness of Labour gave birth to a Toryism unconcerned with consensus, unsentimental about lost homes or lives, uncharitable out of conviction. Mrs Thatcher's new philosophy was really very old – that the economy can only function if the rich are given more wealth and power. It follows that welfare has outlived its usefulness and it is now kind to be cruel. A new morality tale is announced, morally squalid but, it is said, economically inevitable; profit is life's true motive, the market the final arbiter, welfare a corrupting influence on the poor, and respect for law best achieved by force. Any objectors were pointed first to the evident disarray of Callaghan, then to the scale of the world slump, and sweetly told 'There is simply no alternative.'

The newly elected Tory Government had to honour the comparability pay awards, but did not take long to regain the initiative. The industrialists in the private sector were pressing for confrontation: the people who had secretly welcomed the Labour Government in 1974 now felt it had done all the work of which it was capable, and it was now time for the Government to be more decisive in its handling of the unions.

The new Tory approach had three main dimensions. Monetarist economic policies: that is, refusing to protect firms from market pressures and, in the public sector, enforcing strict cash limits, both of which caused an immediate increase in unemployment. Then there were to be carefully timed set-piece confrontations to break the power of key unions; one by one, with the strongest, the National Union of Mineworkers left to last. Finally there was to be legislation to weaken the unions' ability to take industrial action and, by threatening fund sequestration, enforce cooperation with the employers. This three-pronged attack was by no means invincible, but it certainly stood a much greater chance of success because of the atrophy of the unofficial networks which had taken so much of the initiative in the early seventies. Despite Mrs Thatcher's reputation for inflexibility, her ideological enthusiasms did not prevent her from making tactical concessions to the unions when necessary. And, of course, employed workers have continued to keep their wage rises ahead of inflation for most of the eighties. As the economist Dave Beecham rightly suggests, this gives rise to a more complicated picture than the 'worst depression since the thirties' clichés. Instead, argues Beecham,

> it has a unique combination of rapid growth of mass unemployment, continued high rates of inflation matched for a long period by increases in take-home pay, a huge erosion of the heartlands of British capitalism and a persistence of workers' struggle on quite a large scale.[1]

Once Clegg was out of the way, the Government screwed down wages in the public sector, first to 6 per cent and then to 4 per cent. The ambulance workers protested but caved in, and inside the NHS only the hospital electricians fought their way round the edge of the policy. Other unions had fared badly too. The steel strike was faced down by Thatcher and Ian MacGregor as a prelude to massive closures in the industry; the train drivers were quelled with the aid of the TUC, and the civil servants' eleven-week strike produced an inconclusive outcome. The total of days lost (or won) in 1981 was 4.2 million, only a third of the average in the seventies. No one expected the hospital workers to cut up rough, and if they did, Norman Fowler, the new DHSS head, was prepared to tough it out. The Government's reading of the Winter of Discontent was that strike action by the NHS unions was both ineffectual and likely to alienate public sympathy. This confidence was reflected in their response to the twelve health unions' unified 'core claim' of 12 per cent made in early 1982, with a curt offer of 4 per cent for ancillaries and 6 per cent for nurses. The divisive effect of the differential was also entirely intended.

In fact it was the nurses who rejected the offer, under the RCN slogan 'Nurses Need a Living Wage'. They had not taken action since the easy successes of 1947, and 6 per cent wasn't enough. Inflation was still high: 12 per cent per annum; and almost everyone else – miners, gas workers and council workers, let alone judges and the police – had done better. Their mood caught on, and all-union meetings in hospitals all over Britain voted to throw out the offer. What was to happen next was, however, unclear. If the NUM rejects a Coal Board offer, that means an all-out strike. But in the hospitals things are different. There were some immediate selective stoppages in May and a one-day strike in June which was a lot more solid than the union leaders had expected. A London hospital shop steward who subsequently wrote a history of the strike, Jonathan Neale, described the scene at this hospital:

> The nurses were buoyant on the picket line. One of them had been on strike once before in another hospital. One had been a shop steward in a factory before becoming a nursing auxiliary. The rest were on strike for the first time in their lives.
>
> It took a lot to get them out the door. The first five nurses to show up announced that they didn't care if they lost their jobs. They were so fed up with the conditions in there – if management wanted to fire them,

they fucking well could. They were going to stand on the picket line all day, and nobody was going past them.

We began asking passers-by to sign a petition. To our amazement, everybody did. We got together signs asking anybody who supported us to honk their horns. It was a busy road. Many did. We got ourselves a megaphone and stood out in the middle of the road asking people to honk their horns. It got noisy.[2]

What's more, the potential of sympathy action was demonstrated in Sheffield where the local Socialist Workers' Party health workers persuaded a dozen nurses and occupational therapists to go on a tour of the local coalmines. By lunch-time, four of those pits were on strike. It was only a straw in the wind, but it showed that there was a real potential for organised sympathy action. It was also significant because such action was in direct defiance of the 1980 Employment Act, which sought to outlaw solidarity strikes.

The one-day stoppage was followed by a two-day stoppage, or rather two one-day stoppages. This was the TUC's idea of 'stepping up the action'. But, as Neale puts it, the tactic was twice as ineffectual:

They called two one-day strikes: the first on a Friday and the next on the following Tuesday. This was a masterstroke. It was more militant than a one-day strike. It was twice as much striking. It had exactly the same effect on the Government as a one-day strike. (Two times nothing equals nothing.) It lost the members twice as much money. (Two times ten quid is twenty quid.)[3]

At the summer conferences of NUPE and COHSE, there was considerable support for an all-out stoppage, which was strengthened when the second ballot decisively rejected Fowler's improved offer. In Derbyshire there was a complete stoppage of the ambulance service and spirited demonstrations throughout August, when health workers were further enraged by the 10.3 per cent wage rise for the police, who had a wage indexation formula.

Fowler's walk-over was not materialising. Although he claimed that the strike was crumbling, and Mrs Thatcher did everything to give heart to the non-strikers, the action, although indecisively organised from above, was kept going by the grim determination of rank and file health workers. The establishment was becoming unhappy. A leader in the *Lancet* called on Fowler to consider resignation and to 'seek to restore his damaged reputation' by taking the dispute to arbitration. Sir George Godber, former Chief Medical Officer at the Department of Health, was harsher still: 'This hideous confrontation between NHS staff who have certainly been badly treated, and a Government that seems to put obduracy before any attempt to reach an amicable settlement, must be prolonging pain for many patients and shortening life for some.'

By 9 August 1982, most hospitals in Britain had experienced some sort of action as a five-day campaign of intensified pressure began in support of the 12 per cent claim. Over eighty London hospitals were affected, with a vigil outside the DHSS headquarters and a demonstration outside Bow Street police station to draw attention to the size of the pay award to the police. In Cumbria, thirty workers occupied a laundry to stop private contractors being moved in, motorists were stopped and leafleted by health workers as they crossed the Humber Bridge, and in Swindon Hospital workers made a bonfire of the newspaper advertisements issued by the Government and designed, said a COHSE spokesman at the Princess Margaret Hospital, 'to be deliberately misleading and undermine the five-day action.'

With Norman Fowler on holiday in France, his junior Kenneth Clarke was sent to reconnoitre, stating, hopefully, 'Most of the hospital staff are fed up with the present dispute.' He was received by furious health workers in Liverpool, three hundred of whom surrounded him chanting and waving banners outside the Walton Hospital's postgraduate medical centre. At the start of his six-hour visit to Doncaster Royal Infirmary Mr Clarke had to endure chanting of 'Maggie, Maggie, Maggie, Out! Out! Out!' No union member would serve him with coffee, and he had to go to a local pub for lunch because there were no canteen staff. In Glasgow, where angry health workers confronted Norman Tebbit, a chant of 'on your bike' broke out, and the demonstrators also carried a makeshift coffin with the slogan: 'Here lies the body of the NHS – killed by the Tories.'

More sympathy stoppages raised the temperature, with strikes on a construction site at the Grimethorpe Colliery in Yorkshire and in Fleet Street, where Sean Geraghty, leader of the Fleet Street electricians, was put under court injunction for proposing sympathy action with the health workers. The dispute which shouldn't have happened was going very badly for the Government. Mrs Thatcher didn't help things by repairing to the Fitzroy Nuffield

Hospital to have her varicose veins privately seen to. Albert Spanswick, the portly COHSE leader, steamed in: it was 'an insult to the National Health Service and a clear indication of her utter contempt for the principle that health care should be free to all in need, regardless of their ability to pay'.

The TUC September 1982 Conference was dominated by the NHS, and speaker after speaker advanced to the rostrum to make fine speeches about how the whole labour movement must pull together to support the hospital workers. A COHSE emergency resolution calling for 'A National Day of Action in Support of Health Staff' on 22 September was endorsed, with strikes promised by three of the four biggest TUC affiliates, the GMWU, TGWU and NALGO.

What actually happened was not a 24-hour national strike, but it was arguably the biggest national solidarity strike since 1926. 120,000 demonstrators swamped Central London behind the banner 'The TUC demands justice for NHS workers' and took three and a half hours to leave Hyde Park. A million workers in Scotland took some form of action, 750,000 in London, 400,000 in Wales, and 100,000 in Northern Ireland. All but about forty of the country's 197 coalmines were closed by round-the-clock stoppages, and unions claimed that production was low at those which were open. Forty-three of the country's sixty-five ports were closed by stoppages. Shipyards on the Clyde, Tyne, Tees and Mersey were closed. No national newspapers were published and the majority of provincial morning and evening papers also failed to appear. Ulster Television was shut down for three hours, as was Granada. There was massive support in the health service itself, by nurses, ancillary, white-collar and other workers, and in many areas ambulancemen exceeded the TUC guidelines by refusing accident and emergency cover, leaving police and voluntary organisations to cope. Thousands of schools were affected by the action of teachers, caretakers, cleaning and catering staff. Most ferry services were stopped and many urban bus services disrupted. There were marches and demonstrations in most cities and many towns.

Something remarkable was starting to happen in this great pro-NHS surge; the isolation and demoralisation seemed to be breaking down before our eyes. But the awful truth was that nothing less than an all-out strike was going to win. Yet the TUC, by its nature, was not going to call an effective national stoppage (they had tried that in 1926, and look where it had got them). Unopposed, they would simply salve their troubled consciences by calling token action until the hospital workers were exhausted. And yet there was simply no rank and file network in the hospitals which had anything like the authority to move independently; many of those Joint Shop Stewards' Committees that did exist were little more than strike committees of activists, and were even weaker than in 1972 or 1974. So the great Day of Action on 22 September, launched with such volumes of hot air, had a tragic element. On one level it was magnificent in mood and in scale. It was a tribute to the case for the NHS that had been argued for nearly a decade. But like any one-day action, it was becoming weaker from the very moment it began. In London, I remember seeing tears of joy from people united for a cause they believed in and tears of despair from hospital stewards who knew that the wave of protest was disintegrating just when it appeared most magnificent, and that the strike that could have won was ending its run.

Regional TUC days of action continued throughout October. In Liverpool, on 5 October, a long parade of protest was formed through the centre of town and reduced most of the eighty-five hospitals in the Mersey Health Region to emergencies-only service. Banners were displayed on the march from Cammell Laird shipyard, Liverpool City Council, Lucas Aerospace, the tobacco factories and print unions. And in the North-east there were rallies in Middlesbrough, Stockton, Darlington, Carlisle, Whitehaven and Newcastle. Thousands of shipyard employees stopped work for an hour and donated pay to the health workers. Shipyards on Wearside and Teesside were affected by the short stoppages, and in Darlington council workmen drove their refuse vehicles to a lunch-time rally.

But, as Jonathan Neale comments, 'The heart had gone out of the picket line. In May, twenty enthusiastic nurses had hurrahed on the picket line. In the regional one-day strike in October, two stewards stood on the line alone until ten in the morning.'

Then the TUC called a one-day strike by hospital and transport workers but belatedly chickened out of the transport strike. The 1982 pay campaign was effectively over, and the offer on the table, although significantly improved, still fell far short of the claim. The offer to the nurses of their own Review Body was a deliberate attempt to wean them away from hospital trade unionism. It naturally delighted the RCN, for, as a group of Kent nurses put it, it reflected the College's 'total lack of concern for other health service workers who go to make up the caring team – of which nurses are but one part – as opposed to the TUC view that we are in a Health Service dispute which involves members, and where nurses are neither a "spearhead" nor "angels" – but workers who, with other workers, are seeking a decent living wage.'

In the end, most health service union branches voted to accept the pay offer. As the union activists had been arguing all along, the only alternative was an all-out strike with only accident and emergency cover. The trouble was that, after eight months of heroic half-measures, the energy that could have won such a strike and achieved, say, a 10 per cent rise, had been dispersed.

In retrospect, the dispute's true significance can be seen: the Tories were neither invulnerable nor popular and their strategy of confrontation contained high risks. But they could succeed by dividing organised workers against each other and by exploiting their opponents' soft-headedness and fear of the kind of extremism Thatcher relishes. Thus the election of June 1983, which Thatcher won simply by riding out high unemployment and exploiting a divided opposition. Thus, during the great miners' strike, as well as the traditional methods of class war – the police, the courts, the mass media – the Government victory depended on a divided workforce and a Labour Party/TUC performance which was high on rhetoric but disgracefully low in content. But just as in the 1982 NHS strikes, the ingredients for victory were present in the miners' strike, and, at moments such as the threat of the NACODS stoppage in October 1984, the August dock strikes and at Orgreave, were blatantly obvious.

Thatcher's second term

Thatcher's second term brought a blitzkrieg on trade unionism: the banning of the trade union membership at the GCHQ communications centre in Cheltenham in January 1984, the successful legal injunctions by Eddie Shah against the NGA at Warrington, and the defeat of the miners' strike and of the Wapping printworkers. But it was felt indirectly in the NHS. Generally speaking, the Government stuck to the pay awards of the Review Bodies, although they were delayed and had to be partly funded by the local

Health Authorities by service cuts. The pay gap introduced between those assessed by comparability and those decided by Government limits was maintained, with ancillaries getting between 3.6 and 4.8 per cent in 1985 while nurses received between 6 and 8 per cent. Both groups did slightly better in the pre-election year of 1986. Strike levels were low, although they included many disputes about privatisation and action against hospital cuts and closures of a defensive nature. Nevertheless, in contrast to the overall fall in national trade union membership (down 19 per cent between 1979 and 1985) and an even sharper decline in some parts of the public sector (energy and water sector down 29 per cent), union membership in the NHS has remained fairly stable, with nearly seven in ten workers unionised.

But, Review Body or not, the mass of NHS staff have still to escape the low pay quicksand. Only in the late eighties has the problem tended to register negatively: as a failure of the NHS to recruit rather than in positive strikes and protests. As Incomes Data Services comment, 'the test is whether it can recruit and keep staff at the level it is prepared to pay.' By 1988 the answer, at least in nursing, seemed to be no. But given the Government's stated commitments, nurses' pay will be tackled, if at all, by bonuses for specific hard-to-recruit groups (such as Intensive Care Nurses) and the introduction of performance-related pay (NHS District General Managers already have an important 'merit' element).

'Union power' in the hospitals was always a myth, and the unions have been less vocal and influential in resisting cuts and closures in the late eighties than in the heady days of 1969 and 1982. Given the high turnover of NHS staff, many painful lessons, for instance over nurses' striking, will have to be relearnt from scratch. But health service unionism has survived both a baptism of fire and a difficult adolescence, and is capable of much in its maturity. The bravery of NHS nurse union members in 1988 once again inspired the country and gave huge encouragement to other trade unionists.

10
The Cuts

By 1973 it must have seemed to the jubilant nurses who had just won their first decent pay award, to patients who were being treated in the brand new hospitals, to the GPs who had begun to practise in custom-built health centres, that a new era was in sight. Health spending had at last increased, hospital wages were for the first time, at least for some, at a reasonable level. It has proved a mirage, a tantalising glimpse of what could be done rather than the shape of things to come. NHS spending continued to expand between 1976 and 1978, but much less fast. And in 1978 it actually fell in real terms, after the decisive deflation by Denis Healey on terms dictated by the International Monetary Fund.

It is here, under Labour, that the attack on the NHS began and the philosophy of 'nil growth', cash limits and hospital closures originated. And here too was the first angry burst of resistance. 250,000 workers marched through London in 1978 against the cuts – one of the biggest political demonstrations the capital has ever witnessed. And in the small but well-loved Bethnal Green, Poplar, Hounslow and Elizabeth Garrett Anderson hospitals, all facing closure by centralisation, hospital workers were joined by local people and patients to occupy them and keep them open. Even in 1978 it was proving difficult to find the money to pay the staff who were to work in the new hospitals built during the expansion of the early seventies.

The groundwork for the long fiscal squeeze on the NHS in the eighties was laid here. But by the early eighties a thirty-year era, in which both major parties accepted a responsibility towards the steady expansion of the NHS, had ended. Under the impact of the world depression, politicians had undergone an overnight conversion. 'Cuts' is a code word for a social counter-revolution: for a harsher, meaner, less caring Britain, for the return of the Poor Law mentality. A new social philosophy was in the air. 'The welfare state flourished because the growth state prospered,' concluded the Centre for Studies in Social Policy: 'Social expenditure in the past has been designed to encourage customers to raise their expectations and demands . . . In the new circumstances, it could be argued that the emphasis of policy should be to discourage additional demands.' The welfare state is now to be judged strictly in terms of its contribution to productive industry, which turns out to mean profit-producing industry. Judged on that basis, it is being suggested more and more often that the services are positively harmful, creating a mollycoddled indolence among citizens so bombarded with luxuries that they are virtually prevented from finding their way to honest toil.

Worse, under Mrs Thatcher, 'public' has come to mean second rate. While the spending totals appear to record increases, when allowance is made for the rising numbers of the elderly, the costs of medical advances and the underfunding of pay awards, the NHS has been subjected to a steady squeeze. And by the late eighties, with consultants advising their patients to sue the DHSS, this has led to a crisis acute enough to rattle Mrs Thatcher herself.

But, as we have seen, this battle between public welfare and private affluence is the oldest argument in the history of medicine. The amounts we spend on health are not absolute and fixed but the result of political will and public choice. At every stage of the development of our health service, it has been denounced as economically extravagant and morally unsuitable and it has fallen to radicals to defend the budget. Those arguing for the closure of hospitals, the scrapping of services and the reduction of staff in the eighties are the spiritual heirs of the Boards of Guardians whose very parsimony made them immune to human feeling and who became numb to the untended need they witnessed daily. And, like the Victorian moralists, they would never dream of allowing themselves or their relatives to endure the conditions they cheerfully inflict on others.

NHS financing

Since so much high-sounding nonsense is spouted to obscure the realities of the cuts in the health service, it is worth restating some home truths about the financing of the NHS:

- Our health spending remains markedly lower than other comparable countries. France spends 2 per cent more of the national income on health services, West Germany and Sweden 3 per cent more, and the United States 4.5 per cent more.

- The outlay on health care per person in Britain is among the lowest of the industrialised nations. In 1984, only Ireland and Italy spent less.

- In March 1988, the All-Party Commons Social Services Committee called for:
  i an immediate £95 million to make up the shortfall in the current financial year
  ii an additional £1000 million to repair damage done to the NHS by cuts
  iii a commitment to fund all forthcoming pay awards in full
  The committee described the DHSS's failure to monitor the local effects of cuts as 'extraordinary', and calculated a total shortfall of £1896 million.

- The NHS takes a relatively small proportion of the total of public spending. Of a hypothetical 'social wage' of £1000 per year, over half is, in fact, spent on the interest of the state rather than the individual. The NHS gets £134 *per capita*, not much more than the armed forces, who employ far fewer people and whose share increased markedly in the early eighties.

- Britain now has a much *lower* level of taxation than comparable countries, although it is levied principally on incomes as opposed to goods. Austria, Belgium, Canada, Denmark, France, West Germany, Holland, Norway and Sweden all have higher total taxation. Employers make a uniquely low contribution towards welfare in Britain.

- There are high levels of tax relief and capital allowances available to the corporate sector in Britain.

- Britain is thus not over-taxed, nor do the managerial classes do especially badly. Studies show the redistributive effect of sixty years of progressive taxation is not between the poor and the rich, but between the very rich and the rich.

- So Britain not only should but could contribute more finance to its health services. But the NHS has not benefited from the overall growth of prosperity in the eighties. A December 1987 Marplan/*Guardian* poll found that 86 per cent of people questioned wanted more spent on the NHS even if it meant higher taxes. This finding has been consistently confirmed by the annual British Social Attitudes Survey.

And, rather than there being less demand for health care, there is bound to be more, for the following reasons:

- Illness is known to increase in times of economic hardship. The *Sunday Times* reports that 'New research at Johns Hopkins University in Baltimore suggests this startling relationship: the economy gets worse, we all get sicker.' Specifically, the researchers found that about a year after unemployment increases, infant mortality rises sharply. So does heart disease (with about a two- to three-year time lag) and cirrhosis of the liver (with about a two-year lag).

- The old and the very old, high users of medical care, are a growing proportion of the total population, and in many parts of Britain the birth rate is increasing again.

- There will always be an increase in demand for medical atention as science advances what can be treated and people become more knowl-edgeable and demanding about their own health. In every study there is still evidence of reserves of unmet medical need detected. From suicide to kidney failure, lives could undoubtedly be saved if the right sort of medical aid was available.

- The 1986 King's Fund Report *Back to Back Planning* summarised the policies which the DHSS urged Regional Health Authorities to imple-ment, in circulars it issued between 1983 and 1986. Among other things, these included:

    '. . . develop services for kidney failure, coronary artery surgery, joint replacement and bone marrow transplant.' (Health Circular HC(84)2)

    '. . . achieve a target of forty new kidney dialysis patients per one million population.' (Health Circular HC(85)5)

    '. . . plan new services for people with AIDS.' (Health Circular HC(86)2)

    So, far from frivolously wasting money on esoteric specialisms, the money available is at present insufficient to make full use of the potential of medical knowledge which has existed for decades.

The case against the cuts and for an increase of spending on the NHS is straightforward. The problem has been that, until quite recently, the effects of the cuts have been piecemeal and isolated, and the evidence of crisis has been what doctors disparagingly call anecdotal. And the economics of the NHS are hard to comprehend as a totality and easy to ransack for impressive-sounding statistics. Indeed, people like me have been taken to task for years for even using the word 'cuts': 'Don't you realise that the Government spends more each year?' One can point to a boarded-up hospital or a closed casualty department, and one can cite figures for the time waited for outpatient appointments and elective surgery. But it is harder to quantify the effect on morale of non-replacement of staff and neglected maintenance. And because of the dominance of the NHS, we have no ready-made comparisons: we don't know how they treat a stroke in Stuttgart or how long you wait for a hip replacement in Stockholm. Another element in the cuts is inevitably invisible: those services which we could and should be offering but can't afford to. How will we ever know, for example, what scientific breakthroughs might have been made if the medical research budgets hadn't been so sharply restricted?

And probably more important than all these factors in preventing us from getting a clear perspective on the seriousness of the decline of the NHS has been the effective muzzling of the senior layers of the service's management, the Government-appointed authority chairmen and the managers on short-term contracts, who have proved so adept at brushing off anti-cuts protesters as 'rent-a-mobs'. There have also been systematic but, fortunately, less successful attempts to censor clinicians who have made public their anxieties about the impact of the cuts. In December 1987, the BMJ cited twenty such attempts, and the BMA took up the case of a senior doctor in family planning, Gillian Cardy, who was suspended for speaking out publicly against planned cuts in Bath. The spirit of *glasnost* is yet to arrive in British health authorities.

So, for much of the eighties consistent protest was confined to the committed: while all health workers understood and sympathised, most just tried to get on with the job. This feeling of ineffectuality grew much worse after the defeat of the miners, for whom the hospital workers were important fund-raisers: if the miners couldn't win, who could? And, just as in local government, the NHS treasurers produced a series of fiscal improvisations which postponed the impending and inevitable open crisis. Bed use was increased (whatever the cost to the patients discharged in pain). Savings were made by the privatisation of cleaning, catering and laundry (never mind the standards and the conditions for the workers). The relentless closure of small hospitals and the subsequent sale of land buoyed up the capital spending. Internal redistribution of funds meant unevenness. Some sections of the NHS, like the GP services, were indeed somewhat better off.

But the phony war was bound to come to an end, and it did so late in 1987. If a date needs to be put on it, it is 7 December, when the

Presidents of the Royal Colleges of Physicians, Surgeons and Obstetricians and Gynaecologists, the most senior doctors in Britain and almost the most conservative, issued the following joint statement:

> Each day we learn of new problems in the NHS – beds are shut, operating rooms are not available, emergency wards are closed, essential services are shut down in order to make financial savings. In spite of the efforts of doctors, nurses, and other hospital staff, patient care is deteriorating. Acute hospital services have almost reached breaking point. Morale is depressingly low.
>
> It is not only patient care that is suffering. Financial stringencies have hit academic aspects of medicine in particular, because of the additional burden of reduced University Grants Committee funding. Yet the future of medicine depends on the quality of our clinical teachers and research workers.
>
> Face-saving initiatives such as the allocation of £30 million for waiting lists are not the answer. An immediate overall review of acute hospital services is mandatory. Additional and alternative funding must be found. We call on the Government to do something now to save our health service, once the envy of the world.

The importance of this statement cannot be underestimated. What had been argued for years by the humble rank and file cuts campaigners and experienced daily by the users of the NHS was now acknowledged by the high and mighty. In the preceding week, the sociological weekly *New Society* culled the following devastating roll-call of news items over a seven-day period, illustrating the diversity and the seriousness of the problem described by the Presidents:

- The NHS is being propped up by cancer charities because hospitals cannot afford to treat patients, Sir Walter Bodmer, director of the Imperial Cancer Research Fund, told the Lords select committee on science and technology.

- Hospital funds are so stretched that surgeons cannot afford the stringent safety precautions necessary to guarantee protection from the AIDS virus in operating theatres, Andrew Sim, consultant at St Mary's Hospital, Paddington, told a London conference on AIDS and surgery.

- The DHSS is to issue an economy version of the NHS wheelchair even though tests have shown it to be uncomfortable and the makers have misgivings about it.

- Five out of fifteen intensive care cots at St Mary's Hospital, Manchester, are to close because of insufficient funds to staff them properly, according to Malcolm Chiswick, the unit's director. He said that keeping them open without enough staff would raise the risk of saving critically ill premature babies but leaving them handicapped.

- In a letter to *The Times*, C. J. Hinds, chairman of the Intensive Care Society, warned that 'in many centres throughout the country intensive care beds are being closed and the situation is particularly serious in London.'

- The British Medical Association announced a national survey of hospital cuts, to be completed by March, after an angry meeting of consultants' leaders had expressed widespread frustration over the difficulty of maintaining service levels.

- In Newcastle, consultant surgeon John Hawkesford refused to carry out operations because, he told the health authority, of 'unsafe theatre facilities'.

- Thefts from hospitals are costing the NHS millions of pounds because too little has been spent on security, according to Ernest Parkinson, chairman of the National Association of Health Service Security Officers.

- A delegation from West Sussex health authority visited Edwina Currie, the Health Minister, to complain that, despite an impeccable record on putting services out to tender, they still faced a £600,000 deficit this year. They had had to close four wards and put their operating theatres on an 'emergencies only' regime.

- The government should set up a multi-million pound national genetic screening service to diagnose gene defects before birth. This would bring substantial savings on treatment costs, a panel of specialists said in a consensus statement after a three-day King's Fund conference.

- Nurses from St Thomas's Hospital, opposite the House of Commons, presented a 7,300 signature petition protesting at the closure of 130 beds at the hospital to MPs.

- A leader in the *British Medical Journal* said that the proposals for funding the improvements in the family doctor service contained in the primary care white paper were 'ludicrously inadequate'.

- David Barber, the six-week old baby whose hole in the heart operation was postponed five times until last month, died suddenly.

- A report in the *Sunday Times* comparing the health service in Britain and Germany noted that there were 2,431 people on the waiting list at the Bristol Royal Infirmary and none at the Robert Bosch Hospital in Stuttgart.

- Some aspects of antenatal care have not improved in thirty years, according to a survey conducted by the Association of Community Health Councils.

- Two more boys have died after heart operations were cancelled at Birmingham Children's Hospital, an investigation by Granada TV's *World in Action* revealed. Eighty children are waiting for heart operations there.

- An out-of-court settlement has left Hereford and Worcester health authority facing a £540,000 bill for damages to David Woodhouse after an accident during an appendix operation left him brain-damaged. Hospitals paid out £9 million in damages last year, adding to budgetary pressures.

- A poll of scientists in charge of the country's 212 cervical cancer screening labs has shown that only half will be ready to implement full, computerised systems for calling and recalling women for smear tests by a Government-imposed deadline of 31 March and only 10 per cent will have the staff and resources to run the services properly.

- One child a day is being turned away from the paediatric ward at Charing Cross Hospital, according to *Newsnight*. One of the hospital's two paediatric wards is closed because of the shortage of nurses.

- A survey reported that at least 1000 patients a year die because of operating theatre errors.

- A new pay structure to stop nurses leaving the NHS was announced by the DHSS. Trevor Clay, General Secretary of the Royal College of Nursing, said this would not solve the problems without a 'general uplift' in nurses' pay.

Yet only a week earlier the Commons had passed the following government motion:

> That this House welcomes the increased number of people being treated in the hospital and community health services; congratulates the Government on maintaining the NHS hospital building programme and providing a high level of investment in the service next year; reaffirms its intention to continue the promotion of a comprehensive health service; and recognises the Government's achievement in establishing the sound economy necessary to support the continued development of the health service.

Mrs Thatcher had said: 'I shall give the facts. The number of doctors, nurses and paediatric nurses, and the amount of money, have all increased.' The gap between Parliamentary complacency and NHS realities has never yawned wider. But it is, one hopes, no longer necessary to argue with anyone but Tory MPs about whether the cuts exist. In the following chapters I shall review how under-financing affects various aspects of the health service.

11

The Impact: Acute Services and Hospital Closures

Acute services

In general, the UK is still not a bad place to be acutely ill. Access to specialist care through the ambulance service and accident and emergency departments is, within limitations of geography, good. One of the best features of the NHS hospital is the way expert assessment in an Accident and Emergency Department can plug a patient directly into the specialist multi-disciplinary clinical teams. In 1984 the acute inpatient service was by far the biggest item in the total hospital and community budget: £3,188 million out of £9,062 million. But the number of acute medical and surgical beds available has fallen quite dramatically, from 214,000 in 1959 to 167,000 in 1985, mainly in the medical and pre-convalescent departments. To cope with rising demand and shrinking resources, the average length of stay has had to be considerably shortened, from an average of 15.7 days in 1960 to 7.6 days in 1985. Between 1980 and 1985, the authorities have had to increase inpatients by 12 per cent, day patients by 46 per cent, regular day attendances by 11 per cent, and outpatients by 6 per cent. But they were able to spend 11 per cent less per case.

This may have been due to a genuine increase in efficiency, but more often it has meant patients discharged while still in pain or into unsafe or unsuitable home conditions. It underlies the common complaint from inpatients in the era of cuts that they feel they are on a production line, being processed rather than healed, and got rid of as soon as possible. The Government's oft-repeated figures of the increased numbers of cases seen are therefore much less impressive than they may appear. The 1986 report commissioned from the Centre for Health Economics at York University by the Institute of Health Service Management, the BMA and the RCN commented that the rise in the number of patients may not be a sign that the outcomes of treatment have improved. 'It may simply mean that services have to adopt a revolving door policy,' the document stated. Government statistics do not record how many patients are re-admissions, and there are likely to be more of these as the emphasis switches towards care outside the hospital, day treatment, and shorter inpatient stays.

The faster inpatient turn-round inevitably places increased pressure on the Accident and Emergency Departments, which come under virtual siege from prematurely discharged patients, as well as those who despair of getting a hospital appointment in reasonable time, or who are dissatisfied with their GP or want a second opinion. The Casualty Departments also have to deal with patients who are homeless, unregistered with a GP or not bothered to attend, as well as with their *bona fide* emergencies and ambulance work. So a casualty officer's job becomes more and more like that of a receiving officer under the old Poor Law. He or she has to balance a medical assessment against the patient's home circumstances and the relatives' resources. The casualty officer stands at the collision point between the patient's need, the family's worries and the hospital's overcrowded beds. How often have I searched a patient for an upturning big toe or a possible mass in the rectum in order to strengthen the case for admission to a sceptical Registrar, while a knot of relatives, probably now living thirty miles away, cast admonishing glances.

Although there are some fine new facilities, waiting times in Accident and Emergency Departments are commonly several hours long and the staff, often relatively junior, work under tremendous pressure. The massive closure and centralisation process in the hospital service (in 1959 there were 3,027 hospitals, in 1985 only 2,341) means the permanent loss of casualty stations able to cope with minor and moderate injury, with correspondingly greater pressure on the remaining units. Nor are the conditions in those that remain always ideal. There has long been concern about the poor state of the accident services, which cope with 5 million accident victims every year. Sir Henry Osmond-Clarke's Review Committee noted 'insufficient and inadequate staff; inadequate accommodation; lack of rehabilitation departments' and generally low priority. One of the members of the working party noted 'old departments which were dirty and dingy, with patients waiting in corridors, and clean wounds being stitched without any pretence of sterile surgical precautions.' The Association of Casualty Surgeons commented in 1987 on the unnecessarily bad outcome for victims of acute trauma because of delays in getting to the appropriate clinical team for assessment and resuscitation.

There also is considerable concern about the ability of the ambulance service to cope with the increased workload which derives from the increased hospital turnover. Future demand for ambulances will 'outstrip supply', the London Ambulance Service admitted in its 1987 draft strategic plan. Faced with a cut of 5 per cent over the next ten years and higher workloads arising from day patients and community care initiatives, the LAS is warning health authorities that in future they will have to make their own arrangements for getting non-emergency patients to hospital.

In several recent fatal cases coroners have ordered inquiries into the late arrival of ambulances, most recently, in November 1987, in the case of a Hackney man, William Hunt, who died after waiting ninety-three minutes for an ambulance, a delay said to be due to headquarters understaffing. The Emergency Bed Service which, with the aid of medical referees, combs the London hospitals to find vacant beds for patients whose local hospital is full, was itself threatened with closure. The service covers Greater London and London's periphery – the areas most severely affected by continuing reductions in beds. EBS can arrange for hospital admission more quickly than a GP may be able to because the data on hospital closures and restrictions is collected daily. Time thus saved for a GP is available for patient care. The hospital service benefits, too, by the EBS directing admissions away from a health district running short of beds. EBS is funded by the four Thames Regional Health Authorities, and its growing importance is indicative of the failure of the London districts to fulfil their responsibility for emergency admissions of acutely ill patients within their own districts.

There has also been persistent concern about another vital element in emergency medical care, the blood-transfusion service. In October 1987, Professor John Cash argued that the English service was a 'fragmented and disorganised shambles'. And a managerial report in 1987 revealed that 'Alarming numbers of staff are leaving the blood-transfusion service in all areas except the North because of low pay and lack of prospects. Nearly half the basic grade scientists and technicians in the London transfusion centres – the people who process blood and test for AIDS and other viruses – left the service last year.' Cuts affected the transfusion service even more destructively when the DHSS under Norman Fowler continued to import Factor VIII from the commercial blood market in the USA while inadequate finances held back the new British Blood Products laboratory at Elstree. If the advice of the ASTMS in May 1983 to ban all imports of blood from paid US donors had been observed, many of the cases of haemophiliac-AIDS could have been prevented.

So even the assumption that at least the acute service is intact is now questionable in London, which has experienced the sharpest fall in the number of beds anywhere in the UK, and yet whose citizens, because of the inadequacies of the GP services, have traditionally been high users of the Accident and Emergency Departments. A 1986 report from the Association of London Authorities summarised the decline in London's health services and showed that more than 6000 beds and thirty-two hospitals have been closed in the capital since 1980. The report also pointed out that the closure of eight Accident and Emergency Departments since 1980 has increased the burden on the already stretched ambulance services, which are also suffering from a lack of funds.

The severity of the financial pressure on the four Thames Regional Health Authorities is due to the particular effect of the Resources Allocation Working Party. The RAWP proposals, officially a consultative document launched in September 1976, led to nothing short of panic in the four Thames regions, who were expected to absorb a cut, over and above the national stoppages, of £100 million. The concept of redistribution was, and is, entirely right. Indeed, it was the left who insisted on drawing attention to the inequalities in regional spending within the NHS. In 1971 twice as much was being spent on major building south of the River Trent as north of it. The GPs in the industrial North had much bigger lists and worse premises than those in the Home Counties. Oxford had proportionally twice as many psychiatrists as Leeds, London had over twice as many hospital doctors *per capita* as Leicester. Even after the Crossman formula for evening out the regional allocations, the revenue allocations of 1974–75 showed that the same gap still existed between the 'haves' and the 'have-nots'.

RAWP is a classic social-democratic cock-up, joint intellectual brainchild of that school of Labour Party theory which attempts to change society by redistributing it bit by bit until eventually you have socialism, and what one distinguished surgeon has called 'the computer-crazed zombies of the DHSS.' Between its conception and implementation, the biggest economic crisis since the 1930s occurred. And as the *British Medical Journal* rightly put it, 'The fundamental objection to RAWP can be stated in one sentence; when resources are growing reallocation can be equitable, but in a period of recession it makes hardships worse.' The regions who receive money through RAWP are not getting more money, just fewer cuts.

Another basic flaw in RAWP's method is that it takes no account of social deprivation or incidence of disease in awarding resources, relying simply on out-of-date mortality rates. The result is a geographical interpretation rather than a class one, generating the lunacy of designating areas like Tower Hamlets. Hackney and Brent as possessing more than their fair share of resources, which are therefore deemed suitable for siphoning off to East Anglia. RAWP undoubtedly did once embody a serious claim for medical justice, but it has turned out to be just another formula for justifying the cuts. Its first victims, Liverpool and Inner London, have a notoriously high incidence of disease and social deprivation. What started as a great levelling has ended with those who have the least having the most taken away from them. It is worth noting that, according to Robert Maxwell's estimates in *Health Care, the Growing Dilemma*, it would only take another 0.2 per cent of the nation's GNP to even *up* all the regional differences. It is also worth bearing in mind that in Scotland, with its traditionally higher standards of medical care, an average of 25 per cent more is spent per person, which ought once again to indicate the need for a massive overall increase in British regional spending.

Patient migration

The RAWP-induced pressure on beds is intensified by patients imported from outside London to the specialist units of the London teaching hospitals which have a regional, sometimes a national standing. As the 1987 *Tower Hamlets Health Inquiry*, an extensive Report on the conditions of the NHS in East London, argued:

> The competition with regional specialities means that patients who are on the waiting list for acute general medical treatment are rarely given

the opportunity of 'called' admission. As the waiting list increases, not just for general medicine and surgery but for other specialities, there is a knock-on effect. If the percentage of emergency admissions goes up from 50 to 70 or 80 per cent, a planned admission may get cancelled on the morning of a patient's arrival and after complicated domestic arrangements have been made. We were told that on one morning (in 1985) seventy patients were called to come in for admission but only twenty beds were available.[1]

In effect, patients can only be offered an option on a place, a standby ticket, which is nerve racking enough if you are simply taking a plane flight, but entirely unsatisfactory when awaiting a hospital procedure. A rare ovarian cancer patient from Milton Keynes might be found a specialist bed, but at the expense of the further postponement of Mrs Jones of Poplar's hysterectomy. The advice seems to be, if you are going to be ill, make sure you are an emergency. Even if you are in an overcrowded ward with ex-hausted doctors and get sent home before you feel better, at least you've had a bed. The cost of sustaining the emergency admissions is the displacement of routine and planned admission for investi-gation, treatment and elective surgery. Yet the condition which these people on the waiting lists endure may well be semi-acute, causing a good deal of pain, worry and discomfort and lost time from work. A hospital service which routinely gives a four month wait to a first outpatient consultation and a subsequent six month wait for surgery is not a service. As a report from the Industry and Employment Branch of the GLC argued:

> The historic presence of the teaching hospitals has meant that London's acute hospitals have been better funded than elsewhere. But the effect of Government policies to equalise funding between the regions has been that London has suffered more severe cutbacks than elsewhere. The consequence is that services that are already underdeveloped are being particularly damaged. While, in general, facilities for sophisticated medical intervention are being maintained, basic routine health care is suffering, particularly through the closure of the smaller general hospitals catering for older patients with routine conditions.[2]

The smaller hospitals

It was the closure of many of London's long-serving small hospitals which provoked the most active resistance and became the most dramatic symbol of the cuts. As measured on the computer these units are not economic, but they have provided a homely atmosphere and convenient access, which is important for immobile outpatients and visitors, and various specialist facilities. Indeed, Roland Moyle, Minister of State at the DHSS, has said in Parliament: 'I think the homely atmosphere of a small hospital is no less important – it may indeed be more important – in urban community hospitals than in a rural community hospital.' Yet his department has systematically closed over 100 hospitals in the period 1975–77.

One of the first to go was Poplar Hospital, a stately if gaunt dockland hospital, which stands sentry on the East India Dock Road and served the docks of Millwall and the people of Poplar during the heaviest nights of the Blitz. Poplar had only eighty-one beds, but it provided a casualty service to heavy industrial workers on the Isle of Dogs and around the docks. From the staff canteen in the hospital, you could see the dog-men on the crane hooks, tiny boiler-suited figures in the electrical generator station, the ship repair yard and dry docks, and the procession of tower blocks sloping towards Essex. This, if anywhere, was the place for a hospital; the community had served up its burns, fractures, sprains and closing-time fights to Poplar Hospital for generations. The staff at Poplar were horrified by the steady run-down of their hospital and asked for 'a cast-iron guarantee that our hospital be kept fully open. If Poplar closes we lose more than our jobs. The East End loses a hospital which has given good service for years. And the way is opened for shutting down all the small East End hospitals.'

The staff petitioned till they were blue in the face, passed out leaflets and stuck stickers and posters all over the local pubs and streets. They blocked a pedestrian crossing on the East India Dock Road by constantly crossing to and fro. They called special delegate meetings, with pledges from the bus garages, docks, and tenants' associations to prepare to strike. They leafleted twenty-five other hospitals with the aid of the All London Health Workers' Alliance and together invaded the headquarters of the Regional Health Board to demand an explanation. They held marches with heartfelt and heart-rending banners and handmade carnations. The local MPs made it their business to turn up and be photographed at the head of the march; but they could never apply enough pressure to the right place in the new health bureaucracy. Other hospitals were sympathetic but, wrongly, did not see it as their problem. The women ancillary workers at Poplar who led the fight combed the Isle of Dogs for industrial support, barging into rag trade sweat-shops and making fiery speeches to Sikh pattern checkers, addressing railwaymen from a table in a canteen plastered with pin-ups, talking their way past the dock police who made entry and exit to the West India Dock like Colditz.

Somehow, despite the promises, the support never really showed up in one place at the same time. It was murmured that perhaps people did not really like the hospital so much because so many of the doctors were foreign. One by one the facilities froze up. The consultants were bribed away with promises of improved facilities in nearby hospitals. Other small hospitals in East London *were* closed. Poplar became a shell, patrolled by guard-dogs. In 1986 it was finally demolished.

A very similar train of events was started at the Elizabeth Garrett Anderson Hospital in Euston, founded by the first woman to attain, after a considerable battle against male prejudice, medical registration. The EGA did *not* go the way of Poplar: it has stayed open because of a mixture of high-power lobbying by the consultants, effective fund-raising and, above all, the determination of the staff and their supporters, who prevented the authority moving in for the kill. In some respects, the EGA is a rather special example because the goodwill of the senior medical staff, essential if the 'work-in' is to work, has been retained because there is no precisely equivalent NHS work in their specialised 'women treating women' field. In other hospitals, unless new forms are found of organising the medical work, say as a GP-run community hospital, consultants could be offered, and accept, alternative beds in remaining hospit-als, and without them the work-in would collapse. This was one of the factors which worked against the unsuccessful occupation of the South London Hospital for Women in 1986, and assisted the authorities in the closure of the Seamen's Dreadnought Hospital in Greenwich, despite strike action on the channel ferries by the National Union of Seamen when alternative, but much smaller, premises were eventually offered at St Thomas's Hospital.

The extent of support for the EGA was massive, and this was possible because the hospital staff realised they were both a symptom of the threatened programme of London hospital closures, and a proof that active resistance was possible. The campaign had an improvised versatility and fluency about it which proved unstoppable. Anarchists printed leaflets, *cinéastes* made films, GPs stuck up posters in their surgeries, beautifully silk-screened by the local print workshop. EGA badges first sported on radical lapels were soon spotted in the street markets and at the bus stops of London. Volunteers of all political persuasions and of none manned (and womanned) the picket rota. Hundreds of local residents volunteered their telephone numbers as the branches of a telephone tree which could summon an instant picket to block any sudden attack by the authorities. The hospital unions were forced by a determined membership to give official backing and practical support to the EGA, not just the usual hot air at conferences. A caravan from the Women's National Cancer Control Campaign parked outside the hospital giving cervical smears to hundreds of women and showing the need for the Well Woman Screening Clinic which the Campaign wanted to see developed at the Euston site. Outside the hospital, a banner lettered with cycle-handlebar tape said 'EGA stays OK', and another 'We are still open for the treatment of women by women'. A colour film was made of the case for the hospital, and a slide show outlining how the occupation was arranged, aimed at other hospital workers, went the rounds. The porter's office became a veritable library of radical literature. Everyone from Dame Josephine Barnes to the domestic insisted, as was stamped in red on all letters sent from the hospital, 'Treatment for women by women'.

At the time of writing the EGA is still fully functional with forty gynae beds, a busy operating theatre, an early diagnostic unit and facilities for day cases.

Hounslow Hospital was a smaller and still more neglected hospital in industrial North-west London. Overshadowed by the West Middlesex and the Hammersmith, poorly serviced, badly administered, it was the obvious target for a district management team which entered 1976–77 'over-spent' – that is, under-financed – to the extent of £500,000, and with a potential RAWP-tax of £13 million lost revenue to the Area Health Authority as a whole. The Accident and Emergency Department, which saw 6000 visitors a year, and the outpatients – 12,000 customers – were closed simply to save money. Despite this, the sixty-six medical and surgical beds with excellent physiotherapy back-up and a devoted nursing staff would have provided, all agreed, an ideal base for a GP-run community hospital. To prevent closure, the staff decided to embark on a work-in on 28 March 1977. They stated:

In occupying Hounslow Hospital by 'working-in' we are not taking away from the Area Health Authority the responsibility they have in law for the patients and staff at our hospital. We will, however, take no part in staff transfers, closure of beds, refusing admissions or any other activity that leads to the run-down of work at our hospital. We offer assurances to the Community Health Council, the public, and in particular outpatients, that patient care will in no way be impaired, and indeed where possible will be improved. We wish to make clear that it is our intention to continue to provide patient services to those who need them and will draw support from any source where it can be obtained.

The second-ever occupation of a hospital was under way, beginning the painstaking, patient task of building up local lines of support and an atmosphere of trust, overshadowed all the time by the authorities' death sentence. And they obtained not only 30,000 petition signatures but the practical support of the doctors, the ambulance service, their trade unions, local councillors, and the local MP. But on Thursday 6 October 1977, the administration decided to put a stop to this. In what was described as a 'Gestapo-type raid' they hired a fleet of private ambulances and carted the patients to the West Middlesex Hospital. Many patients were distressed and shocked. Many were old; three were over 90. But that did not bother the Area Health Authority, for the hospital occupation had to be broken at all costs. Not content with this, they broke up the beds with hammers, removed the springs, threw mattresses and furniture around, leaving the hospital in a sorry mass. Sister Cynthia Scott, who was on duty when the officials arrived at the hospital door, said simply: 'There is no hospital left. They have destroyed it.' Staff invited the public to inspect the damage caused by management representatives, touring the streets with billboards saying starkly: 'Your hospital has been wrecked. COME AND SEE.'

The effect on local supporters of the campaign was profound. Stan Hunt from the nearby West London Hospital told an emergency meeting of ninety shop stewards from thirty-four London hospitals, convened jointly by *Hospital Worker*, the EGA Campaign and CLASH, the unofficial London-wide NHS shop stewards' committee, of his own feelings:

We have been down to the Hounslow work-in several times. It was always peaceful. We'd have a joke. Then this happened. What was on the TV was bad enough. But when me and the stewards went down, well, it shook us. We had a good look. The whole place had been turned upside down. The nurses who witnessed it were still in a state of shock. It's hard to put it in words. Now, some people might say, oh well, it's all right, maybe, if they've got alternative beds ready. But they hadn't. The patients they kidnapped from Hounslow went into makeshift beds in the corridors and the middle of wards.

After seeing the mess, we went straight back to the members and recommended open-ended strike action from Wednesday until they reopen that hospital. We have to strike while the iron's hot. If we wait for some government inquiry, we're dead.

Hospital workers have got to start it themselves and then call on other workers to back them.

The wave of anger washed through the London hospitals and over 3000 people besieged the afternoon meeting of the Area Health Authority on 12 October. As the Authority licked its wounds inside the Town Hall, banners and placards draped the closed front entrance and speaker after speaker mounted the concrete steps to denounce the conspirators within. Middle-aged gentlemen from NALGO, jiving NUPE cooks from Hammersmith, solid determined bodies from the West London hospitals, large delegations from hospitals like the Royal Free and Charing Cross, which had held emergency meetings, small but vitally important knots of stewards from local industry like Heathrow Airport and the Park Royal railway repair yards who, although not immediately affected, had risked their jobs to show their solidarity; all were there. On the suggestion of John Deason, Secretary of the Right To Work Campaign, the protesters marched down to Hammersmith Broadway to spread the word, rather than simply await the verdict. But the cars went on whizzing past above, on the flyover.

For, in truth, people still did not want to know. To win a future for Hounslow would only have cost peanuts in financial terms, but it required a change of policy at Cabinet level. Try as we did, there was not yet the degree of awareness and confidence required to force a change of national policy. The 'Social Contract' had done its numbing work. Ennals stood his ground, effectively condoning an action many suspected him of having authorised in the first place. The Fleet Street printworkers, the airport maintenance staff had their hearts in the right place but their fists were in their pockets.

Meanwhile at the Plaistow Maternity Hospital, in the Newham District of East London, which was experiencing particularly severe cuts, another work-in had started on 15 July 1977. In an interview with *Women's Voice*, Dot Potter, Pat Varney and Elsie Brooks explained the reasoning behind London's third work-in:

> We started the occupation because it was the only answer. Something has to be done to save this small service we have in Newham. If this hospital goes, others will as well. Other closures are already planned. We live here, we've had kids in this hospital, we want to save the hospital for the people who live in Newham.
>
> There are no buses to Forest Gate on Sundays and public holidays. But the Minister for Health doesn't travel on buses, so he doesn't know that. They say there's no money, but you can't weigh up lives in terms of money. We're running a service, not a business. We're just a pawn in the economists' devious game. They've chosen hospitals to cut back on, rather than other things, because they think we are less likely to go on strike.
>
> They expect hospital workers to keep quiet – we've never fought back before. But this time we've given them a shock. We've learnt from the failure of the Poplar Hospital Campaign, and we've had help and advice from the EGA and the Hounslow campaigns. Now we need to get together and draw up a blueprint to fight all hospital closures.[3]

And on 1 July 1978, after a ten month campaign to keep Bethnal Green Hospital open, the first-ever casualty work-in began. The run-up to the work-in had included one of the largest postwar political meetings ever held in the York Hall, the famous boxing venue, a petition signed by 20,000 people and 9 thirteen-point statement of objection signed by 102 East End GPs, a march of 500 people in wheelchairs and bandages and a two-hour protest strike for which workers from all five local hospitals were joined by brewery workers, printers, postal workers and strikers from other local industries.

At 8 p.m., the time of official closure, the hospital staff, applauded by a crowd of local people and filmed by the *News at Ten*, put up a notice stating 'Casualty *Open* Under Staff Control'. Detailed arrangements were made between hospital doctors and the ambulance and Emergency Bed staff to guarantee the safety of patients and the first casualty work-in in history began, with its first patient arriving at 8.02. On the following day, Mrs Cox of Bethnal Green Hospital NUPE addressed a special London-wide trade union meeting against the hospital cuts which voted to 'take immediate industrial action in the case of any attempt to close the Casualty Department at Bethnal Green.'

Later the same week, Bethnal Green campaigners joined people outside twelve threatened London hospitals in a torchlight vigil to celebrate the thirtieth anniversary of the NHS. The success of the work-in forced Roland Moyle, Labour Under-Secretary for the Department of Health, to finally see the delegation he had refused to meet on several previous occasions. He left abruptly for a banquet without giving them an answer. Two weeks later, Moyle announced to the press, without informing the delegation, that he would not intervene, that the decision had been 'soundly based and properly taken,' and urging the staff 'to co-operate with the Authority.' On 30 July, managers removed nursing staff from Casualty and threatened the senior doctor involved with dismissal and legal action. The work-in was called off after having treated 1,100 emergency patients.

The overall experience could have been heart-breaking. The consultants who had supported the work-in, especially Jon Thompson, one of the most gifted and inspiring teachers of undergraduates ever to have worked at the London Hospital, paid a considerable professional price. For the secretaries, laundresses, staff nurses and porters who had discovered new abilities and eloquence during the battle, the outcome was hard to take, especially the hard-faced rejection by 'their' Labour Minister of Health. But the battle of Bethnal Green will be remembered in East London long after Roland Moyle has been forgotten. For as the Chairman of the Campaign wrote prophetically in 1980:

> The most important thing is that, like the Elizabeth Garrett Anderson and the Hounslow Hospital, Bethnal Green became a symbol of resistance, not compliance. The Battle of Bethnal Green gave a warning to Londoners of what lies in store in a Health Service they too often take for granted. If we have awoken the general public to the seriousness of what lies ahead for the London NHS, we will have achieved something of real importance. It is better to have fought and won a partial victory than never to have stirred at all.[4]

In January 1988, Labour's front-bench Health Spokesman Robin Cook issued figures which showed a 13 per cent drop in acute care beds in England since 1979. This reduction, from 147,000 to 128,000, represented beds available on an average day for short-term medical treatment or operations, not the long-stay sector, where policy is changing in favour of community care. The closures reflected financial pressure and could be linked to lengthening waiting lists. In general surgery 4,000 beds had gone, while the figures showed that 34,000 people had been waiting over a year for treatment. In orthopaedics, 1,500 beds had closed although 40,000 patients had been waiting over a year, and in ear, nose and throat, 800 beds had shut – one in six – with 22,000 people waiting over a year. London had lost 5,000 beds between 1979 and 1988, and 500 in 1987 alone. The largest bed losses were in North-west Thames (24 per cent) and Mersey (20 per cent).

Cook, an apostle of the 'new realism', did not mention rank and file resistance to this decimation which was, despite all the set-backs, still alive, and was bound to be awoken by the sheer irrationality of the new cuts. Cuts, as the President of the Royal College of Physicians put it, not into the tissues or fat but into the very bones of the service.

In Paddington, in October 1987, the highly praised and cost-effective twenty-two-bed GP Unit in Chepstow Road was abruptly closed, to the distress of the local GPs and the anguish of nursing staff and patients. And in Cornwall in late 1987, supporters of the Bolitho Maternity Unit in Penzance occupied the home's kitchen and draped the building with a huge banner saying 'Save Bolitho, Save the NHS'. It was the old story, a convenient and popular small hospital suddenly declared unsafe when it suited the authorities' closure plans, and that closure putting still more dangerous pressure on the remaining facilities: in this case, some forty miles away by road. As one non-pregnant mother put it, 'Those of us who haven't got bumps will fight for those who have.'

In December 1987, over a thousand people, many of them nurses in uniform, marched through Truro against health cuts in Cornwall. The General Manager of nearby Torbay District said: 'We have probably reached saturation point as far as Torbay Hospital is concerned.' Torbay had seen itself as pioneering the kind of cash-raising schemes favoured by the Minister, renting space to florists, for example. They raised, after three years, nearly enough to pay for one whole nurse!

Even Cheltenham, not a stronghold of the loony left, saw a

march of 400 nurses, ancillaries, consultants and administrators against the cuts on 9 January 1988.

But in general in the eighties, the closures were endured and resented rather than resisted. The significant case of the Tadworth Children's Hospital in 1984 indicated that a new Government strategy, the formula of charitable funding, was to be used to enforce unpopular closures.

Tadworth

Tadworth Hospital was known as 'the country branch' of the world famous Great Ormond Street Hospital for Sick Children. Set in sixty-two acres of grounds on the edge of the North Surrey Downs, it had 106 beds for children in three main groups; the mentally handicapped, children admitted for orthopaedic operations and those being treated for the lung condition cystic fibrosis. The quality of the service it provided the young chronically sick and those who cared for them was first class, and the hospital had an enviable informality: I have seldom heard parents and patients speak with quite such affection of a hospital. As Eileen Childs, the Administrator, said: 'The parents of our children deserve medals too. Mrs Thatcher should have had a handicapped child . . . perhaps then she would understand.' But high quality intensive or respite care for mentally handicapped children or for those who will die young is, inevitably, uneconomic. It is more 'economic' to let them be looked after at home by their parents or to store them away out of sight in rural institutions.

The Great Ormond Street group of hospitals (which includes the invaluable Queen Elizabeth the Second Hospital for Sick Children in Hackney) was itself under severe financial pressure, not least due to the growing cost of treating premature babies and cardiac surgery. Although the total annual cost of Tadworth was only £1.4 million, under 5 per cent of the group's annual budget, the Board of Governors came close to closing the unit and commissioned a confidential report by the London estate agents Gould and Co. to advise on the division of the site into three 'development parcels'.

In fact, a noisy public outcry prevented the sale, and the hospital was rescued by a group of children's charities, spearheaded by the Spastics' Society, who took over the management from the Great Ormond Street trustees. Tadworth Court Trust took over in April

1984 and immediately removed negotiating rights from the trade unions, who had been active in the fight to save the hospital. Sale of part of the site raised over £16 million for Great Ormond Street, and the number of beds at Tadworth shrank to fifty-six. But the hospital has developed some innovative services for the rehabilitation of young accident victims and in the schooling of children with profound learning difficulties. It also offers a hospice for very ill children. Barry Hassell, Chief Executive of the Tadworth Court Trust was emphatic in January 1988 that the hospital should *not* be seen as a pioneer example of 'the voluntary sector taking on the responsibilities of the state. Rather, we are sub-contractors, providing innovative services in a unique environment.' Still, Tadworth was bound to sound a warning: the first NHS hospital handed back to charity since 1948. The implications have been pithily described by Captain Hazel Wilson of the Salvation Army in Whitechapel:

> The Salvation Army was set up in Victorian times to deal with a society like that. We pioneered social work and handed it over to government agencies. Now they seem to be handing it back to us. I have the feeling this is where we came in.

The approach had set a precedent. When Great Ormond Street itself became engulfed in a major financial and staffing crisis in late 1987, it attempted to raise £30 million through slickly solicited private donations, an endeavour which was doomed to failure and which weakened rather than strengthened the pressure on the Government to provide the funds.

Waiting lists

Potentially, hospital waiting lists are of great utility in objectively assessing the impact of the cuts on patient services, because they demonstrate so starkly the extent of unmet need. Waiting list lengths express the delay between diagnosis and treatment which represents the NHS's most effective means of rationing. However, evaluation of waiting list statistics is complex. They can be reduced by striking off patients who do not respond to a check letter (as was done in the 1985 'validation exercise'), or can increase as a consequence of industrial action (as in 1975, 1979 and 1982). There are wide regional variations (with Wales doing especially badly), and there have been several changes in the way in which the statistics are collected. Trend data have to be treated carefully, and it is easy for Government statisticians to show an apparent improvement in waiting lists by contrasting the best year of the eighties with the worst of the seventies.

There is little doubt that the overall situation remains very unsatisfactory. As outpatient waiting list times are not centrally collected by the DHSS, the BMA sent a questionnaire in 1984 to all Health Districts in England and Wales asking about waiting time for a first appointment in several specialities including general medicine, general surgery, gynaecology, ear, nose and throat and orthopaedics. They found a 20 per cent increase between March 1983 and March 1984, a deterioration subsequently confirmed by the Health Services Management Centre at Birmingham. The Birmingham inquiry discovered but did not reveal thirty-six Health Authorities which in 1984 had waiting lists of over ten weeks for four or more of the listed specialities. The College of Health, a consumer-orientated health pressure group, published a guide to waiting lists in 1985 which suggested that well over 650,000 people were waiting to be admitted to hospital. This estimate was subsequently confirmed by DHSS figures of a total of 791,000 people on hospital waiting lists on 31 December 1985 (excluding those waiting for geriatric and mental handicap beds or expecting babies). This represents over fourteen people waiting per thousand population, or nearly five people waiting for their turn to occupy each hospital acute bed. Although there have been ups and downs in the waiting lists throughout the eighties, the total still represents a rise of about one third over that recorded in 1974, and nearly two thirds in excess of that in 1959. The increase in waiting list size was most marked in traumatic and orthopaedic surgery. Clearly the mathematics of increasing demand and decreasing beds have not been overcome by even the most energetic and efficient efforts of doctors and nurses.

Staff morale

Another window through which to observe the discrepancy between Government rhetoric and the realities of NHS cuts is the morale of the service's staff. Here again, Government claims are highly misleading. As part of his triumphalist speech to the 1986

Tory Party Conference, for example, Norman Fowler stated: 'The fact is that more doctors and nurses are working for patients than at any stage in the history of the NHS – over 70,000 more than when we came to office.' Certainly nurse numbers have increased, but at least half of that apparent expansion was simply made to meet the shortened working week needed to implement Clegg (and also to comply with EEC rulings). And when one bears in mind that the number of whole-time equivalent ancillary staff fell by 17.5 per cent between 1978 and 1984, inevitably creating more work for nurses, that the intensity of nursing work increases with shorter hospital stays and that more senior nurses are involved in training and administration, things look less rosy for the ward nurse. The advances won in 1982 proved short-lived.

Nursing Times commented:

> Nurses come off badly whichever way you look. Nurse earnings are just 58 per cent of the average male non-manual earnings and even com-pared with other public sector staff they appear desultory. After fifteen years, a police constable (that is, an officer who has not been promoted) can expect to earn £14,000 – the unpromoted staff nurse will earn barely £9,000, even taking special duty payments into account.
>
> To the uninitiated, this sorry state of affairs is puzzling to say the least. There is no doubt that nurses are held in high public esteem. Politicians extol the profession's virtues at every turn. Organisations such as the Royal College of Nursing have grown in power and influence and even the columns of this journal are scrutinised by decision-makers. Above all, the wider media are enraptured, some would say obsessed, by the plight of the profession.
>
> And yet, in spite of all this and the existence of an independent pay review body, low pay, low morale and low retention are the hallmarks of nursing in Britain today.[5]

The reason was as much the cuts as the wages. A nurse at the London Hospital wrote to her local anti-cuts bulletin *Siren*:

> TLC. What does it mean? Well, nurses use this abbreviation in their care plans. It stands for Tender Loving Care. It is a cynical reminder of what the nursing staff are there for and what has come out of the good intentions at the end of the day: little more than good will and giving basic care, like washing patients, feeling pulses, taking temperatures, giving bedpans and handing out meals.
>
> The rest is just wishful thinking. Reality is not tenderness and love, but understaffed wards, shortage of linen, clerks being threatened with the sack, cuts in the District Health Authority's budget.

Let me just quote two examples to show how bad the situation is already in the London Hospital:

1 Some wards are incredibly short staffed at the moment. There is no way the needs of the patients in a normal twenty-seven-bed ward can be met when one staff nurse and two student nurses only staff a whole shift. This is no exception. It is the norm!

2 New linen often does not come up from the laundry until the early afternoon, but beds of course are made in the morning. There is never enough linen to replace soiled sheets anyway. The laundry at the London Hospital is catering for all Tower Hamlets Health Authority and it is working to capacity. But knowing that does not make much difference to the patient who needs to have his or her sheets changed and gets the answer, 'Sorry love, we are out of linen at the moment and so is next door.'[6]

Nor are the NHS doctors, although better off financially, happy about the way they have to practise medicine in the era of the cuts. In a sober survey of 'How the NHS Economies Affect MDU Members', the Medical Defence Union stated in the winter of 1985 that several doctors contacted them each week about the low level of medical cover:

Typically, juniors are required to work twice the recommended number of hours; consultants are concerned about the distance between two, three or even four hospitals where they are supposed to provide emergency cover concurrently.

Nursing cover is also a problem: surgeons are concerned about the lack of theatre assistants: both surgeons and physicians about the shortage of nurses: they waste valuable time looking for a nurse to act as a chaperone when a female patient has to be examined.

Doctors of all disciplines are held back by secretarial shortages too, caused largely by the low salaries paid by the NHS (though somehow the money is found to pay agencies for expensive, supposedly temporary help). X-ray reports are delayed or handwritten; the patients' records are mislaid or are in the wrong place; reports to GPs are not typed up and dispatched.

But even more recurrent than manpower shortages are poblems arising from shortages of facilities: surgeons have no choice but to use theatres that have been declared unsafe if they wish to continue to operate; blood of the right type is not to hand; and of course beds are in short supply, leading to long waiting times before treatment can begin. These are shortages of basic tools, nothing that could be described as an extravagant diagnostic toy.[7]

Doctors under particular pressure were identified as casualty officers, expected to deal with simultaneous and often unprecedented acute problems with only the normal facilities and cover, psychiatrists facing emergency admissions without approved social workers or secure beds, and paediatric doctors forced to refuse admission to gravely ill babies because of lack of cots.

Sometimes the problem is clearly about the NHS's low wage levels. Basic grade pharmacists are leaving the NHS at such a rate that some hospital dispensaries are having to close. But it is hardly surprising when high street chemists can earn nearly £5,000 per year more. Intensive care nurses are snapped up by the private hospitals, who increase their salaries by £2,000 and still find them a bargain. The low pay levels for medical secretaries are a constant problem.

But something more insidious is rotting the morale of many others who leave the NHS: the highly frustrating experience of trying to produce high-quality work in a chronically short-staffed workplace. The first, and best disguised, cuts have been achieved by freezing existing, inadequate staffing levels. The negotiated establishment for a ward or department has been concealed or replaced with an 'in post' estimation. Long-advertised consultant posts, especially in the less popular and more socially useful specialities, have been quietly abandoned. Managements were generally successful at pressing people to cover up, even though the strain of being constantly short-handed and depending on poorly trained personnel is nerve-racking for the staff and dangerous for the patient. Further wage savings have been made by hastening the departure of staff, especially those over retirement age, and cutting back on the guaranteed overtime which alone makes hospital wages possible to live on. Further shedding of staff is achieved by centralisation of catering, laundry and laboratory facilities, forced through despite the inevitable decline in efficiency.

It is hard for people who have not worked in the NHS to appreciate quite what a difference staff shortages can make. Yet those of us in it have become so habituated to them that to make a fuss now seems self-interested. It is not just the extra workload but the now lost possibility of acting like one human being to another, rather than as clock-watching automatons processing people called 'patients'. That brief but reassuring chat between the ward auxiliary and the shaved and dazed patient waiting to go into theatre, the spare moments for a nurse to talk to a patient who never has people to visit him, the chance for a junior doctor to really explain what an operation entails before a bleep heralds a new crisis, warm ward meals, individual rehabilitation, proper training – in short, the human touch – require time and staff. Another pair of hands can really alter the whole atmosphere in a ward, department or surgery. Staffing makes all the difference but it is the first area in which financial savings are made.

12
The Impact: 'Cinderella' Services

The problems caused by the NHS's under-financing are seen most poignantly in the 'Cinderella' services: the high workload, low-glamour care of the mentally ill and the physically and mentally handicapped. With the right resources, there is much more potential for progress in these areas than was recognised even ten years ago. For example, the special furniture designed by Ron Moon, a nurse at the Royal Earlswood Hospital in Redhill, Surrey, as an alternative to the standard NHS wheelchair produced significant improvements. Spastic patients were no longer crying and moaning because of the sheer effort they expended to hold themselves upright. They began to laugh and smile, even to answer questions with electrical signals. The work of Andreas Peto, a Hungarian doctor, has proved that spastic children can be taught to achieve control over their disordered limbs. And it is universally recognised that the stigma of institutionalisation can be reduced if the mentally ill can stay in small community-based units and retain social contacts with the outside world. There is a real challenge here, to devote real curative resources to people isolated and imprisoned from us by an accident of birth. Not to store them out of sight but to care for them generously, imaginatively and in public.

Instead, something cynically and shamefully different is happening, in the name of 'care in the community'. The statistics about community care show, with some exceptions, a financial growth throughout the seventies which either slackened or ceased in the eighties. What was described in 1980 by the Health Ministers as 'growth in the amount of voluntary care, of neighbourhood care, of self-help' has in reality been a dramatic expansion of private nursing homes and hostels and a huge increase in home nursing by usually unpaid, often female relatives. Social services support to people living in their own homes had been further limited by local authority spending cuts and rate-capping. As the Audit

Commission very accurately predicted in their 1986 report, there did exist a

> window of opportunity to establish an effective community-based service to provide the care needed for frail elderly, mentally ill, mentally handicapped and physically handicapped people. If this opportunity is not taken, a new pattern of care will emerge, based on private residential care where appropriate. The result will be a continued waste of scarce resources and worse still, care and support which is either lacking entirely, or inappropriate to the needs of some of the most disadvantaged members of society and the relatives who seek to care for them.

The cuts mean that the opportunity was largely squandered.

The bitterness subsequently felt by people who have chosen to work in these demanding areas is entirely justified. They and we have been hoaxed. A teacher of children with special needs wrote about going on strike for the first time:

> I used to think that units like ours were intended to be better for children than special schools because we enable children to mix together, to be educated in their own area, and because we are beginning to break down prejudices about handicaps among the normal population – and because we also save money in the long term by helping to keep children within the normal system.
>
> Now I see that the Government actually intends to save money on our children several times over – no specialised equipment, no extra resources in buildings, no concessions whatsoever to their 'special needs' in terms of money.
>
> I've been conned. The harder we work, the less help we get. The more children we send out successfully, the easier it will be for them to say that we are no longer needed. The more equipment I make, the less they will spend on us.
>
> I went on strike because it isn't only my salary the Government is skimping on. I want a fair deal for the children too, but I'm not prepared to get it for them on my hard work alone as my reward for that was even less funds.[1]

Cinderella never even got to the ball.

The old and the very old

The composition of the population by age and the structure of families within it has changed constantly over this century, with important implications for the health service. In particular, the growth of the old (those of pensionable age) and the very old (over 75) as a proportion of the total population presents a considerable challenge to the NHS which it has had great difficulty in meeting. The considerable rise in the average expectation of life (from 48 years in 1901 to 70 in 1981 for males, from 52 in 1901 to 76 in 1981 for females) has largely been achieved by a fall in mortality in childhood and early adulthood. People are not living a lot longer, fewer are dying young. But because of the fall in infant mortality, people are having much smaller families and so the number of the old, as a proportion of the population, has increased: by 2001 the over-75s will form over 40 per cent of the total pensionable group.

The present generation of the old have fewer potential carers (because their own immediate families are smaller), and relatives who do exist characteristically live at some distance. Age Concern calculate that one in three does not have a close relative anywhere. Many pensioners live alone. In the 1981 Household Census, 14.2 per cent of households consisted of one pensioner living alone. Such people are likely to be very poor by general standards. Poor means cold, fed out of tins, surrounded by shabby furniture and with the only prospect of a real holiday being a stay with relatives or perhaps a council seaside hotel. It means no new clothes, few excursions, no car of their own. It probably means fear of violence and resentful proximity with new neighbours who are younger, noisier and more unruly. It inevitably means they will, or should, be high users of the NHS and the statutory services. This is all the more important because many will be suffering from undiagnosed mental illness and confusion due to physical causes, as well as memory loss, confusion and mild dementia which can suddenly become acute and dangerous.

The geriatric and psychogeriatric hospital services have definitely improved in medical status, attitude and quality of care. The inhumanity and occasional cruelty in the inactive long-stay wards, well documented in the fifties and sixties, seems to have been alleviated, with much more emphasis on active management and the maintenance of independence. Dr Peter Horrocks, ex-Director of the Hospital Advisory Service set up by Richard Crossman after the Ely scandals, wrote optimistically in 1987:

While there has been considerable progress, inhumanity and inadequate care have not been eradicated from every ward where old people are treated and the need to encourage a positive approach remains constant.

But what the cuts and closures have done is to shift the problem from ill-treatment inside hospital to neglect or even abuse at home. Responsibility for the old in the community is unclear and often passes backwards and forwards between social services, hospitals and GP. The halt in council building has meant still longer bottle-necks in getting a place in sheltered or group homes. And changes in the state earnings-related pensions moved the BMA to describe the discretionary Social Fund as 'the less acceptable face of Victorian moral values' and express the fear that the elderly could be forced to rely on charity, 'or even be forced to beg'.[2]

There have been many closures of old, gaunt and hard to heat geriatric hospitals, and partial replacement with modern units. The problem is always a net loss of beds and capacity. And while it is right that the elderly sick should be returned to their homes when well, there will inevitably be a group, notably the senile demented, who require long-term inpatient treatment. In affluent areas, private nursing homes may take up the slack and make a pretty profit in the process. But this is not often an option in the poor inner urban areas.

In Enfield in April 1983, for example, the psychiatrists in charge of a new psychogeriatric centre boycotted its official opening by the Minister of Health because of this loss of beds. Dr Suman Fernando, Chairman of the psychiatry division in Enfield, said:

> All four consultants who run the ward – it hardly deserves the name centre – feel very strongly about the minister's visit, which seems to be just for publicity.
> Originally, we were promised an 84-bed unit at Chase Farm Hospital in Enfield. So far we have only a 28-bed unit with 18 beds in use and no community services. We are left in the position where we can only take very desperate cases. Other people are being turned away and their relatives are having to seek private care to get them into hospital.[3]

Dr Elizabeth Hocking, consultant geriatrician to Swindon Health Authority, went further, suggesting in May 1984 that cuts in hospital services were putting elderly people at risk of abuse, occasionally fatal, from their frustrated carers. Dr Hocking, who had had three such cases which ended in the death of the old person, said:

Sadly, by the time it has got to the stage of physical abuse, relief stays in hospital aren't enough. The person needs admitting permanently, but because of bed shortages all over the country, they are having to stay at home.[4]

The anguish and strain when senile dementia affects one partner in a long-standing relationship, who then becomes unpredictable, sometimes imbecilic, sometimes violent, sometimes just incoherent, can also lead to violence. CPNs for the elderly, alarm systems and day centres can do a lot, but there is often no substitute for a secure old people's home with professionally qualified staff. Yet places in such homes are like gold dust. Although I have been fortunate as a GP to have worked with a committed and well-organised geriatric department, there have never been fewer than five elderly demented on my list waiting for appropriate sheltered accommodation, who are at risk and a constant source of worry. It has proved unadvisable to be either old or to be sick in Mrs Thatcher's Britain. To be both is extremely risky.

Paediatrics

At the other end of the age scale, the intensive care of the newborn has been prominent in discussions of the cuts. Here it is not a simple question of services lost, but rather of new and important medical advances which are inadequately financed. It is impossible not to be proud of and excited by the achievements of the paediatricians in the seventies, which mean that premature babies delivered as early as thirty-two weeks now stand a very good chance of survival without handicap. And one is awestruck by the good survival rates at birthweights between 1,000 and 1,500 grammes, and remarkable results even below one kilogramme are now achievable.

By current standards, much postwar neonatal care was rudimentary, arbitrary and not very scientific. Nowadays we have units which are not only superb examples of applied science, but which have managed to retain their humanity and allow open visiting, put the tiny babies into tiny baby clothes and encourage the mother and father to begin being parents at the side of the gasping ventilator and blinking monitors. Well-applied neonatal care is something that the NHS should make absolutely no apology for: the premature baby who might have survived anyway will achieve a much better quality of life, and the very precious baby of an older or sub-fertile couple will live to be loved. And, again quite rightly, the better the results, the greater the referral rate of small babies; a classic example of better health facilities producing an increase in demand rather than its elimination. And it is entirely right that consultants who trained as senior registrars in the regional units practise their skills in the hospitals to which they are appointed – that is what they are paid for. But, because of the cuts and advances which are under-financed, it works out as an either/or situation. As Dr Jeffery Bissenden, a Birmingham paediatrician, puts it,

> The League of Friends' ventilator goes on the blink and the technician will not come until Monday. Disaster strikes, the consultant is burned out and those larger babies who used to do well are not getting the attention they had before because overworked nurses have been concentrating their efforts on tiny babies who should not be there . . . The spirit is willing but the support staff is weak.[5]

Academic medicine

Considerable play has been made of Mrs Thatcher's science degree, perhaps unwisely, since its only application seems to have been a brief period investigating protein polymers which would enable ice cream to hold its configuration in the cornet for longer, hardly a major contribution to scientific knowledge. However, the Somerville College graduate's three terms of Prime Ministerial office have had an impact on British medical research which is, in the words of Sir Christopher Booth, Director of the Medical Research Council's clinical research centre, 'catastrophic'. As Booth wrote in September 1986, 'The Government is increasingly reluctant to support science in Britain as effectively as is necessary to maintain the country's scientific position in a competitive world.'[6]

The academic branch of the medical profession has been treated even more harshly than the NHS doctors. Over three years to 1984 there had been, reported the Commons Social Services Committee, a net loss of more than 200 clinical academic posts as a result of university cuts, and many medical schools faced an annual deficit of more than half a million pounds. Yet the Medical Research Council budget was cut by a further £3 million in the same year, and the cuts have continued. In 1986, five further professorial/

consultant level posts were lost along with four senior lectureships and eight lectureships. In a review by the National Association of Health Authorities, it was calculated that universities, which had suffered a real decline in income of 20 per cent since 1981, generally faced another 2 per cent reduction in resources per year, adding up to a 30 per cent cut by 1990.[7]

The problem for academic medicine is a good deal worse than those figures alone suggest. This is because simultaneous NHS cuts have forced the academics out of the laboratories and back to the wards to keep the service going. And because the undergraduate population has remained relatively constant in medicine, which remains a very popular career choice, the same teaching load is being carried by a smaller number of doctors. Time for research inevitably suffers. 'I have only one and a half days a week set aside for research, and the rest is clinical work, including as much on-call duty as my NHS colleagues,' reported Dr Colin Smith, the Chairman of the BMA's academic staff committee and a senior lecturer at Southampton University, in 1986; and this is an increasingly typical experience. The rise in the private practice commitments by 'part-time' consultants further aggravates the problem.

There is also the loss of talent by emigration. It is calculated that at least 617 experienced British scientists and engineers working in biochemistry, chemistry, earth sciences, electronic engineering and physics, left Britain between 1975 and 1985. And then there is the waste of the talent which remains. Writing in the BMJ in 1987, John Rawles, senior lecturer in medicine at Aberdeen University, described the impact of the cuts:

> Many, many academic man hours have been spent in debates, in meetings, in committees, in lobbies, in coffee rooms – man against man, department against department, us against them. Months have been spent relocating departments, laboratories and libraries, retrenching into less space. Rooms are now shared, making private study impossible; telephone extensions have been removed, making communication less efficient; laboratories are now dangerously overcrowded; new books and journals are not now affordable by the library. Morale is at a nadir, and we are now being invited to accept early retirement from the age of 50. Where is the sense in making retirement financially rewarding with attractive severance payments? Is our expertise such a liability to society that we must be encouraged to withdraw it?

> The position is worthy of *Alice in Wonderland*. We are invited to retire, to our financial advantage, at a time of high personal productivity, to obviate punitive measures by the UGC [University Grants Committee] based on an arbitrary assessment that is unrelated to the quantity or quality of our research work.[8]

The overall result has been well summarised in two separate studies carried out for the Advisory Board for the Research Councils by the Royal Society and the Science Policy Research Unit at Sussex University. Their conclusions were that British scientific research is starved of money compared with every other industrialised nation, has lost its most distinguished practitioners to other countries, and does less research than many other countries, with the results that are obtained having less of an impact on the international community. The results of this folly are not measured simply in Britain's declining standing as a centre of original research, but in the loss of skills and the decline in morale.

The quality of undergraduate teaching itself is bound to suffer. As a report of the Royal College of Physicians rightly emphasised:

> The training of a doctor is not limited to passing on a repertoire of established skills, though that forms part of it. The more important part is to create an understanding of health and disease so that even after years in practice the doctor remains competent to assess for the benefit of his patients the many advances in medicine which are certain to occur, if not in this country, then elsewhere.
>
> But this openness of mind cannot be achieved by an education based on rote and dogma; the whole process must be informed by awareness of the growing edge of medicine, part of which will in due course be essential in sound practice. Yet it is just this research-based outlook which is most threatened by academic poverty, and by staff shortages.[9]

The danger then is, as Abe Guz, when Professor of Medicine at Charing Cross and Westminster Medical School, warned, that 'gradually we will produce doctors without a spirit of enquiry. They will become the victims of the best advertiser.'

Care of the newborn

There remains a shortage of neonatal cots which is conservatively estimated at a 25 per cent underprovision. This is partly due to overlong use of the out of date formulae of the 1971 Shelton Report, but mainly to cuts and nursing staffing difficulties caused by low pay and low morale. The House of Commons Social Services Committee Follow-Up Report on Perinatal and Neonatal Mortality warned that there now exists a danger that 'paediatricians working in small units will be compelled to attempt intensive care without adequate resources; some of the infants they treat may well be left handicapped for life.'

Yet neonatal intensive care is much cheaper than is popularly thought, and only a fraction of the cost of lifetime care of individuals with long-term handicaps.

Physical disability

The intensive rehabilitation of disabled persons not only helps them make the emotional leap from being a patient to being a person, it can make them economically self-sufficient.

Yet, despite the Tunbridge and Mair Reports of 1972, specialist care is both limited and unevenly distributed geographically. Where it does exist – the Spinal Injuries Centre in Stoke Mandeville, Mary Marlborough Lodge, Ritchie Russell House and Rivermead Rehabilitation Centre – results have been outstanding. Public response to the International Year of the Disabled was strong. Yet there are simply insufficient NHS funds available to staff existing posts, let alone expand the speciality. Instead, disc jockeys raise the money by charity stunts. And the victims of stroke, head injury, multiple sclerosis, motor neurone disease, Parkinson's Disease and severe rheumatic disorders must soldier on in desperate dependence. It may appear to 'save money'. And the disabled and their relatives are in a poor position to make a fuss. But it is an entirely false economy.

Child abuse

The disabled live and die conveniently out of sight. But the death of children by non-accidental injury and adult abuse is highly public. Over the last few years it has glared at us from the newspaper front page, reproaching us all and, one hopes, impelling our society to act effectively to prevent it.

A decade ago many more children known to be at risk were taken into care, but changes in policy and the cost of care has resulted in a much higher proportion of these children being maintained, under observation, in the community. But effective monitoring of at-risk children requires high staff levels and considerable experience and skill. It also needs teamwork, notably close liaison between social workers, health visitors, GPs and paediatricians. But the squeeze by central Government and local authority finances, rate-capping and the continual attacks on social workers themselves by right wing loudmouths who wouldn't last a week in the job, has depleted exactly the resources which could prevent the continuing toll of child deaths. Certainly this was the verdict of the DHSS's own inquiry into eighteen serious cases of child abuse between 1973 and 1981, commissioned by George Young in the wake of the Maria Colwell case.

The report found a lack of co-ordination between services, unqualified, untrained and inexperienced social workers handling cases, inadequate supervision of parents and children, staff shortages, heavy caseloads and low morale. And almost every study finds poverty, bad housing, high rates of unemployment and dependency on welfare benefits in the families of abused children. Abuse is a social and class problem. But adequately staffed, properly organised, well co-ordinated units could still do a lot to prevent abuse when it is recognised or reported. Instead, social workers are leaving the job in droves and new vacancies are unfilled. The conditions everyone pretends to abhor are thus worsened . . . and further victims are guaranteed.

Possibilities

Medical breakthroughs create rather than abolish demand. And for that we should be glad. Scientific breakthroughs gain social meaning when they can be applied by ordinary mortals through an organised and planned health service. In the ten years to 1980, hip replacements trebled to 31,000 a year, patients on a kidney machine or with a transplant rose from 1,300 to nearly 8,000, and coronary bypass operations rose from 250 to 5,000. Yet the waiting lists were longer at the end of the decade than at the beginning. The report commissioned by the DHSS from Brunel University on heart transplants at Papworth and Harefield Hospitals, published in 1985, confirmed that the procedure is now successful in terms of quality and quantity of life. Yet Magdi Yacoub at Harefield and Terence English at Papworth have watched sixty-eight of their patients die, according to the transplant report, because they did not have the money to treat them. Yacoub and English have had to turn away sixty-five donated hearts between them because they did not have the resources to give them to patients.

Robert Sells, who runs the kidney transplant unit at the Royal Liverpool, calculated in 1985, when he was President of the British Transplant Society: 'Nationally we only did 1,400 kidney transplants last year and 2,500 new patients needed treatment.'[10] In January 1988, the British Cardiac Society released a report that suggested that the number of cardiologists per head of population in Britain is about one tenth of that on the continent, even though heart disease is the biggest single killer in the country. The United States had thirty-two times as many cardiologists per head. Thousands of people are dying prematurely every year because of a shortage of heart disease specialists, the report claimed.

And even when Ministers have bestowed crumbs on the lucky few units, they fail to mention that this is not new money but is taken from the total health budget: each Health Authority gets correspondingly less to finance the specialities which have not had a visible crisis that year. Likewise the schemes for a national cervical screening programme with effective call and recall at three-year intervals, and the national programme for regular breast cancer screening by regular examination and mammography. These techniques are now proven successes in halting cancer deaths and are recognised as such by the Government, which nevertheless denies the finance or the political push to set them up properly.

The skill is there, but the political and economic will to apply it is not. One almost feels that the Treasury wishes that Charnley hadn't invented his brilliant artificial hip joint or Christiaan Barnard not performed his damned cardiac transplant or pioneered coronary artery bypass surgery.

What we stand to lose lies not simply in the failure to apply existing knowledge, but in the loss of the next generation of medical advance. In Denmark Hill, the Harris-Birthright Unit are slowly transforming the terms on which we approach foetal medicine. But will fetoscopy, the sampling of foetal blood and infusion into foetal circulation, remain a research procedure or become an everyday test and therapy? The answer lies in the funding, or lack of it. Could angioplasty, an operative technique for dredging clots in the cardiac arteries, replace artery and vein bypass operations if our radiological equipment was better and hospital referral for angina was earlier? It is the accountants rather than the cardiac surgeons who have the answer. Will the Magnetic Resonance Scanner technique developed at Velindre Hospital in Cardiff provide a blood test that tests for cancer? The *Guardian* is right when it argues:

> Unless help is forthcoming from British sources, it could end as so often before with a valuable technique originating in the inventive brains of British scientists, only to find resources for full development abroad.

At this point, someone will inevitably say that, of course, if you provide a service free, demand is likely to be infinite. And if we go on in this way, by the year 2045 the NHS will take up the entire GNP. But health care is not a commodity which people desire in endless profusion for its intrinsic utility, but one which they seek when they are unwell. Certainly the slope of the demand curve is infinite at the present inadequate level of supply. What should be considered is what higher level of supply would provide equilibrium with demand. That would be the point at which further supply led to unused or underused facilities. It might be 25 per cent more for the NHS (which would bring us to German levels of funding), or even 50 per cent more (equivalent to American spending, but, because of the NHS, likely to be much more effective). But that is the level we can and should attain.

It is my conviction that in a better society, no longer class-divided and profit-driven, many of the medical problems which now present would not exist. I'd like to think there might even be a lot fewer doctors, social workers and do-gooders because good would be done by society itself. But in this imperfect and worsening world we desperately need our doctors, our hospitals, our nurses and our ancillaries. We need them to be given the finances to use their skills to the full. The cuts must be stopped and spending increased to a level at which the NHS can function properly again. Unless this is done, decline, disillusionment and a multitude of private tragedies will continue. Until it is done, we – health workers, patients and citizens – must raise our level of dissent.

Endnotes

Chapter 1

1. C. Newman, *The Evolution of Medical Education in the Nineteenth Century* (Oxford University Press, 1957) p. 59. Cited in Brian Abel-Smith, *The Hospitals 1800–1948* (Heinemann, London, 1964).
2. E. P. Thompson, *The Making of the English Working Class* (Penguin, Harmondsworth, 1974) p. 295.
3. R. A. Lewis, *Edwin Chadwick and the Public Health Movement 1832–38* (Longman, London, 1952). Cited in John Robson, *Quality, Inequality and Health Care* (Marxists in Medicine, London, 1976).
4. Frances Cobbe, 'The Sick Poor in Workhouses', *Journal of the Workhouse Visiting Society*, 1861, p. 487. Cited in Abel-Smith, *op. cit.*
5. Commission Report, *Lancet*, 27 April 1866, p. 34.
6. Robert Roberts, *The Classic Slum* (Penguin, Harmondsworth, 1973), p. 108.
7. Danny Abse, *Medicine on Trial* (Aldus, London, 1967) p. 12.
8. S. and B. Webb, *The Poor Law Medical Officer and his Future* (London, 1909).
9. S. and B. Webb, Report of the Royal Commission on the Poor Laws 1905–9, *Minority Report*.
10. Report of the Royal Commission on the Poor Laws 1905–9, Appendix.
11. Charles Chaplin, *My Autobiography* (Bodley Head, London, 1964).

Chapter 2

1. Cited in G.D.M. and M. Cole, *The Condition of Britain* (Gollancz, London, 1938) p. 101.
2. See Michael Foot, *Aneurin Bevan*, vol. 2 (Davis-Poynter, London, 1973) pp. 100–26.
3. D. S. Murray, *Why an NHS?* (Pemberton, London, 1972).
4. John Campbell, *Nye Bevan and the Mirage of British Socialism* (Weidenfeld and Nicolson, London, 1987) p. 376.

Chapter 3

1. Michael Kidron, *Western Capitalism Since the War* (Penguin, Harmondsworth, 1970) p. 11.
2. C. A. R. Crosland, *The Future of Socialism* (Cape, London, 1956).
3. J. Tudor Hart, 'The Inverse Care Law', *Lancet* 1971; i: pp. 405–12.
4. *British Medical Journal*, 12 July 1986.

Chapter 4

1. *World Medicine*, December 1984.
2. Griffiths NHS Management Inquiry: First Report of the Social Services Committee 1983–4 (HMSO).

3. *Guardian*, 8 August 1984.
4. *Observer*, 25 October 1987.
5. Richard Titmuss, *Commitment to Welfare* (Allen and Unwin, London, 1968).

Chapter 5

1. J. Tudor Hart, *World Medicine*, 1984, p. 11.
2. J. S. Collings, 'General Practice – England Today', *Lancet*, 1950, p. 555.
3. A. Cartwright and J. Marshall, 'General Practice in 1963', *Medical Care*, 1965, p. 69.
4. Report of the Royal Commission on the NHS, Cmnd 7615 HMSO, July 1979, paras 7.58, 7.62, 7.63.
5. Rhodes, Prashar and Young, *Primary Health Care in the Inner Cities: After Acheson*. Foreword Abel-Smith. (Policy Studies Institute, London, 1986).
6. J. Robson, 'Primary Care for the 1990s'. Evidence to the Tower Hamlets Health Inquiry, September 1985.
7. *British Medical Journal*, 28 June 1986.
8. 'The Future Organisation of Primary Care', MPU, August 1987.

Chapter 6

1. A. Watt, 'Overcrowding in the Mental Hospital', *Lancet*, 1956.
2. Cited in G. L. Cohen, *What's Wrong with Hospitals?* (Penguin, Harmondsworth, 1964).
3. Jack Tizard, *Community Services for the Mentally Handicapped* (Oxford University Press, 1964).
4. See J. A. Baldwin, *The Mental Hospital in the Psychiatric Service* (Oxford University Press, 1971).
5. See *Psychiatry in Practice*, April 1985.
6. Malcolm Weller, *World Medicine*, November 1984.

Chapter 7

1. DHSS, *Priorities for Health and Personal Services in England* (HMSO, London, 1976).
2. *Lancet*, 1959, p. 584.
3. *Guardian*, 10 December 1984.
4. *Listener*, 16 February 1984.
5. Monopolies Commission, *A Report on the Supply of Chlordiazepoxide and Diazepam*, HCP197 (HMSO, London, 1973).
6. Ron Lacey and Shaun Woodward, *That's Life: Survey on Tranquillisers* (BBC Publications, London, 1984).
7. See James Erlichman, 'Drug Makers Get a Tonic From Mrs T', *Guardian*, 19 August 1986.

Chapter 8

1. Griffith, Rayner and Mohan, 'Commercial Medicine in London' (GLC, London, 1985).
2. Cited in the *Guardian*, 20 February 1982.
3. Cited in Samuel Mencher, *Private Practice in Britain: The Relationship of Private Medical Care to the NHS* (Occasional Papers on Social Administration No. 24, London, 1967).

4. *Guardian*, 1 February 1984.
5. *Guardian*, 25 October 1984.
6. *Guardian*, 22 February 1984.
7. *Guardian*, 23 March 1984.

Chapter 9

1. David Beecham, 'Updating the Downturn: the Class Struggle Under the Tories', *International Socialism* No. 14, Autumn 1981.
2. Jonathan Neale, *Memoirs of a Callous Picket* (Pluto, London, 1983) p. 91.
3. *Ibid.*, p. 103.

Chapter 11

1. *The Tower Hamlets Health Inquiry Report*, May 1987, p. 53.
2. *London Industrial Strategy: Health Care* (GLC, London, 1985) p. 11.
3. *Women's Voice*, August 1977.
4. Jane Salvage and Kambiz Boomla, *The NHS in East London: What Lies Ahead?* (Save the Bethnal Green Hospital Campaign, London, 1980).
5. *Nursing Times*, 18 December 1987.
6. *Siren*, October 1986.
7. *Journal of the Medical Defence Union*, Winter 1985.

Chapter 12

1. *Guardian*, 9 April 1985.
2. *All Our Tomorrows* (BMA Publications, 1986).
3. *Guardian*, 13 March 1986.
4. *General Practitioner*, 25 May 1984.
5. *General Practitioner*, 24 February 1984.
6. *BMA News Review*, September 1986, reported in the *Guardian*, 8 September 1986.
7. *University Funding and the NHS: The 1986 Review* (The National Association of Health Authorities, Birmingham, 1986).
8. *British Medical Journal*, 1 August 1987.
9. *The Problems Facing Academic Medicine*. Policy Statement, Royal College of Physicians, July 1982.
10. *Guardian*, 20 February 1985.

Further Reading

Brian Abel-Smith, *The Hospitals 1800–1948* (Heinemann, London, 1964)

Danny Abse, *Medicine on Trial* (Aldus, London, 1967)

The Acheson Report: 'Primary Health Care in London' (HMSO, London, 1981)

Dennis Altman, *Aids and the new Puritanism* (Pluto, London, 1986)

Duncan Blackie and Ian Taylor, *Aids: The Socialist View* (SWP, London, 1987)

Sarah Boston, *Will, my Son: The Life and Death of a Mongol Child* (Pluto, London, 1981)

M. J. Butts, D. Irving and C. Whitt, 'From Principles to Practice' (Nuffield Provincial Hospitals' Trust, London, 1981)

Alex Callinicos and Mike Simons, *The Great Strike: The Miners' Strike of 1984–5 and its Lessons* (SWP, London, 1985)

John Campbell, *Nye Bevan and the Mirage of British Socialism* (Weidenfeld and Nicolson, London, 1987)

Barbara Castle, *The Castle Diaries 1974–76* (Weidenfeld and Nicolson, London, 1980)

K. Coates and R. Silburn, *Poverty: the Forgotten Englishmen* (Penguin Harmondsworth, 1970)

Vernon Coleman, *The Medicine Man* (Temple Smith, London, 1975)

Richard Crossman, *The Crossman Diaries* (esp. vol. 3: *Secretary of State for Social Services 1968–70*) (Cape, London, 1977)

Leslie Doyal (with Imogen Pennell), *The Political Economy of Health* (Pluto, London, 1979)

Barbara and John Ehrenreich, *The American Health Empire: Power, Profits and Politics* (Vintage, New York, 1971)

Barbara Ehrenreich and Deidre English, *Complaints and Disorders: The Sexual Politics of Sickness* (Writers' and Readers' Publishing Co-operative, London, 1976)

Barbara Ehrenreich and Deidre English, *Witches, Midwives and Nurses: A History of Women Healers* (Writers' and Readers' Publishing Co-operative, London, 1976)

The Ely Report: 'The Report of the Committee of Enquiry into Allegations of Ill-Treatment of Patients and Other Irregularities at the Ely Hospital, Cardiff' (HMSO Cmnd 3975, London, 1969)

Michael Foot, *Aneurin Bevan*, vol. 1 (MacGibbon and Kee Ltd, London, 1962), vol. 2 (Davis-Poynter, London, 1973)

Paul Foot, *Stop the Cuts* (Rank and File Centre, London, 1976)

Michel Foucault, *Histoire de la folie* (Librairie Plon, Paris, 1961)

Derek Fraser, *The Evolution of the Welfare State* (Macmillan, London, 1973)

Lesley Garner, *The NHS: Your Money or your Life* (Penguin, Harmondsworth, 1979)

Jonathan Gathorne-Hardy, *Doctors: The Lives and Work of GPs* (Weidenfeld and Nicolson, London, 1984)

George Godber, *The British National Health Service* (US Department of Health, Education and Welfare, Washington, DC, 1976)

Linda Gordon, *Women's Body, Women's Right* (Penguin, Harmondsworth, 1977)

Germaine Greer, *Sex and Destiny: The Politics of Human Fertility* (Secker and Warburg, London, 1984)

Ben Griffith, Geoff Rayner and John Mohan, *Commercial Medicine in London* (GLC, London, 1985)

Ben Griffith, Steve Iliffe and Geoff Rayner, *Banking on Sickness: Commercial Medicine in Britain and the USA* (Lawrence and Wishart, London, 1987)

Chris Ham, *Health Policy in Britain* (Macmillan, London, 1982, 1985)

Paul Harrison, *Inside the Inner City* (Penguin, Harmondsworth, 1983)

Tom Heller, *Poor Health, Rich Profits* (Spokesman Books, Nottingham, 1977)

Steve Iliffe, *The NHS: A Picture of Health?* (Lawrence and Wishart, London, 1983)

Ivan Illich, *Medical Nemesis* (Calder and Boyars, London, 1975)

International Journal of Health Services, quarterly (Baywood Publishing Company, Johns Hopkins University, Baltimore)

J. C. Kincaid, *Poverty and Inequality in Britain* (Penguin, Harmondsworth, 1973)

Patrick Kinnersley, *The Hazards of Work* (Pluto Press, London, 1973)

Alan Klass, *There's Gold in Them Thar Pills* (Penguin, Harmondsworth, 1975)

Rudolph Klein, *The Politics of the NHS* (Longman, London, 1983)

Elinor Langer, 'Inside the Hospital Workers' Union' (*New York Review of Books*, May/June 1971)

Martin Loney, *The Politics of Greed: The New Right and the Welfare State* (Pluto, London, 1986)

Melanie McFadyean and Margaret Renn, *Thatcher's Reign. A Bad Case of the Blues* (Chatto & Windus, London, 1984)

Nancy Mackeith, *Women's Health Handbook* (Virago, London, 1978)

Vincente Navarro, *Medicine and Capitalism* (Croom Helm, London, 1977)

Vincente Navarro, *Class Struggle, the State, and Medicine* (Martin Robertson, London, 1978)

Vincente Navarro, *Crisis, Health and Medicine. A Social Critique* (Tavistock, London, 1986)

Jonathan Neale, *Memoirs of a Callous Picket* (Pluto, London, 1983)

David Owen, *In Sickness and in Health* (Quartet, London, 1976)

Tony Parker, *The People of Providence* (Hutchinson, London, 1983)

Tony Pinchuck and Richard Clark, *Medicine for Beginners* (Writers' and Readers' Publishing Co-operative, London, 1984)

Radical Statistics Health Group, *In Defence of the NHS* (London, 1977)

John Rentoul (Ed.), *Who Cares? The Future of the NHS* (NS Reports, London, 1984)

Gerald Rhodes, Usha Prashar and Ken Young, *Primary Health Care in the Inner Cities: After Acheson* (London: Policy Studies Institute, 1986)

John Robson, *Quality, Inequality and Health Care* (Marxists in Medicine, London, 1976)

John Robson, *Take a Pill . . . The Drug Industry, Private or Public?* (Marxists in Medicine, London, 1976)

Michael Rose, *The Relief of Poverty 1834–1914* (Macmillan, London, 1972)

Ken Rosenberg and Gordon Schiff, *The Politics of Health Care: A Bibliography* (Committee for Human Rights, Boston, c. 1972)

Sheila Rowbotham, *New World for Women: Stella Browne, Socialist-feminist* (Pluto, London, 1977)

Royal Commission on the NHS: Report (HMSO Cmnd 7615, London, 1979)

Jane Salvage and Kambiz Boomla, *The NHS in East London: What Lies Ahead?* (Save Bethnal Green Hospital Campaign, London, 1980)

Jane Salvage, *The Politics of Nursing* (Heinemann, London, 1985)

Wendy Savage, *A Savage Inquiry* (Virago, London, 1986)

Peter Sedgwick, *PsychoPolitics* (Pluto, London, 1982)

Elaine Showalter, *The Female Malady: Women, Madness and English Culture, 1830–1980* (Virago, London, 1987)

M. Sissons and P. French (eds), *The Age of Austerity* (Penguin, Harmondsworth, 1964)

Richard Smith, *Unemployment and Health* (Oxford University Press, 1987)

Richard Smith, *Prison Health Care* (BMA, London, 1984)

Joan Sohn-Rethel and John Carrier, *Private Practice within the NHS* (Socialist Medical Association, Birmingham, nd)

Peter Tatchell, *Aids: A Guide to Survival* (Gay Men's Press, London, 1986)

Colin Thunhurst, *It Makes You Sick: The Politics of the NHS* (Pluto, London, 1982)

Richard Titmuss, *Commitment to Welfare* (Allen and Unwin, London, 1968)

Peter Townshend and Nick Davidson, *Inequalities in Health: The Black Report* (Penguin, Harmondsworth, 1982)

Julian Tudor Hart, *The National Health Service in England and Wales: A Marxist Perspective* (Marxists in Medicine, London, 1976)

Steve Watkins, *Medicine and Labour: The Politics of a Profession* (Lawrence and Wishart, London, 1987)

J. Westergaard and H. Resler, *Class in a Capitalist Society* (Penguin, Harmondsworth, 1976)

Margaret Whitehead, *The Health Divide: Inequalities of Health in the 1980s* (Health Education Council, London, 1987)

Elizabeth Wilson, *What is to be Done About Violence Against Women* (Penguin, Harmondsworth, 1983)

Elizabeth Wilson, *Women and the Welfare State* (Tavistock, London, 1977)

Jock Young and Victoria Greenwood, *Abortion in Demand* (Pluto, London, 1976)

Statistical sources

Unless otherwise cited my principal statistics are derived from the 1987 *Compendium of Health Statistics* (Office of Health Economics, London, 1987) and *Facing the Figures* (Radical Statistics Health Group, London, 1987)

Relevant pamphlets

'Abortion: Our Struggle for Control' (National Abortion Campaign, London, 1980)

'Abortion: The Struggle in the Labour Movement' (Labour Abortion Rights Campaign, London, nd)

'Deprivation and Ill-Health' (BMA Board of Science and Education Discussion Paper, London, 1987)

'General Practice: A British Success' (BMA, London, 1983)

'Liverpool's State of Health', Katy Gardner and Steve Munby (eds) (Merseyside Communist Party, Liverpool, 1980 and 1983)

'No Pass Laws to Health' (Conference Report 12 December 1982)

'Taken Bad. The State of Health in Tower Hamlets' (THIRRC, London, 1985)

'Tower Hamlets Health Inquiry Report' (London, 1987)

Useful Publications

British Medical Journal (weekly, BMA House, Tavistock Square, London WCI)

BSSRS Newsheet (British Society for Social Responsibility in Science, 9 Poland St., London W 1)

Medical World (bi-monthly, ASTMS, 79 Camden Rd, London NW 1)

Medicine in Society (quarterly, Central Books, 14 The Leathermarket, London SE 1)

Politics of Health (Intermittent bulletin of the Politics of Health Group, 9 Poland St, London W 1)

Radical Community Medicine (quarterly, 5 Lyndon Drive, Liverpool)

Science for People (quarterly, BSSRS, 9 Poland St, London W 1)

Self Health (bi-monthly journal of the College of Health, 18 Victoria Park Sq, London E 2)

Socialist Worker (weekly, PO Box 80, London E 3)

Index